Situations

A Southern Boy's Journey into Madness

Shane

Situations
A Southern Boy's Journey Into Madness

© 2022 copyright

To everyone who experienced these situations with me and came back out of the madness. I love y'all!

To those who didn't take these journeys with us but were on the outside looking in—thank you for still loving us. We love y'all!

Contents

1. NO WASTING TIME 5
2. THE SITUATIONS BEGIN 11
3. THE MADNESS BEGINS 45
4. THE ART OF NEEDLEPOINT 79
5. LIVIN' ON TULSA TIME 117
6. THE RETURN 141
7. SAME AS IT EVER WAS 149
8. THE BEGINNING OF THE END 189
9. THE END 217

Afterward: The New Beginning 237

A List of Revolutionary Artists 243

1   NO WASTING TIME

If I had twenty dollars for every time I stuck a needle in my arm, I'd probably be able to look at my bank account and breathe a sigh of relief, but that shit ain't the case. It's not that I claim bragging rights to how much of a junkie I was, it's just the truth. It wasn't just me, though. It was the whole lot of us. Some of us may have been worse off than the other, but we were all completely fucked in our own way.

My part in this story started thirty years ago when I moved back to Little Rock, Arkansas from Londonderry, New Hampshire. I had moved to New Hampshire to live with my biological father after getting into a little trouble my first eighth grade year. Yes, I had to repeat the eighth grade. So, my mom and I thought it would be good to do that in New Hampshire, but it turned out it wasn't such a good idea.

Although, on a side note, my relationship with my biological dad has started seeing light after many years of no communication, and I look forward to continuing to grow that relationship.

After completing my second eighth grade year in New Hampshire, I moved back to Little Rock to be with my mom. It was the summer of 1990 when I made it back home, and my mom was about to marry the guy whom, over time, I would come to call Dad.

Believe me, calling him dad didn't happen overnight. In fact, it took many years before we were to see eye to eye. My parents had known each other for years and had dated once before in the mid 1980's, but it didn't work out the first time. Needless to say, I had known the man for several years before they married and had played with his two adopted kids over the years, Walter and Roman. In fact, I was there during Walter and Roman's adoption ceremony, years before my mom and dad married, when dad was still married to a different woman.

Anyway, about two weeks after I moved back from New Hampshire, my mom and dad married. That's when the chaos began. Walter, dad's oldest adopted son, who was sixteen when I moved back, started taking me out with his friends that summer, showing me the ropes of how to socialize in his environment, which was nothing but a party environment. I had smoked weed for the first time when I was thirteen, but I only did it a few times, which was during my first eighth grade year, and never touched it again until I was fifteen, which was how old I was when I moved back to Arkansas from New Hampshire. Needless to say, I was quickly learning how to live this new lifestyle that I jumped into headfirst. I started drinking, smoking weed, and smoking cigarettes. I even took acid for the first time that summer. Have you ever taken acid? For those of you who haven't, let me just say that it's a wonderful drug and hard to explain to someone who hasn't experienced a trip.

It has always been better than mushrooms for me. Many will argue that, but I like the intensity of a trip on acid versus mushrooms.

I remember it vividly. It was just white blotter, but it was really good. Walter and I were heading out to have a good time on that hot and humid evening, and we were going to a school parking lot to meet some friends of his and then over to a small, wooded area attached to the parking lot behind the school. Even though it was behind a school, the wooded area was secluded and unused. We didn't have to worry about others being there, and if there were others, they were within our group. We hadn't planned on tripping that night, but someone showed up unexpectedly with some. Walter and I put our money together and bought four hits along with enough skunk bud to roll us a couple joints after the trip was done.

Trust me, when you've been frying all night, nothing is better than some weed to put the cherry on top. Hell, it's good during the trip as well.

We both took two hits and started our evening. As soon as I put it in my mouth, I tasted it. I felt the chemicals soak into my body. I was really nervous about taking it, but excited also.

I had always heard about acid and what it did but was never around anyone on it and had never seen it until that moment. Never gaining my right mind back ran through my thoughts. I was thinking about all the "Just Say No" commercials and the scary interviews that I watched as a child of those that had met or exceeded their drug lifestyle. The feeling of mystery, of not knowing what the night would entail or what the final result would be, was thrilling. Everyone hanging out that night knew it was my first time, and it seemed as though they were just as excited for me as I was, reassuring me that I was going to have a great time.

After 30 minutes I started feeling the overwhelming sensation of entering my trip. I had a good body high, but my brain, my thoughts, were on a whole new level. During that first hour, I found myself laughing uncontrollably. It wasn't that anything going on was really funny, it was just my brain adjusting to the intensity of the acid. After about an hour, I was well into this new realm, this new situation I put myself in. The first hour after taking acid sometimes gives insight into how your trip is going to be.

Keep in mind, not every trip is the same. Sometimes the feeling leading into a trip is calm. It doesn't mean that you're not going to have a good trip, it just means that it might be a calm or very smooth one. It may be that the acid you have is really clean or it could be the mindset you have going into the trip. Then, after that hour passes, you may start frying your ass off. Of course, other times leading into a trip can be very intense. Maybe your mindset could be in an aggressive mode or maybe you just have good acid, and you're about to fry your ass off. Then again, it might be that after that first intense hour of what you thought was going to be an intense trip could turn into a calm one. You just never know.

That night my first hour was very intense. I think it was a combination of good acid and the unknown. After about two hours, I wasn't speaking any longer. I was frying my balls off! There were tracers and shadows everywhere, and everyone's face was offset or vibrating.

At some point during that evening behind the school, some girl was leaving the parking lot and ran right into a chain that someone had put up during the time we got there and the time she tried to leave. It was the only way in or out of that particular parking lot. Laughter and excitement paused for a minute when we heard the loud collision. We didn't know what the fuck had just happened. There may have only been two of us tripping, but when we heard what turned out to be that girl's car hitting that chain, we all started tripping, especially me and Walter. There was probably about ten of us there at that time, and all of us but two ran to where that awful sound had occurred. At that point, the girl and her friend were out of the car and the girl driving was already crying, wondering what the fuck just happened. When we got to the scene, we saw that she had fucked her car up pretty bad, but it wasn't totaled by any means. She was not only trying to figure out who chained the gate but how she was going to explain to her parents that she ran into a chain that was blocking the entrance of a parking lot behind a school where she wasn't even supposed to be. What I was trying to figure out, and what everyone else was trying to figure out, was, one, how she didn't see the big fucking chain dangling between the two posts it was connected to, and two, who the fuck came and put the chain up. After the initial shock of what had happened was over and we unhooked the chain for that poor ruined girl so she could continue her journey to wherever, we started walking back to where we were originally stationed, and we just started laughing. "Dumb bitch!" Walter said, laughing. It was at that point that we decided to leave and go elsewhere. Someone, probably someone working at the school, had put that chain up, so we thought it was a good idea to get the fuck out of there.

Six hours later I finally started coming down and found myself at someone's house with a bunch more muthafuckers than what we started with. The drinking and smoking continued until sunrise. That was an interesting night. In fact, I had a blast that summer and knew right away that I wanted to make this new-found fun a full-time thing. You see, I saw an atmosphere of fun-loving people, good people that watched out for one another and loved to have a good time. Living in

Little Rock during those times meant that you needed people like that around if you were going to be out in the streets because Little Rock was a very dangerous place. The murder rate and overall rate of crime and violence in the city was approaching an all-time high during the eighties and nineties, so it was comforting to know that rolling deep and with such loyal and watchful individuals could make the difference between making it home or pulling into the emergency room. Of course, being out in the streets meant that you were putting yourself in those situations to begin with, which is something that I didn't realize until many years later.

The summer of 1990 in Little Rock was just the beginning. It was almost like going to a school with a curriculum of street knowledge and taking classes like "partying," "drugs," and "learning the game." I was fascinated and got caught up quick.

We thought we were living like adults and doing what we thought were adult things, which was furthest from the truth. Compared to what our peers were doing, which was following the rules like going to school, being active in sports and the community, and taking care of family.... we were acting like fools. Be that as it may, we thought we were on a higher level because we were at the adult parties hanging with people who were in college and oftentimes much older, who were already in the professional world, which was a scary thought. The people we were hanging with in Little Rock just liked to have a good time and talk about the same things, and they shared the same ideas and philosophies, which were ways to revolutionize anything that was part of a system against us. What were we against? Fuck, I don't know. They were your typical teenage angst thoughts. For example, politics, religion, the legalization of weed, and just the overall attitude of mainstream society were big topics for us, as they still are for the majority to this day. We didn't like the mainstream approach or thought process. Although, besides talking about it, bitching about it, or debating about it, no one actually did anything to change it or make any sort of difference. Don't get me wrong, I'm not saying you have to be on drugs or apart from society to think for yourself. I'm just saying that you can still be part of society and conduct yourself professionally, ask questions and make intelligent decisions that aren't based on the current trend and what the cattle are doing but rather what is ethical, moral, and a righteous action or idea to take. It is a mode of thinking that will separate you from those that mean to do you harm, who really don't give a shit about you or your best interest. You know, fake ass muthafuckers. Of course, it's the same thing we have today, a bunch of fucking cattle out to graze, following what the political, educational, religious, and authoritative entities say is the right way. Moo along! There's nothing to see here!

When I think back on those earlier times in Little Rock, I often wonder why the fuck those people, sometimes twice our age and older, allowed us to hang with them. Who the fuck wants thug teenagers hanging around, who don't have a clue of what life is about? The only answer I ever came up with is that regardless of age or life experience, everyone still had something in common with each other (besides drug use). Our commonality was simple. It was a similar thought process and questions about life we all wondered about. Was life good or did it suck? Was society getting worse or better? Were the politicians doing what the people wanted?

We felt life and society were getting worse. We wanted to change what was because we saw how things could become, which, unfortunately, now are. We all had ideas of how that could be achieved. Like I said, regardless of age and experience, the older folks wanted to be around those who were likeminded, if for nothing else than comfort and approval. As older versions of us, they were not receiving what is essential for human beings, which is fellowship. Basically, we were living and thinking outside of the box, avoiding what was popular and trendy, doing what we thought was right for us. Actually, that's not too far from the way myself and the others, meaning my peeps, feel now. The difference now is that we don't participate in the thug or criminal way of things, at least not what we consider criminal. We're not out stealing, dealing, and carrying illegal guns anymore; put it that way.

2   THE SITUATIONS BEGIN

The journey began after my parents said, "I do." Oh, if only I knew the journey I was about to take.

The things I'm writing about have been heard before. We've seen it all before. It's not the strangest, most dangerous, or craziest journey ever told. In fact, it's far from it. But for small-town boys living in small-town America, it was a hell of a ride. You would expect to hear this kind of shit coming out of the big city, or from famous people in Hollywood, or from the music industry—but not necessarily in a place the size of Russellville, Arkansas. Here's the deal: I didn't write this for recognition, pity, fame, or fortune. I couldn't care less! I'm writing this for the people who took the journey with me and for the ones that were sitting on the sidelines wondering what the fuck we were doing and why. This is for my family and friends. And it's for me. It's therapeutic. I'm able to put this shit on paper in order to take a look at myself, to find out who I was, what I did, and who I am now. I think about the past all the time, but it's different when I write it out. Writing it forces me to slow my thinking and to take my time and really reflect. This memoir has allowed me to do that. It has allowed me to look at myself, my life—and everyone in it—with fresh eyes and thoughts. I've been able to see things in a new light because writing this has allowed me to look at my story from the outside in. Just so you know, my childhood was wonderful. I was never mistreated. I grew up surrounded with love. My mom, brother, grandparents, aunts, and uncles were all very close. We were and still are a tightknit family. I decided my path. The decisions I made about my life are mine.

One more thing to keep in mind while reading this story: it's not about expanding minds, thoughts, consciousness, or any of that silly, hippie-ass bullshit. This story is about getting fucked up, doing fucked up shit, having a good time, and pushing it to the edge as often as possible.

Did we expand our minds and all that shit during the process? Yes! But we didn't set out to accomplish that. We may have thought about that shit for a brief moment (mostly when we were taking acid, although even that lost its value). Mainly, we were doing what we did to get as fucked up as we could. That's it. Period. We were Generation X! It's part of our culture. We loved and still love to party. I think Ice Cube said it best: "Generation Triple X...we all about the weed smoke and the kinky sex."

My parents were working for an energy company, and the employees in Little Rock were being transferred to the nuclear plant in Russellville. However, the parents didn't move us up to Russellville with them until the weekend before school started. That gave Walter and me plenty of time to live it up in Little Rock before we moved. Russellville was only an hour outside of Little Rock, but that hour drive meant the difference between the city and the country, at least what we thought was the country.

Actually, I'm leaving an important person out of this: Dad's other adopted boy Roman, who was 14 at the time. Roman didn't hang out with us. He stayed with his adopted mom for most of that summer, and he ended up going to Russellville a little before Walter and me. He and Walter were blood brothers and were separated as children. They were shuffled in and out of different foster homes before Dad adopted them both in the mid-eighties. Roman didn't join the dark side until years later. We'll get to him soon enough.

So, we show up in Russellville, and, of course, my parents, being the wonderful people they are, had our bedrooms all set up and ready for us.

The parents initially thought to keep us where our friends were, where we had something to do for the summer. They knew what Walter and I were up to, but they thought it would be horrible for us to be in a new city, not knowing anyone, sitting at the house for three months, cooped up going crazy. Walter didn't have a car yet because he kept fucking up and pissing off Dad. I didn't have a license yet because I was only fifteen, but that didn't matter; I was not legally allowed to get my license because I "stole" a car when I was thirteen and wrecked it. So, the state of Arkansas and the insurance companies wouldn't insure me until I reached seventeen. It wasn't a "steal" per se, it was a joy ride. A buddy and I took his mom's car out. The problem with that was that I wrecked the car. Not bad. I just scraped the back end of the car against a dumpster while we were doing donuts at my old elementary school playground, and I ripped some of the bumper off. It was horrible. Anyway, that's why I couldn't get my license until I was seventeen.

It's not that the parents were alright with us getting fucked up all the time and doing thug shit. The plan was to start being a family once everyone was in Russellville, to start fresh in a new environment with new friends and new people around us. Unfortunately, things just got worse. Much worse. My parents didn't understand that it didn't matter where they put me: I was looking for a specific lifestyle, and I was going to make it work no matter what. My parents could have put me in a church (which would have been appropriate), and it wouldn't have made a fuck. None of us knew, however, that Russellville was full of the kind of people and things we wanted to get into.

Russellville is a small town with big-city problems. To put Russellville, Arkansas on the map for you: it was the town where Ronald Gene Simmons killed sixteen people in 1987. It made national headlines because a crime of that magnitude had never occurred in Russellville. Of course, something of that magnitude would make top headlines anywhere. It's also the hometown of former Arkansas Razorback and NBA star, Corliss Williamson, who played for the Sacramento Kings, Toronto Raptors, Detroit Pistons, and the Philadelphia 76ers.

Within the first two weeks of school, around September of 1990, Walter and I had managed to find several people engaged in our way of life.

By the way, Roman was in the eighth grade, I was in the ninth, and Walter was in the tenth grade.

Although we had not yet found a consistent hookup for weed, we had found some of the smokers, which was a good start. Walter had also established a ride to and from school with some of the people he met.

They were in high school, and it was an open campus, which meant you could leave campus at lunch. That was awesome because neither of us had to ride the bus any longer. Roman, however, was on his own. Like I said, he didn't cross over until years later. Besides that, Walter was an asshole to Roman and wanted nothing to do with him. The feeling was mutual for Roman.

The first person that Walter introduced me to was a guy named Heath. "What's up bro?" he asked, as if we had known each other for years. Heath had given Walter a ride home that day, which became one of our regular rides. I was already home because I had taken the bus. I think that was the last time I ever rode the bus. Heath was a crazy muthafucker! And I mean that in a good way. Heath loved to have a good time. He would do anything for you. We started hanging out with him full time.

Donovan was the next person I met. He also gave Walter a ride home from school within the first two weeks of us being in Russellville. Donovan's family was also transferred to the nuclear plant, but from Texas. I'll never forget the first time I met Donovan. Walter had brought him up to the front door, which was weird because we never used that door as the main entrance of the house. The main entrance for us was the side of the house, where the driveway was located. From the den watching TV, I noticed an old, ugly, brown Chevrolet step-side pull up in the front of the house. I went to the other side, and there Donovan stood—with long, red, ratty hair. Walter was taking a music class at school and met Donovan there. Walter and I had wanted to start a band once we got to Russellville. Walter played bass in a band before we left Little Rock. I had always wanted to play drums but didn't have a set yet. Actually, Walter didn't have a guitar or bass at that point either. Nonetheless, the plan was to start a band, and Donovan played guitar. Donovan and I hit it off right away. We thought alike, and we both had long hair. His hair was longer, but I was not too far behind, and that was a big deal in those days—especially in Russellville.

There weren't many guys our age, or any age for that matter, in Russellville that had long hair and dressed the way we did. Back then, we were referred to as hoods. The other side of that label were the preps. Looking the way that we looked in Russellville, we were outnumbered, to say the least. Back then, when one saw someone who looked and dressed similar—long hair, jeans, t-shirt—one tended to migrate to that herd, where there was acceptance, which was very hard to find in a small town, looking the way we looked. Appearances spoke loudly back then. I mean, think about it: we both had moved from bigger cities that had a bunch of people who thought and looked the way we did. Now all of a sudden, we're living in the quiet town of Russellville, population 21,000. It was a place where it was acceptable to miss a couple days of school when deer season started. You understand what I'm saying to you? It was a complete culture shock.

Another big thing that Donovan and I had in common was the music we liked: rock and metal! You know, Metallica, Megadeth, Mötley Crüe, and so on. I actually went to my first concert with Donovan. AC/DC, baby! Thunderstruck Tour! Donovan and I started hanging out together full time. Even though Donovan and Walter met first, Donovan quickly became *my* friend, and from that day we were together, we became brothers. Donovan started picking me up every day from school, and we'd go straight to his house.

We deemed ourselves brothers not only for us to recognize the bond we were creating but for others to recognize it as well. You fucked with one of us, you fucked with all of us, and that's just the way it was. The brothers were always around each other, and folks would rarely find one of us without at least another one of us around. A lot of people will be mentioned in this story, but that doesn't mean they were necessarily brothers, just friends who would hang out with the brothers. It wasn't the drugs that kept us together, it was the amazing love, respect, and loyalty we had for one another. We all had so much in common and thought the same way. Because of the bond and fellowship that we acquired early, we still hold that same bond and love for one another to this day, without hesitation.

In the beginning, we were just hanging out in parks, on the move, or at someone's house that Heath knew, which was awkward for me, Walter, and Donovan. Heath knew of other places to hang out, but Walter and I didn't think they were cool or fun enough, being that it was Russellville. Plus, Donovan was in the same situation as Walter and me: he didn't know anyone except for us. And Heath was looking for something different anyway, which he found it with us. We quickly decided to go down to Little Rock on the weekends to party. Well, I say we went down on the weekends, but actually we were hauling ass down there on Friday nights and hauling ass back up—to get home by midnight. Nonetheless, we all made the decision to go to Little Rock as much as we could to hang out with all of Walter's friends.

On a side note, two of the other people we first met besides Heath and Donovan were Theresa and Kristie. I don't mean to dismiss that part. Those two were around us for many years. They actually took me and Walter cruising one of the first weekends we were in Russellville. We were ridin' in Theresa's badass Chevy Nova. Anyway, I love them both and miss them dearly. They come back into the story later.

I'm not sure how in the hell we made it to Little Rock and back all those times without killing ourselves, but we did. We would always take Heath's car for the simple fact that Walter still didn't have a car, and Donovan's big ass old truck, hell, I don't even know if we would have made it in that thing had we tried. Plus, Heath's Toyota Corolla was inexpensive to fill up (when we actually paid for gas).

I remember one of the times we went down to Little Rock. In fact, it was the first time we all went. It was probably late September or early October. We would usually leave Russellville after we had talked to the parents and told them some lie about what we were doing that night; so somewhere between five and six in the evening. Heath comes and gets me and Walter, and we all go get Donovan. We hit the interstate a little before seven. It was close to dusk, and we were hauling ass. We hit Atkins, which was about ten minutes outside of Russellville, and we heard a pretty scary *boom*! We had blown a tire on the rear driver side. Heath's car was a very old, blue Toyota, and the car had problems. Well, not the car's problems but more so Heath's, and, of course, anyone who rode with him. The two problems of major concern: constantly needing tires (good ones at least) and gas. Normally, those problems would be fairly easy to overcome, but we were teenagers, and jobs were out of the question.

Walter did acquire a job eventually, which helped with things like gas, but it really came in handy when we needed money to get fucked up. And money eventually ended up not being a problem, but that's later in the story.

So, there we are on a mission to Little Rock and tragedy strikes. We all knew right away what happened when we heard the quick sound of our dire situation. "Shit," and "fuck," I think were the words echoed inside the car as we pulled off the Atkins exit onto the shoulder. Following the echoes of profanity was a deathly silence that hovered stagnantly between us. It was a very limited silence, though. It was a quick silence, then, "Oh, shit! Now what are we gonna do?" I'm sure the immediate next thought was, "Oh, shit! We're not gonna get to party and get fucked up!" Well, that wasn't our fate, because the next thing that was spoken after that horrible brief silence was about to fix everything. "Dude!" Heath said excitedly, "we're gonna steal a tire!" He said it rather matter of fact, as if that were all there was to it. You can imagine the puzzled looks on our faces when he said that. I mean, c'mon. It's past seven at this point. It's now dark, and we're in Atkins, Arkansas, population 3,000. Walter inquired as to where the fuck we could steal a tire. Heath quickly explained that he had recently been looking for a new car and found another Toyota that was the exact make and model of his current Toyota. Again, you can imagine the look of confusion and thoughts of doubt as we sat there processing what he was saying. When I asked how he knew it was still there, with a grin on his face, he said, "Because I came and looked at it yesterday." Keep in mind, all of this happened in about a 30 second time period. The four of us quickly got out of the car so the spare could be put on, and about five minutes later we were on our way to steal a tire.

This was the first time we were with Heath and a tire blew, but it wasn't the last time—for damn sure. Little did we know at the time that Heath was very familiar with his tires blowing and had turned into quite the IndyCar pit man, and he was really good at changing his tires in a very timely manner, which was extremely amusing to watch.

Heath drove us deep into Atkins, where the car was supposedly parked. I had no idea where the fuck we were. Heath was the only one who knew where we were. As we turned another corner in a neighborhood, sure as shit, there it was. It was parked in a front yard with a for-sale sign on it. It looked as though it was a heavenly gift, like it was meant for us to use at our disposal. For a minute, I thought I saw a gleaming light shining on the car from above, separating itself from the cold dark that smothered the rest of the landscape around us. If I didn't know better, I would have sworn I heard a choir of angels. I couldn't fucking believe it! The man was right, exact make and model. Hell, I think it was even the same color. Blue. We all just started laughing in disbelief and excitement. I knew at that moment that we were about to acquire a new tire to continue our journey. Heath asked if someone was going to help him take the tire off. Donovan was laughing, but I could see he thought the situation was crazy. Walter made it clear he wasn't going to help. Reinforcing his stance, Donovan stated, "I'm waiting here." I sat quietly knowing that I was next. I was on deck. Heath was already getting upset, as if he couldn't believe everyone was saying no. In a last desperate attempt for support, he turns to me. "Fuck it, man! Let's do it," I quickly replied. It was exciting! I was excited!

If you remember, the last time I had stolen anything was that car several years earlier, but I really didn't consider that stealing because as you know, it was my friend's mom's car. We were just borrowing the car, you know, doing a little joyriding. Yes, it was wrecked in the process, while doing donuts in a school playground, but that happens sometimes when you're joyriding. Although, it wasn't really wrecked. The passenger side bumper and fender were dragging the ground from hitting a dumpster, but other than that, the car was fine.

This instance however, I considered stealing. I had no ties whatsoever with the owner of this car, who, within a matter of a few minutes, was about to hold the title of victim. I had to step up. I had to prove that I wasn't a bitch. I had to do some dirt to earn respect, at least that's what was going through my idiotic teenage mind. We parked about ten yards from our sitting treasure. Heath and I exited his car with the jack and tire iron in hand. We ran up to the other car on the driver side. Heath quickly put the jack underneath, and I started loosening the lugs on the driver-side front wheel. He had the car jacked up quickly, and I continued to take the lug nuts off. All we heard was laughter from

Walter and Donovan in the other car, and it was making Heath and me laugh. I'm surprised the laughter alone didn't get us caught. It was just after seven, and anywhere else we wouldn't have gotten away with it, but we were in Atkins, and the neighborhood was shut down like it was midnight. We must have been in a neighborhood full of old people, or something. We had that tire off the car in less than two minutes. Hastily, I asked Heath what we were going to put the car back down on when we were done. It's not like I wanted to ruin the car. Heath looked at me like I was crazy for asking. His intention, based on that look, was to bring it back down to the ground on the rotor. I was just trying to be a thoughtful criminal. He grinned at me because he knew where I was coming from. He looked around and saw a big brick laying in the current victim's yard. He ran over, picked it up, and ran back over to the car to lay it under the rotor as I was bringing it down. It sat nicely on that brick. We ran back to our car, barely making it because we were laughing so hard. We threw the new tire in the trunk of his car and proceeded to get the fuck out of there. "Y'all are fucking nuts," Donovan stated, laughing, as we were getting back in the car. As we were pulling off, we all looked back at the car we had just vandalized and started cracking up. It was the funniest shit to see that car sitting there, missing the rim and tire, the rotor resting on a brick. Although, I don't think the owner of that car thought it was too funny. The theft was reported the next day, and it was also reported in the *Atkins Chronicle* at some point. After we left the scene of the crime, we headed back to the interstate and stopped at the on ramp to put the tire on. Then we continued our journey to Little Rock. I think the entire episode took about ten minutes—from the time the tire blew until the time we were back on the interstate.

Now that I'm thinking about it, it seems that every time we went down to Little Rock, we had an adventure, either on the way there or on the way back. I remember another time we were headed back to Russellville from Little Rock: it was the weekend after the tire incident, and if I remember correctly, we only had about forty-five minutes to get back to Russellville—to meet the midnight curfew that Walter and I had. We were a solid hour away from our destination. The situation is a little blurry, but I remember being drunker than shit and getting in the car, and Walter saying we had to hurry because we had less than an hour to get home. On top of that, we were about to run out of gas and had no money—at least none that we were planning on using for gas. Donovan and I were in the back seat, and both of us were about to pass out from intoxication. I remember fading in and out at points during the drive. I suddenly woke up in a panic, tried to open my eyes and lift my head up; Walter was yelling at Heath, "Look out! Be careful!" I slowly looked out the window to figure out why Walter was in such a panic. I noticed we were passing people on the shoulder of the interstate at high rates of speed, and several times we apparently came across situations involving death. I'm only making that assumption because of the panic indicated in Walter's voice during those moments, and, of course, there was the abrupt weaving and stomping on the brakes that kept sending me and Donovan in various directions in the back seat. During those moments I actually had the energy to try and lift my head and open my eyes: I saw that we were going so fast that it seemed as though we were travelling through a science-fiction warp-tunnel, lights quickly passing by like tracers. Of course, I was drunker than shit, so I'm sure that had something to do with it. You can only go so fast in a Toyota Corolla. We were passing cars like we were in the fucking Indy 500 as we tried to make curfew. In between all that, I would look over at Donovan to make sure he was doing alright, but there was nothing going on over there except a deep, drunk sleep. I thought to myself, "Fuck it! If we die, we die." I was too fucked up to worry about it. I passed back out.

The next thing I know, I hear the car door shut. We're parked at a gas pump. I was confused. It was one of those situations where you remember you're in one location and what seems like seconds later you're in another location. In our case, it had been a matter of thirty minutes. Walter was already headed inside the store to get some munchies. I asked, "Where are we?" "We're in Atkins," Heath stated. When I inquired as to what time it was, Heath started laughing. As he was getting out to pump gas, he stated that it was about fifteen minutes before midnight, which really confused me. I was trying to figure out if we had actually made it to Atkins from Little Rock in thirty minutes. Apparently, we had. I looked over at Donovan and grabbed his arm, telling him to wake up. The look of confusion on his face was the exact feeling I had when I woke up and saw that we were at a gas station. "We're in Atkins getting some gas," I stated before he could ask. It had already soaked into my drunken thought process of where we were and what we were doing. Just a week earlier we were in this town stealing a tire. Now, we're here getting gas fifteen minutes before Walter and I had to be home. That may not raise an eyebrow for most of you, but what you don't understand is that seventy-five percent of the time that we were at a gas station, we were "pumping and jumping." We usually had money to get things like gas and snacks, but why would we use the money for that? Apparently, gas was supposed to be set aside as free for us. It just so happened that this was another one of those occasions.

Walter came walking out of the store, and Heath was still putting gas in. I knew right then what was about to take place. I knew that Walter hadn't paid for the gas. Walter never walked into a store back then and walked out with only what he had paid for. Not only were we about to steal gas, but I knew Walter had a pocket-full of shit because he had spent too long in there to only walk out with a Coke and some fucking chips—but that was the idea, or plan. Heath needed time to get some gas in the car. Ya see, the thing about pumping and jumping: it's all in the technique and timing. Walter was the distraction for the gas station attendant and was also the deciding factor on how much gas Heath was going to pump because he couldn't stop pumping until Walter came out of the store. At the same time, if you start pumping too early, you can fuck everything up because then you might be awkwardly waiting. You can't steal gas, get back in the car, wait on your friend to come out, and then drive off—especially when the friend in the store hasn't paid for the gas or anything else in his pockets. That looks too suspicious. You have to wait until that person comes out, and then finish pumping. That way, as the one person is walking quickly back to get in the car, the person pumping finishes up and gets in the car right before or at the same time the other person is returning. Then you drive off quickly! Got it? Does it make sense? Although, we didn't always use that system. Sometimes we just pulled up, everyone would sit in the car while one person pumped, and then we would drive off. It just depended on how busy the gas station was or if one of us needed to go inside the store.

At fifteen minutes until midnight in Atkins, we were the only ones there. Walter jumped back in the front seat, and as he did, Heath finished pumping and jumped back in. "Go dude," Walter said, frantically. Heath turned the key in the ignition, and the thing that you would not want to happen in that situation happened. Nothing. All we heard was *click*. The car wouldn't start. That is about the time one would start throwing profanities about. You know, things like, "Oh Shit!" or, "What the Fuck!" Heath nervously kept trying to start the car, but it just wouldn't turn over. I looked towards the store to see what the clerk was doing. He was staring intensely, definitely trying to figure out the situation. Time was running out. I looked back over; the gas station clerk was walking out from behind the register and out the front door. "He's coming out! Let's go!" I shouted. "I'm trying!" Heath stated, anxiously. By that time, I was ready to get out and start running. I sure as fuck wasn't going to be popped for stealing gas, and I could see by the look on Donovan's face that he was ready to jump out with me. I said, in a panic, "Let me out!" All of a sudden, with the gas station attendant about twenty feet away, the car started. We got out of there with the quickness. I guess the gas station attendant didn't think about getting our license plate. Or maybe he couldn't see it from where he was. Or maybe it was just too much trouble for him to fuck with. Believe it or not, we made it back home by midnight, and I immediately went to bed. As I laid there with a smile on my face, with thoughts of the evening, I shut my eyes and faded to black.

For some reason, it reminds me of another situation in which I found myself on the way down to Little Rock one night. It was a couple of weeks after the gas situation. It was quite disgusting, but it's important to write because it speaks to the debauchery taking place in my life. It was just me, Walter, and Heath on that trip, along with two girls. Heath fucked one of the girls on the way down. Walter was driving. On the way back, after a night of drinking at the dam, Heath was driving, and Walter fucked the same girl. How special was that? I guess that girl liked being fucked in moving vehicles travelling at high rates of speed. She was actually a pretty girl. I couldn't help but think about what a dirty bitch she was. If she knew the kind of nasty, dirty muthafucker Walter was, maybe she would have rethought the situation.

About Walter: this is a muthafucker that didn't take a shower for about two weeks during that summer we were in Little Rock, before we moved to Russellville. He not only didn't take a shower during that time, but he fucked multiple girls during that time and never cleaned himself. Do you see what I'm saying? Nasty muthafucker!

Then again, she fucked two different people the same night. Gross. At the same time, I was thinking about how fuckin gross Walter and Heath were. Nasty muthafuckers! They would pretty much fuck anybody. As I was thinking about all of that, I was thinking about how naughty and sexy the whole situation was. What the fuck was wrong with me? I definitely didn't want to be the third victim that night. There was no jealousy that I felt. Although, make no mistake about it, I was most definitely judging the situation. I couldn't believe two ugly, nasty fucks like Walter and Heath could get so lucky. Wait, lucky? Why would two different people fucking the same girl in one night be considered lucky? Why would fucking a girl that engages in such behavior be an awesome experience? What the fuck was wrong with me? But, at the same time, I couldn't help but think about my own sexual fantasies being fulfilled one day. Were mine to be similar to what I had experienced that night? If someone else was on the outside looking in, watching me fulfill my fantasies, would it be just as gross? Or would it be just like I always fantasized it would be: pornolicious? Wait, what the fuck was wrong with me? Am I normal to be thinking about such things? Or was I just as sick and twisted as everyone else? Wait, does thinking about such things make one sick and twisted? Maybe. It really didn't matter, though. I loved the entire situation!

I guess I had been exposed to that kind of behavior early in life. The friends I had growing up in Little Rock had exposed me to porn pretty early. When I say early, I mean I watched my first porn by the time I was in sixth grade. Hell, I had already watched two kids having sex before I even saw my first porn. I say kids because they were kids. It was in Missouri, when I was visiting my biological dad one summer. They were military brats living on the base as well. For some reason they decided to tell me that they would have sex from time to time. Of course, I told them they were full of shit. So, they decided to show me. They actually climbed a tree that was in the backyard, pulled their pants down, and started having sex. I couldn't fuckin believe it. They were maybe a grade ahead of me, and I was going to start the sixth grade that year. I don't know. For some reason, I was just exposed to that shit early. Fucked up, ain't it?

As the weeks went on, we continued such behavior. It was only about a month after the tire incident that Donovan's parents left the state because of work, which was sometime in late October. So, we just started hanging out and partying at his place full-time. Yes, his parents left the state. His parents actually left their two teenage sons behind to live in and care for the house while they were gone. This wasn't just a week at a time or something like that. This was their parents being gone for the entire school year and not returning until the following summer. Jaxton, who was Donovan's older brother, had just started his first semester in college. (Cool guy!) Donovan's place became the official spot. And my mom and dad bought me my first drum set because they had bought Roman a four-wheeler a month earlier. My first drum set was a Powersonic. Donovan and I quickly moved my drums to his place after his parents left so we wouldn't have to practice in my parent's garage anymore.

By the way, this is a good time to tell you who the biggest influences in music were and have been throughout my life—in the realm of rock, metal, and rap. This will give you an idea of what bands, groups, and artists inspired me to play drums and write music. Whether it was the whole band, group, artists, or drummers that inspired me, these musicians have carried me through the years. And three of the drummers just happen to be a part of three of my favorite bands. The lists are in the order that I first heard them. And as far as ranking the drummers, they are all number one in my opinion because I feel they are the best drummers in the world. Therefore, it would be impossible to rank one over the other. Does that make sense? One more thing: these lists aren't to suggest that I don't like other musicians or artists, because I do. There are many. These are just my early favorites. And I'm being specific about the genres because I grew over the years with my music. The drummers won't change as far as influence and style, but the music will change in that my taste and catalog have evolved. I'll do two lists for you, drummers[1] and bands[2].

---

[1] My list of drummers that have inspired me over the years goes as follows: Tommy Aldridge, Lars Ulrich, Tommy Lee, Randy Castillo, Steven Adler, Sean Kinney, Danny Carey, Morgan Rose, and Josh Freese.

It was spring of 1991 when I officially met Christian. We were both in 9th grade and the same age: sixteen. I had seen him around before, but I never met him. He and Phillip, his best friend at the time, would hang out together. I had already been told who they were and that they were the two badass muthafuckers in the school that you didn't fuck with. They were the only hoods that would actually walk over to the prep's side to hang out.

I say the prep's side because the social division was literally set up so that the preps would hang out on the right side of the school, the nerds and geeks in the middle, and the hoods—or what I like to refer to as real muthafuckers—would hang out on the left side.

By that time, we were getting close to school being out for the summer, late March or early April. It was lunch time. Usually, the first thing the smokers did when lunch started was make their way to where everyone else would hang out after eating lunch, which was the front of the school. We liked to get a quick cigarette in before the rest of the cafeteria emptied out into that area because, by that time, not only were other students out there but teachers were also.

The school sat on one of the main strips in the business district of Russellville, so, literally, there was nothing to block the rest of the world from seeing you. If you left the front yard of the school, then you would be walking into traffic on a very busy road. It wasn't like schools are today, secluded in the back parts of neighborhoods or parks. This school was right in the middle of everything, with no place to hide while you were smoking. In fact, the businesses across the street were in cahoots with the school, and they would sometimes report that students were out front smoking. Of course, I got caught smoking a couple times and got detention, but I didn't give a fuck. I just needed a cigarette. And yes, I was already addicted to tobacco at sixteen.

---

2 My list of bands, groups and/or artists, looks like this: Ozzy Osbourne, Guns n Roses, NWA, Ice Cube, Alice in Chains, Jane's Addiction, Dr. Dre, Snoop Dogg, Nine Inch Nails, Tool, Korn, and Sevendust.

So, there I was by myself during lunch on a low brick retaining wall, smoking a cigarette. It just so happened that I was the first one out there. Or maybe I was the last one out there, and everyone else had already smoked. Either way, I was alone and hot-boxing one down as quick as I could. Christian came walking around the corner. He came around the side. He walked right up to me, sat down, and asked if I had an extra cigarette. I quickly replied, "Hell yeah." He introduced himself, as did I, and he replied that he knew who I was. "You're part of that Little Rock group," he stated with confidence. I smiled and said, "That's right." Smirking, he replied, "Shit, it ain't hard to pick y'all out." We continued to finish our cigarettes and talked the remainder of lunch. We discussed his best friend/bro Phillip, who had just moved back to Texas where the rest of his family was so he could finish out the school year. After several minutes had gone by, the front started filling up with students who were done eating lunch. Eventually, the bell rang for everyone to go inside and resume class. We both said our nice-to-meet-ya's and proceeded to whatever class was after lunch.

Just over an hour later, as I was walking to my sixth-period class, I ran into Christian again. My sixth period class was either gym or a study hall class. I can't remember which one. Regardless, I had to go outside the main part of the school to get to my next class. As I was walking there, he was headed in the same direction. He walked right up to me and said he was going to the house, and then, laughing, he asked if I wanted to go with him. I couldn't believe it.

Now keep in mind that this was only the third time in my school career that I had been asked to skip school, the first time being in seventh grade when I was still living in Little Rock. I was twelve. That didn't turn out to be a very good experience. We ended up walking to the mall that day, and on the way, we got caught by the vice principal of our school as she was walking out of a restaurant during her lunch. The second time was earlier this school year, in ninth grade. That didn't turn out good either. We obviously got caught and received in-school detention for a day.

When Christian asked if I wanted to go to the house with him, I had an array of quick thoughts. It was a mix of being scared to leave for fear of consequences the next day with being scared to say no because I didn't want Christian to think I was a bitch. At the same time, I was thinking about the excitement. I had this guy that I just met—one of the most popular kids in school—who asked if I wanted to skip the rest of the day and go hang out. Ya gotta understand, the pure-and-simple fact that he thought to extend the offer to my dumb ass—a person that was not popular at all and a person he just met—was pretty fuckin cool. Obviously, I decided that it would be good if I were to take the rest of the day off. We proceeded to bail out. We walked to the back of the school where Christian's mom, Cheryl, was waiting for us in her car. I couldn't believe it. His mom was actually there to take us to her house to skip school the rest of the day. Well, she wasn't originally there to get my dumb ass. She was pissed when I walked up with Christian and angrily asked him who I was. Christian stated, "This is Shane. Shane, this is my mom." I nervously said, hello. Christian proceeded to tell his mom that I was one of the new kids that just moved from Little Rock. "Do your parents know you're leaving?" Cheryl asked. Again, I nervously replied, "No." She looked at Christian with great anger. He just started smirking. I eagerly assured her that I would handle my parents and that no one would be the wiser about how I departed school. I then thanked her for letting me come along. Christian, of course, couldn't help but giggle the entire time. When we got to Christian's house, he and I went to his bedroom and started smoking some weed. Cheryl ended up taking me home later that day before my parents got back from work.

You see, Cheryl was, and still is, one of the coolest moms on the planet. Over time, I considered her my second mom. She and her husband, Miller, eventually took me in after the parents finally kicked my dumb ass out. But we'll get to that later.

The next day at school, Christian and I, of course, were called into the office. It had surprised me that the school never called my parents to ask where I was the remainder of the previous day. Nonetheless, the school knew where I was supposed to be and knew that it wasn't an excused absence. The principal punished our unexcused absence with in-school detention that would begin the next day. However, that same day during lunchtime, we were out there smoking again and one of the teachers from the school came running across the street from a local business to bust us. The teacher busting us was none other than the civics teacher who had just gotten back from serving in Operation Desert Storm. I can't even remember his name. There were at least five of us out there smoking when we saw him running across the road. It didn't matter. He saw all he needed to see at that point. By the time he got to us we were trying to put the cigarettes out, and he was pointing at the ones he targeted. "You, you, and you come with me," the civics teacher said. He was pointing at me and Christian. I can't remember who the third person was and have no idea what happened to the others out there. I do remember what happened to me and Christian, though. We got three days of SDC (student discipline center). Since we were already scheduled to have in-school detention, the principal thought it best if we get sent to SDC.

SDC was at the high school. It was a room with about ten different cubicles that was located above the high school gym. You would have to sit in there the entire day of school and do whatever homework was sent over from your teachers. Of course, before you were given the privilege of actually being able to sit down, you had to write, standing up, about why you were there and why it was wrong. Then you had to write three to five pages, if not more, of the act you committed, saying you won't do it again. For example: "I won't smoke on school property." That phrase would be repeated until you filled the pages you were assigned. SDC was the same place the high school students would go as well for doing something bad. At the junior high, they called it in-school detention, and at the high school it was called SDC. The ones that were always in trouble at the junior high were sent to the high school for discipline, for some reason. I'm not sure why or what difference it was supposed to make, but, regardless, that's where the constant troublemakers would go. If a person continued to fuck up, obviously, they would be suspended.

At that point, my parents knew what was going on because the junior high called and told them. They had learned about my skipping and detention. Although, I didn't get in trouble with my parents. All I got was the disappointed look. I didn't give a fuck.

I was never one for trying to be sneaky with what I was doing. Mainly because it was a rebellious and in-your-face sort of thing to do. Plus, I felt I was old enough to make my own decisions (which was furthest from the truth), and if I wanted to smoke, skip school, drink, and whatever, I would just do it. Though, I think also it was an influence thing as well. Each one of us influenced the other. Simply put, we were all teenage thugs that were out of control and unstoppable. Even if our parents wanted us to stop, there was no stopping any of us. We were gonna do what the fuck we wanted to do. Walter and Roman were sneaky and rarely got caught. But for some reason, I just didn't give a fuck, which is the same behavior and attitude I saw from my friends. If my parents asked, I was brutally honest with them. That was one of the things they came to appreciate over the years. Regardless of my constant fucking up, they knew I would be honest with them. I was very honest with them. Of course, after a while they were afraid to ask for fear of what I would tell them.

Anyway, I was being sent to SDC at the high school the next day, so I just rode in with Walter and Heath. Christian's mom had dropped him off at a park about a hundred yards off from the school.

If you were in high school, a smoker, and didn't have a car to leave campus at lunch, that's where you would go to get as many cigarettes in as you could in a thirty-minute time period. The high school couldn't do anything about it because we were on public property.

As I was walking up from the parking lot to the school, I saw Christian coming up on my left. Walter told me that he was walking up to the side of the school where students would get the last of a few drags in before first period started. It was a side glass door that took you right back into the halls of the school, but teachers were not prone to hanging out on that side during the day because it was on a side where there wasn't that much activity between classes. It was the gym side of the school. We were out there hot boxing a couple down with some other high school students, and once we were done, we headed inside with the rest. And wouldn't ya know it, the principal was standing inside waiting for us. He had been watching all of us smoke. Now, I'm not sure why the other students weren't picked out, but Christian and I were apparently the only ones on his mind. Maybe he picked us out because he knew we were his two junior high students there for SDC due to skipping and smoking. And here we are, smoking outside with the high school students, yet again, on school property. Whatever the case, the principal had us targeted. We walk in from smoking and the principal says, "You two, come with me. Since you guys think it's ok to smoke out there, we're gonna see about getting y'all some more SDC time." Christian and I both looked at him like he was smoking crack. Christian immediately and angrily asked, "What? What about everyone else out there smoking?" He continued, "You're gonna single us out while everyone else out there was doing the same thing?" "Don't worry about everyone else," the principal said. This conversation was happening as we were walking to the front of the school where the cafeteria and office staff were located, as well as the entrance to the gym, above which the SDC room was located. "Fuck that," Christian exclaimed. Defending what Christian just said, I backed it up with, "Yeah, no shit! What's up with that?" "Hey, you watch your mouths and don't talk like that," the principal said as he was getting more irritated. By the time these things were said, we were at the principal's office. As he was opening the door to escort us in, Christian said, "Fuck that, I'm going to the house!" "Shit, I'm going to," I quickly said. At this point, the principal had the door open, expecting us to go in, but we quickly turned our direction to the front door, which was just a few feet away from us. The principal frantically walked after us, and as Christian was opening the front door to walk out, the principal grabbed the door and forced it shut saying, "Y'all ain't going nowhere." Christian tried forcing his way out the front door again, but the principal was just too strong. He was a pretty big guy. Well, big compared to two sixteen-year-olds, anyway. Immediately, Christian turned around and bowed up on the guy. "You better let us the fuck out of here," Christian stated, aggressively. He turned to try and get out again, and the principal was still successfully holding the door shut. Then, I started helping Christian push the door open, and with the two of us pushing, he could no longer hold on to it. As we finally broke through the door, looking back at the principal, I shouted, "Muthafucker!" Christian turned around and shouted at the principal, "Fuck you!" We both just stood there looking at him like, "Now what, bitch?"

I could tell that the situation had made the principal a little nervous. I'm sure he thought he was about to get into a physical altercation. Hell, I was nervous as well and definitely thought we might just throw hands. The morning school bell had just rung, so there were still people scattered everywhere watching all this go down. Everyone's adrenaline was running strong at that point, as well as egos. We were both ready to take it to the next level. I think the principal realized that as well. I guess he hadn't expected us to respond the way we did. I think he originally thought we were just going to put our heads down in shame and quietly follow him to his office. Then, I guess he thought he was going to physically keep us from leaving the school property. I reckon that whatever was going through that brain of his didn't work out as he had originally planned. Although, his plans weren't the only ones that had changed. Both of us showed up as we were supposed to and were ready to start our three days of SDC. Just like everyone else out there that morning smoking, we were just trying to get in as many drags off a cigarette as we could before we were locked away the rest of the day. Why did he have to try and shame us and belittle us like he did? There're ways to go about things, and then there's ways to go about things. I guess he picked the wrong way.

The principal nervously said, "I'm calling the police." I couldn't believe it. We both responded simultaneously, "Fuck you!" It was actually quite funny. "Call the police, muthafucker," Christian said, grinning. Smiling, I said to Christian, "Let's get the fuck out of here." I was smiling because, at that point, I felt we won. The principal was left with the only threat he had, which was calling the police. And I was smiling because I thought the whole situation was fuckin badass. Two sixteen-year-olds just told the high school principal to fuck off while being threatened with the police and physically having to force our way out of the school. Ya see what I'm saying? The whole situation lasted about three minutes, but what a three-minute rush that was. As we were walking off, the principal thought it would be good to threaten us one more time with calling the police. We both just started laughing—as we were lighting our cigarettes.

As we got to Hickey Park, we started wondering what we were going to do. It's not like we had a cell phone we could use to call someone to pick us up. As we debated the long walk to Christian's house, wouldn't you know it: the police arrived. Hickey Park was off school property, so we weren't worried about that part, but I didn't know if what we just did was illegal or not. The principal said he was going to call the police. But I wasn't sure if he was just saying that to scare us or if he was saying that because what we did as minors was illegal. Turned out, we didn't do anything illegal. The cop was just checking on us to make sure things were alright. He was actually cool. I don't normally say that about cops, but this guy was okay. He asked that we don't go back on school property the rest of the day. That wasn't going to be a problem. We told him we were going to Christian's house. He told us to be careful and left. Like I said, he was a pretty nice guy. Another cool part of that situation is that we didn't have a ride and were going to start walking to a payphone so we could call Christian's mom, but then this car came pulling in after the cop left. It was Heath! He said someone had told him what had happened, so he left school, picked us up at the park, and took us to Christian's. It was so awesome! After all that chaos, one of our boys had us taken care of. Kick ass!!

When we showed up the next day, we both received two extra days of SDC, which gave us a total of five days apiece. Of course, Christian didn't make it past the first fifteen minutes—when we were told what we had to write and how much we had to write before we were able to sit down. He left and went back to the house. Put it this way, I was standing for almost two hours before I was able to sit down. Christian ended up coming back the next day and did his time and completed SDC a day after I did. That was the last time I got SDC that year, but it wouldn't be the last time. Another thing that was certain: I was done participating in school, for damn sure.

It was about this time when I met Jacob and Dane. Jacob and Dane were cousins and were childhood friends of Christian. Jacob was eighteen and had already dropped out of school. Dane was the oldest out of all of us, twenty or twenty-one at the time. Jacob and Dane had the same mindset as the rest of us: fuck the world. Get fucked up. And do fucked up shit. Along with Christian, Jacob and Dane were two other people you didn't fuck with; they were well known in the community and loved to have a good time. It only took the first introduction, and there was no separating the three of us. I say the three of us because it was Christian, Jacob, and I that did the extracurricular activities together. You know, the hardcore fun. Donovan did also, but he didn't run the streets with us. He didn't really have to. Afterall, he had an entire house to himself. No worries, we'll get into that shortly.

Jacob took to me quick, like Christian had. There weren't a lot of hardcore muthafuckers in the area like them, and when they met me, there was an immediate connection. We were like-minded folks. Christian and Jacob took to me so well because I was part of what they considered to be a well-off family. In Russellville, well-off people would usually not have anything to do with folks like Christian and Jacob, much less be getting fucked up like they did. They couldn't believe someone could live in the house and neighborhood that I lived in and still have the same thoughts and like the same things that they did. Don't get me wrong, they liked Walter also, but over the next year or two nobody liked Walter—because he became a dick. He was an asshole. A big asshole!

Eventually, everyone just tolerated Walter, especially Jacob, Christian, Dane, Donovan, and Liam (Liam shows up later. I met him through Christian). In fact, most of the time, Jacob, Christian and Dane would put Walter in his place when he tried bullying me or acting like a dick. I was weak in the beginning and had lost the ability to stand up for myself. For some reason, Walter seemed so large and scary at the time, but as time went on, that changed. I guess it took watching Christian or Jacob stand up for me before I found my heart. What an awesome thing to do, standing up for someone getting treated badly. Christian, Jacob, and Dane may have belonged to the "unders," but one thing they were all about among each other was respect and honor. Well, respect and honor for those they considered friends. They couldn't stand bully muthafuckers.

Anyway, Jacob, Christian, and I started hanging out daily. One of the first nights we were all out together we had been drinking heavily and were on our way up to Donovan's. We had this other guy with us that we were dropping off somewhere along the way. He was in the same grade as Christian and me, and he had asked earlier that day at school if he could get a ride somewhere. Well, apparently, Jacob didn't like this guy. We didn't know at the time that Jacob didn't like him.

So, there we were, making our way to Crow Mountain where Donovan lived. Walter was driving. Jacob, Christian, and I were in the backseat, and that other guy was riding up front because we were dropping him off right quick anyway. We were laughing and having a good ol' time when the guy that Jacob didn't like started laughing with us for the same reason, which really didn't involve him; it was about something we had been doing a few hours earlier, before he was with us. That guy started laughing and agreeing with what we were talking about, like he had been there with us the whole time or something. All of a sudden, from the back seat, Jacob slapped the shit out of him in the back of the head and shouted, "Not you, muthafucker!" You can imagine the awkward silence that followed. That guy's only defense was to keep laughing as if Jacob were joking. That made things even more awkward because Jacob didn't like that. When Jacob was drunk, you should tread lightly around him—unless you were close to him. Needless to say, that guy didn't make it to his destination. Walter pulled over and let that guy out. Christian had made the comment that we had better pull over. He knew Jacob was about to beat that guy to death. Turned out, that guy had been dating one of Jacob's cousins and had been abusing her. I guess you could say that Jacob was telling him that it was over and that he better leave his cousin alone. After that night, that guy was never seen again in any of our circles.

A couple of weeks later, Walter and I started looking for some acid. I asked Christian if he knew where to get any. He asked Jacob, who then pointed us to Dane. Of course, Christian already knew Dane because the three of them grew up together. So, Christian sent Dane to our house to drop off the acid. We were told to meet him at the top of the hill in our neighborhood because Dane wasn't getting out of the car—especially in that neighborhood. It was to be a drop-and-go deal. Hell, we were lucky he was even giving us the time of day. The only reason he gave us the time of day was because Jacob and Christian vouched for us. Looking back at it, I think Dane wanted to lay eyes on us because he'd heard about us from Jacob and Christian. I'm sure he was feeling out the situation. Little did I know that it would be the beginning of a new friendship.

This old beat-up car pulls up to the top of our hill, and Dane is in the passenger seat. I had no idea who was driving him and still don't.

"What's up," Dane said. He reached out of the car, dropped the acid in Walter's hand, and I handed him the money. "Alright, appreciate it," Dane said. Then they drove off. That was it. That was the first time I met Dane. I can't remember taking the acid or if that acid was any good. That's not the point. The point is that Christian, Jacob, Dane, and I started kicking it. About a year later, the summer turned out to be an acid fest. (We'll get to that later.) Dane was the hookup. Actually, Dane was the hookup for most things, as you'll see shortly.

We were partying at Donovan's place ever since his parents had left the state. Keep in mind that all of this was happening within the first year of us being in Russellville. Like I said earlier, I moved my drums over to Donovan's so we could practice there without being bothered. After word got out that Donovan's parents were gone—and that there was a nice house with a pool table and a swimming pool up on a mountain—well, it was on. We had parties there every weekend. We didn't even have to invite people. They would just show up. If I wasn't at home sleeping or at school fucking off my education, I was at Donovan's.

One time on a Friday night, we were getting ready to party at Donovan's. Walter said he had invited a few people over to hang out with us that night. Donovan and I didn't think much of it because one of us was always inviting new people to come kick it with us.

We didn't invite just anyone. We would invite people we thought were cool and safe to hang out with. I say we because Donovan and his brother, Jaxton, had given us permission to pretty much do whatever we wanted. For example, I didn't have to knock when I came over. We didn't have to ask for something to eat. We would just eat. We didn't have to ask to stay the night. We would just crash. See what I'm saying? Donovan and Jaxton trusted me and knew I wouldn't bring shady people into the environment, at least not intentionally. Christian was a big help in this category because he lived in Russellville his whole life and pretty much knew everyone, and everyone knew Christian. He would have been able to tell us right away if someone didn't need to be there.

Anyway, we were getting ready to go to the liquor store to get supplies for the evening. Heath and his ol' lady at the time, Betty, had come over to give us a ride.

A quick note about Betty: she was one of the sweetest people I ever met. How she had hooked up with Heath I never understood. That's not anything against Heath or Betty. It's just that they were opposites. She was in her first semester of college, and Heath was in his senior year at high school. Regardless, it didn't matter because they loved each other and were about to have a kid. Betty liked to have a good time also, but she was much more responsible about it than the rest of us were. She was a voice of motherly love and reason. Obviously, she wasn't drinking with us because she was pregnant, but she loved being with Heath and hanging out, nonetheless.

So, Donovan, Heath, Betty, and I jumped in Betty's car to go to the liquor store. We agreed that Walter would stay behind to wait on people showing up. We pulled into Blackwell, and, as always, we picked up as much alcohol as we could. We would always try to get enough not only to get us through the party but to last through the week as well.

Russellville is in Pope County; it was and still is a dry county. The closest place for us was Blackwell, and that was about fifteen to twenty minutes away. We would get as much as we could every time we went. Although, stocking up rarely worked. We usually did a good job of destroying ourselves and pushing the limits on every occasion.

As we left Blackwell, Donovan and I immediately dipped into our goodies, starting with a liquor called Cisco.

If you're not familiar with that drink, in the early-90s it was causing some concern because people were dying and going into chaotic and violent episodes from it. I guess folks were mistaking it for wine coolers because it was kind of sweet and fruity. If you drank too much of it, you would be subjecting yourself to possible alcohol poisoning or even worse. In fact, the federal government had to get involved. They either made the company change the formula, change the labeling, or both. I'm pretty sure they had to change the labeling, letting people know it wasn't a wine cooler. Heath had actually introduced us to it. It was cheap and effective. It would fuck you up! You could get a twenty-five-ounce bottle for two or three bucks. Donovan and I took a liking to it for a short time.

By the time we hit the Russellville exit, coming back from Blackwell, we were both done with our bottles. Yes, we bought ourselves one each to get us started. Can you believe that shit? A sixteen and an eighteen-year-old were drinking this shit down like it was nothing. Well, it was nothing. Like I said, that just got our evening started. Yes, at sixteen I was a social alcoholic. We all were. That summer we would become full-blown, but we'll get to that later. As we're pulling down Donovan's driveway with a car full of goodies, we notice something odd. Ya see, Donovan's driveway was long. It was about one hundred yards long before you got to the house, and as soon as we turned into his driveway and got about twenty-five yards down, we see car after car lined up alongside the driveway—going all the way down to the house. "What the fuck?" Donovan asked. Heath just started laughing. I was thinking what Donovan was thinking and reading his behavior. He wasn't mad, just shocked, surprised, and confused. Walter said he was inviting a few people over, not the whole fuckin town. Somehow, Walter had instructed people to not park in the actual driveway in front of the house, which is where we pulled into, and Donovan frantically exited the vehicle. Walter was standing there smiling, "I'm not sure what happened. Don't be mad, bro." "I said a few people—what the fuck!" Donovan said, grinning. I just smiled and followed Donovan into the house to see who the fuck was there. Some of the people there we knew, but most we didn't. There were people everywhere. The living room, bedrooms, pool room, kitchen, and outside were packed with muthafuckers. It was quite hilarious. There must have been seventy-five to a hundred people there. That may not sound like a lot of people, but for a house party in Russellville, it was pretty epic. I was quickly assigned a role to help keep people out of the bedrooms. We didn't want people in the bedrooms doing shit that only the select few were allowed to do. When Christian showed up and was assigned the role of keeping people in order, there wasn't much left to do at that point. If Christian said to keep your shit together, then you kept your shit together and didn't fuck shit up or cause problems. In fact, one of Donovan's old childhood friends from Texas came to live with him. His name was Connor. With Christian and Connor keeping watch over things, it was all good.

Connor became one of the brothers. It took him a while to adjust to the rest of us. Well, not me so much as Christian and Jacob. Mainly it was Jacob. Christian really never had a problem with him. Christian just had to make sure that Connor knew that it didn't matter that he was bigger than himself—that he would fight whoever, whenever. Although, whenever Jacob got drunk, unless it was me or Christian, Jacob had a problem with everyone. I had to stand my ground with Jacob when I first met him. There really wasn't much to it. Jacob was pushing this girl around I dated at the time, and I had to get in-between him and her. He said a few drunk things trying to engage me, one of which was, "Yinz want some?" That translates to, "Do you want some?" I just laughed because it was the first time I ever heard the word you *pronounced that way, which I think helped break the immediate tension because Jacob started laughing, too. Plus, Christian had told him to stop, which helped the situation as well. However, Jacob's first interaction with Connor got physical. Yes, Jacob was drunk. I can't even remember what was said to piss Jacob off. The next thing you know, Jacob took a swing at Connor. It was nothing for Connor. Connor blocked the attempted hit, and suddenly Jacob was in a full-nelson with Connor telling him to calm down. I couldn't believe it. Not only did Jacob try to punch Connor, but Connor didn't even try to hit back. He just put Jacob in that full nelson and wouldn't let go until Jacob decided to calm down, which took about thirty seconds. Usually, when someone tries to punch someone else and misses, the other person comes in swinging, not grabbing them, telling them to calm down. That was Connor. He was actually one of the responsible ones. I say one of the responsible ones because—besides Betty—he was the only other one that actually gave a fuck. He was a voice of reason for the rest of us. It's not that he didn't like to have a good time, but he did it responsibly. And since Betty only showed up here and there, Connor was a good person to have around so the rest of us fuck-ups could keep doing what we did best: have a good time! Connor didn't do drugs. He only drank, and I think that's why I actually took to Connor so quickly. He reminded me of how I had been only a couple of years earlier and how I still liked to think of myself: as rational, loving, and with common sense. The rest of us had those qualities, but we just kicked them to the side for the most part. Connor kept those qualities, which was no small task for the rest of us to be around. I would like to think our behavior was caused only from the drugs and lifestyle we were living, but that isn't the truth. I'm sure the drugs and lifestyle had something to do with it, but the fact-of-the-matter was that we just didn't want those qualities in our lives at that time. We enjoyed doing and selling drugs. We just wanted to keep getting fucked up and having a good time.*

The partying at Donovan's continued pretty aggressively over the next couple of months—then tragedy struck. As usual, I had gone over to Donovan's after school to practice. He got out of his classes early from the high school and would come to the junior high to wait for me to get out. Although, by the time his parents left the state, Donovan decided to drop out of high school. Nonetheless, he would still get me after school. Anyway, we always practiced for a couple of hours, and then he would take me home. Since the day I had met Donovan, whenever we would meet up or say goodbye, we would always shake hands or hug. You know, show love. We all did it and still do. I remember that the sun had just gone down when we pulled up to the front of my house. Only a tiny sliver of light from the sun was penetrating the overcast sky. It was that tiny sliver of light that demanded my attention. I gave it none. Instead, I reflected on the darkness and gloom that was consuming me. When I think back on it, it was quite appropriate. Our lives were about to change. Where there was once light, now darkness. For whatever reason, I didn't shake Donovan's hand as I was getting out of his truck. I wasn't mad at him; as usual, we had a good afternoon playing music together. And for some reason I was in a foul mood by the time we pulled up to my house. Random teenage anger, I guess. I don't know. There was only one other time after this situation that I didn't show love, and that was when I moved to Tulsa. That's neither here nor there at the moment. Besides, we'll get to Tulsa shortly. As I got out of the truck, I said, "Alright bro, we'll see ya tomorrow." He just looked at me like I had forgotten something or like we had been fighting, like we were still trying to heal from words that were spoken. He waved his hand and said, "Alright man, see ya tomorrow." He drove off, and I walked inside. Do you think it bothered me? It did. I remember that as I was walking inside, I had asked myself why I didn't show him love.

Nonetheless, I didn't, and that was that. I walked inside and started grabbing something to eat.

Meanwhile, Donovan had made his way back to his house. About thirty minutes later, Heath came busting through the door saying that Betty was in the car about to have their baby and asked if Donovan and Connor would like to ride to the hospital with them. I know what you're thinking: why the fuck would Heath take the time to pick Donovan and Connor up in the middle of Betty going into labor? Well, that wasn't the original plan. Heath and Betty were already on their way to Donovan's to hang out for a while, and as they were coming down the driveway, Betty's water broke. As crazy as Heath was, I guess he thought, "fuck it. They were already there—might as well see if the guys wanted to ride along." So, that's what happened. Donovan and Connor wasted no time and jumped in the car, which was Betty's car, and they all drove off to the hospital. As they got into town, they were driving down Arkansas Avenue, and I'm assuming they were going to cut across Parkway to get to the hospital, as that would have been quicker, and as they got to the Parkway and Arkansas Avenue intersection, a car pulled out in front of them from a grocery store parking lot. Not having anywhere to go and trying to avoid the collision, Heath veered left into the opposite lane to try and miss the car. Unfortunately, a truck was already in that path, and it immediately smashed into the passenger side of the car—where Betty and Donovan were sitting. The impact killed Betty instantly and almost did the same to Donovan. Thankfully, Heath and Connor walked away. The person that pulled out in front of them was never located. They fled the scene. The person driving the truck that hit Heath was heartbroken. Obviously, it wasn't their fault. One minute they're driving down the road, and the next thing they know they're hitting a car that came out of nowhere. The only fault to be had was the motherfucker who fled the scene. To this day, no one knows who that was.

Walter and I got word of the accident shortly after it happened. I have no idea how we got that info. It's not like we had cell phones back then. Maybe Connor called, or maybe it was Heath who called us. I'm not sure. For some reason, I want to say it was some random person who knew all of us, who saw it go down and knew we would want to know and called our house to tell us. All I know is that we're sitting there watching TV, and the phone rings, and Walter picks it up, and that's how we got the news of the accident. It was about nine at night. We rushed out the door and hauled ass to the hospital to figure out what was going on. We didn't know Betty was dead at this point or, for that matter, the condition of anyone involved. We were just told that there was an accident, that people were taken to the hospital. We were there within ten minutes. As we walked into the emergency room, Heath walked up to us and said that Betty had been killed. I couldn't believe it. It seemed as though I went deaf at that point and couldn't hear anything around me. I guess I was just trying to process what I had just been told. I remember asking for clarification, not because I didn't *hear* what Heath just said but because I couldn't *believe* what he just said. I asked for clarification, trying to make sense of it, "Betty is dead?" My next questions were, "Where is Donovan? Where is Connor?" Heath, with a look of defeat on his face, stated that Donovan wasn't doing so good and that Connor was calling Donovans' parents. He went on to explain what had happened. By the time I came out of this foggy, confused, unorganized moment—and my brain had finally processed everything—it was apparent that Heath was done explaining what went down. The look on his face told me there was nothing else to be said. He was just looking at me, waiting for me to respond. Nothing was said. What could I say? For some reason, I don't remember seeing Heath the rest of the night. Maybe he was there, but I can't remember. I do know that he was in complete turmoil and grief. Maybe he resided with his family the rest of the night or went home. Whatever the case, I couldn't imagine how he must have felt at that point. Pain? Anger? Guilt? Hate? Complete hopelessness? All the above? I know that's what I was feeling. I know something else too: that night took something out of Heath, and it was never to return. That something was love. He was still crazy and was always having a good time, but there was an attitude and behavior change. He lost the woman he loved and his child. I think his goal became what ours was: fuck it all off and keep going. I didn't blame him.

At some point during the chaos, I heard Donovan screaming in pain behind the ER doors where the doctors were working on him and asking him questions to figure out what all was wrong with him. Walter and I decided to wait outside for a while so we could smoke.

Besides, I didn't want to hear my friend screaming in pain any longer. When we were outside smoking, people brought Betty's body out to take to the morgue or funeral home. I'm not sure, but they were taking her somewhere. She was in a body bag, and we knew it was her from the huge bump in her belly—from the baby. I broke down once again. I was also pissed that they were being so slow about putting her in the transport vehicle. It was like they were torturing us. I said something to Walter, but he told me to calm down, that they were trying to let us view her one last time before they took her away. They knew who we were because we were crying and saying bye to her as they rolled her away. Maybe Walter was right. Regardless, it was the last thing I wanted to see. I threw my cigarette out and went back inside to wait for the status of Donovan.

After a few hours of surgery, the medical staff finally let us go back. They would only let one or two go back at a time, so Connor went first. He was back there about five minutes and came out crying. Walter and I went back next. When I laid eyes on him, I was shaking and in tears. That was the first time I had ever seen anything like that. There were tubes and wires coming out of him everywhere. I didn't know what to do. A nurse said to go ahead and touch him, talk to him, to let him know we were there. I rubbed his head and arm and told him that everything was going to be alright and that I loved him. That was about all I could handle before I lost it. I had only experienced trauma like that one other time, in sixth grade when one of my buddies took a shotgun and killed himself. I wasn't sure what to do or how to act back then, and I didn't know what to say or how to act at that moment either. One of my best friends was lying there lifeless with massive amounts of injury. Sure, we had only known each other less than a year, but like I said, we took to one another very quickly. All of the brotherhood did. It was like we were all soul mates. We were all supposed to be together, as we still are today. Needless to say, Walter and I got the fuck out of there. As I was walking out, I saw the doctor that had done all the work on Donovan, and I asked him what the overall scenario was. He told me his condition was not good and that he was in poor shape. It didn't take a doctor to tell me that shit, but as I later realized, they couldn't really tell us anything because none of us were immediate family. I can't remember exactly all the injuries he had, but they were significant. Put it this way, it took right at a month, or a little over before he was released.

Heath was nowhere to be seen at this point, and it was about one in the morning, so Walter, Connor, and I bailed out. As stated earlier, Connor was living with Donovan, so we drove him to the house. On the way there, Connor told us that Donovan's parents would be there the next day. We just kind of looked at each other and knew that it was going to be a long night. As soon as we got to Donovan's, we divided up the tasks and went to cleaning. Let me tell you, there was a lot to be done. The house was a fuckin mess. What would you expect with teenagers left to their own devices, especially teenagers on drugs? We cleaned for hours. It was about five or six in the morning when we finished. Well, we thought we were finished, as finished as teenage eyes thought were finished, but the reality was that the house needed much more work. Fuck, compared to what it looked like when we started verses when we finished, we thought we had done a good job of concealing the evidence from the past few months of debauchery. That wasn't the case.

Betty's funeral was within the first week she died. I didn't mention this earlier, but she actually picked me up from school a few times. She was a really sweet person. Did this just get awkward? Look, there's not a whole lot to say. Betty wasn't what I'd consider a real close friend, but close enough that I liked her and enjoyed her company. Close enough that I would pay my respects at her funeral. However, I never went back to visit her after that day. I don't know why. As of writing this, I still don't know why I've never gone back to see her. I do know that she didn't deserve what happened. I hope her family and friends were able to move on. Whatever the fuck that means. How do you move on from losing a child or close friend? Well, I'll tell you how in a little while.

Heath will also exit this story for now, but he will show back up later. He was still around here and there for the next year or so, but he slowly faded out of the circle and started doing his own thing, which was fine because the relationship had run its course—for everyone.

Over the next month or so, I would visit Donovan regularly. After about a week, he was able to talk. Of course, he asked about Betty, and no one would tell him that she had passed. The doctors wouldn't let us. Smart. Everyone just told him that everyone was fine. Although, I'm sure he figured it out on his own before he was officially told. I mean, for fuck's sake, everyone that was involved in the accident was coming to see him regularly, except Betty. He was hurt, not brain dead. Donovan came home after a month or so. I was really excited! There was an adjustment period for him, obviously. There was also an adjustment for his mom and dad. They could finally express how disappointed they were in all of us. Hell, after he got home, we weren't even allowed back at Donovan's house for at least the first two weeks. Donovan finally demanded to see his friends, and we were allowed there for about an hour at a time. Finally, his parents just gave in after they realized there was no getting rid of us. I say us—it was mainly me.

As the healing progressed and summer rolled in, well, the fun was just getting started. Donovan's family sued someone over the accident, and it ended up that Donovan got a little over $100,000. He bought an RT twin-turbo Dodge Stealth, a new guitar, and an amp. We finally started playing again! Although, we were back at my house in my parents' garage. That was fine. I was just happy Donovan was back and that we were playing music. Thus, ended that chapter in our lives. That run was officially over. It was time to get into new situations.

3   THE MADNESS BEGINS

The summer of '91 was a drunk summer. Donovan was home and healing nicely, and the rest of us were out of school for the summer. For some reason it was really dry in Russellville that summer. When I say dry, I mean there was no weed to be found. The weed we did find was homegrown bullshit. It got the job done, but it wasn't what we were used to. I think that whole summer we found all of an ounce. That sucked! And when I say we, I mean me, Jacob, Christian, and Walter. Donovan didn't do much that summer. We went to his house now and then, but he didn't feel like going out much at first, and with his parents back it was hard to do any real visiting. Plus, Donovan wasn't ready to get things going again on account that he almost died. So, we decided to drink our summer away—we drank and drank and drank. By the end of the summer, we were drinking no less than a fifth of whiskey a day. That doesn't even take into consideration all the beer we drank. We pretty much hung out at Christian's pond the whole summer or drove around with Lizzy. Ah yes, Lizzy. Lizzy had been around for most of the previous school year. I haven't mentioned her because she hasn't really been a significant part of the story yet. Jacob started dating Lizzy that summer. I don't even think it lasted past the summer. Lizzy came from a very rich family. Jacob did not. Nonetheless, the union took place. It wasn't a good union. Jacob was abusive to Lizzy. Actually, we were all abusive to Lizzy. I have no idea why she put up with our shit for so long. She was a sweet girl and didn't deserve the abuse. I never physically abused her, but I did verbally. Walter and Christian were the same. Regardless, she would just come back around to hang out with us. There were many times we drove down the road in her car throwing out her cassette tapes because we considered them to be bullshit music. She must have replaced her Chicago album at least twice because—if she was playing that bullshit—that bullshit got thrown out the fuckin window and replaced with some Ozzy or Mötley Crüe.

No offense to the band Chicago. We were young and stupid. Chicago is actually a badass band that I wish I would have taken the opportunity to see live.

Pretty mean, right? Yes, it was. We didn't give a fuck. Hell, she paid for a lot of our alcohol, which is why I think we allowed her to keep coming back. Nobody had money, and if we did it was already going to drugs and alcohol. It didn't matter. She was with us to have a good time and get fucked up, and fucked up was what she got.

We were at our house one day getting fucked up while the parents were at work. Jacob got so abusive that day that Lizzy called one of her friends over to beat his ass. Her name was Brenda. Brenda was one of those chicks you didn't fuck with, and for some reason Jacob was afraid of her. I've never seen Jacob back down from anyone except Brenda. She never got her hands on him, but if she had, it would have been a sight to see. Shortly after, Lizzy and Jacob separated. It didn't matter because she would still come and hang out. Walter actually started fucking her after that. Not dating. Just fucking. Hell, she consented to it, so I guess she didn't mind getting fucked and left all the time. If there wasn't another woman around that Walter had the opportunity to fuck, then he would just turn to Lizzy as backup. Fuck that shit!

Anyway, like I was saying—we drank a lot that summer. We had many nights at Christian's pond with party balls or kegs, good music, and women. Speaking of kegs: what happened to having keg parties? You just don't hear about them these days. We'd go to keg parties all the time. That shit was a blast! And what ever happened to cruising? Man, we went into town all the time and just cruised. Shit, if you weren't at a kegger, you were cruising. Good times, baby! By the end of the summer, we would have withdrawals if we weren't drinking. I would get very anxious and even violent and angry until I drank something. But as the summer came to an end, the dry spell ended as well—thankfully! It seemed easier to stop drinking as much once we had some weed. Shit, we had to put the whiskey away for a few weeks just so we could get our shit together as school started back.

A quick side note: At some point during that summer break, a couple more people entered my life who are still a part of it today: Robert and Kelly. They were actually part of the crew well before me. They grew up with Christian, Liam, Jacob, and Dane. The two of them only came around a few times at first. They had been doing their own thing. I met both of them through Christian. Robert actually came up to my parents' house when Christian was there one day. We smoked out. That was the first time I met Robert. I met Kelly a couple weeks after meeting Robert. He randomly showed up at Christian's place one night. We smoked out. Luckily, both Kelly and Robert started hanging out all the time after I met them.

As Christian and I started sophomore year—and Walter started his junior year—we were ready for fun. Not school. Fun. By that time, we were sitting good with our peers. Everyone knew who we were and knew who to get with to have a good time. The first year of high school was pretty laid back. Not a lot happened besides the same old partying and getting fucked up. Although, by the spring of '92, things were starting to take a different turn.

Liam had started hanging out with us full time. Like I said earlier, I met Liam through Christian one day after school. Liam smoked us out. I finally got my driver license, which meant none of us had to depend on Walter for a ride any longer. (I got the car Walter was driving, and dad and mom got him an old Honda Prelude to drive around.) I also got a job washing dishes at an Italian restaurant. Dane started hanging out with us more, which meant that—between him and a few others we knew—we were good to go on weed. We were able to start dealing to others and put a little cash in our pockets. Mainly, we were able to get most of our weed for free, which was of greater importance than money. On top of all of that, Donovan and I were pretty much playing full time again, and he was back partying with us. Oh, and his parents left the state again for work. So, you know what that meant.

Of course, before Donovan's parents left, they gave strict instructions that nobody come over and, especially, to not have any parties. In order to help facilitate those instructions, Donovan's brother, Jaxton, moved back home. He had dropped out of college. Connor had gone back to Texas at some point but returned around the summer of '92. At first, we were only allowed to go into the bottom part of the house, which was basically a huge studio apartment. It was where we practiced, and it was Donovan's bedroom. But, after a while, Jaxton stopped acting like a warden and let people like me, Walter, and Christian into the main part of the house. However, Jaxton wasn't there long and moved back out, which meant we had the house to ourselves again—just in time for summer, which leads me to the next situation.

I think it was the first week of summer break in '92 when Walter, Christian, Dane, and Jacob decided to go to Little Rock to hang out. It had been nearly to a year since anyone had been down there. Donovan and I decided we weren't going on this run, and Liam had gone on the road with his dad for most of that summer.

When the four of them got to Little Rock, they drove to the dam. All the old spots in Little Rock had been compromised with too much heat around. Heat meaning the cops. Hundreds of people would go to the dam to hang out and get fucked up. Apparently, it was one of those nights where many people were there drinking and hanging out. Jacob and Christian had been before, but it was Dane's first time. All was going well until Dane spotted this hottie.

She had arrived with another guy. At the time, the only ones that didn't know that were Christian, Walter, Jacob, and Dane. According to all four of them, this guy looked like the biggest nerd on the planet: skinny, clean cut, with glasses. I'm not saying that someone who looks like that is a nerd, but, according to the guys, he looked like the character Waldo.

Dane decided that he wanted to dance with her. It's important to note that the hottie who Dane was going to dance with was standing in the vicinity of that nerdy guy. It's also important to note that Dane didn't dance. That meant he was drunk as shit. So, he started dancing with the girl, and, according to the guys, the girl was having a great time. They said she was smiling and laughing, like it was no big thing. Well, apparently, it was a big deal to the nerdy guy because the next thing you know, that nerdy, Waldo-looking guy used his beeper to send a message out.

Now keep in mind that Christian, Walter, Jacob, and Dane all have the same story about this whole situation. As they were telling it to me, each one would finish and add to the other one's story.

According to the guys, about fifteen minutes later, as Dane was dancing the night away, about five cars slowly pulled in. As the cars pulled in, Walter, Christian, and Jacob noticed everyone else moving out of the way.

Now, these weren't just ordinary people coming to enjoy the party. In fact, they were straight-up gangstas and thugs. These folks were coming to take care of business. The business they had on their agenda? Dane.

These folks got out of their cars, started walking toward Dane, and made a circle around him while he was dancing. Christian, Walter, and Jacob described it as the sea parting when these folks walked up. It seemed as though everyone knew what was about to go down, except Dane. At that very moment, Christian, Walter, and Jacob realized what was happening, but it was too late. About twenty people surrounded Dane. By the time Dane realized what was happening, they rushed him. Dane barely made it out with his life. Although, he did take some licks before getting out. Dane fought his way out of the vicious pack that encircled him and narrowly made his way into the woods surrounding the dam. Dane had managed to escape, but the vicious circle that once encompassed him had quickly turned its attention from Dane to Christian and Jacob. Walter, at that point, had made his way deep into the rest of the crowd to blend in and keep from getting attacked, hoping to appear as if he was just one of the regular people out there having a good time. Christian and Jacob, however, knew they were in trouble. They didn't blend themselves into the crowd like Walter had while Dane was being attacked.

Although, I don't know if Christian or Jacob would have been able to blend in with the rest of the crowd had they tried. They didn't look as if they belonged. It would have been easy to pick them out of the crowd.

As they got rushed, both Christian and Jacob took hits. Somehow, as Dane did, they managed to get the fuck out of there before it was way too late. They made their way to the woods as Dane did. Although, all three went in different directions. Walter never got recognized or attacked. It turned out that this nerdy, white guy was a somebody—affiliated with a gang or something. He may have not looked like much, but it was very evident that he was in good with some dangerous folks. The guys definitely learned a huge lesson that night. It's a lesson that everyone has come across at least once in their lives. Don't judge a book by its cover.

That nerdy white guy was no joke, and neither was the entourage he called in. Do you see what I'm saying? This guy was in so good and tight that all he had to do was page a motherfucker and people came rolling in five cars deep. It takes a lot of pull and power to have five cars full of Black Americans come rolling in to take care of what this guy needed. Black Americans with that kind of status wouldn't normally fuck with white guys like that unless deeper shit was going on. Do you see what I'm saying? That guy didn't say one thing to Christian, Walter, Jacob, or Dane. He just sent a page, and that's all it took. Dane and his buddies didn't even get a warning from that guy to leave his ol' lady alone. That's how this muthafucker was rollin. G status, my friend. Those folks in the car already knew who their target was when they pulled up. That's why—when they were done trying to get Dane—they went after Christian and Jacob. I suspect Walter would have had the same outcome had he not walked away when he did.

Walter immediately jumped in his car and drove off to look for everyone. He found Christian first. Christian said it only took about thirty minutes or so. It took three hours to find Dane and Jacob. They found Dane first and then Jacob. They were hiding, and nothing in the world was going to bring them out of hiding until they heard the calls from Walter and Christian. That was after three hours of looking. Needless to say, that was the last trip Dane and Jacob took to Little Rock. It didn't really matter, though, because the summer was about to get really good in Russellville, so there was no reason to go anywhere. Oh, and real quick, after that night, Dane was wanting to kick Walter's ass for doing what he did…which was, in Dane's eyes, "bailing out on them".

I'm not sure where it all came from, but the summer of '92 was a trip. Literally, a two-and-a-half-month trip. There was acid everywhere. I knew where we were getting our acid from, but I just wasn't sure where Dane's guy got it from.

You gotta understand, acid was one of those drugs that came around few and far between unless you knew someone who dealt it. And there weren't many people in our parts who knew anybody who dealt it. Not to mention, the time you would get for getting caught dealing acid surpassed most, if not all, other drugs at that time. Law enforcement didn't measure it in just quantity but in weight also. For instance, being caught with ten hits of acid (each hit containing about one hundred micrograms of LSD, at 0.05 grams including the paper) was considered trafficking. They would get you on having five grams of acid because they're also counting the weight of the paper the LSD is on. That's no less than five years in prison for a first offense. You see what I'm saying? It's bullshit. So, that's why it always amazed me when we would come across large quantities of that shit. I loved it, but I always wondered how the folks who made it or dealt it were able to be at peace knowing that their lives could be over with one bust. Of course, now that's the case with things like meth because it has become such an epidemic, which we'll get into later.

I don't remember the name of the acid we started our summer off with, but each of the hits were huge hits of acid. I would say each hit was damn near the size of two hits combined. Each hit had an image of a black ant on it. The shit was powerful. I didn't have a lot of experience with acid as to accurately compare it with other acid except the two times I had already tripped. But I can tell you that I've taken hundreds of doses since then, and I must say that it was some of the best acid. We were eating that shit like candy. Hell, it wasn't just us. It was everyone that liked to get fucked up and do fucked up shit.

Yes, I use that line a lot because it's one of my favorite lines from House of 1000 Corpses, but mainly because it describes the history of our drug induced lifestyle very well.

The first time I took it I ate two hits. Oh, goodness! It was me, Christian, Jacob, Donovan, and Walter. We started off going to

Blackwell, which, if you remember, was the liquor store for Russellville and surrounding areas. We had to make sure we had some cold beer for the night. Thankfully, we didn't drop until our way back from Blackwell. When I say thankfully, I mean it. We didn't get ten minutes down the interstate before someone said, "I'm getting fucked up." Meaning, they started feeling the effects of the acid. I don't remember who said that, and until that was said—besides the music that was playing—nobody was saying a fuckin thing, which is usually a good indication that you're about to get fucked up. As soon as it was said, all of us started dying laughing. That was absolutely a correct statement.

Keep in mind, from Russellville to Blackwell is about a fifteen to twenty-minute drive. We all dropped the acid as soon as we were driving out of the Blackwell parking lot. In our defense, acid usually doesn't start taking effect until about twenty to thirty minutes after you ingest it. And that's good acid. We were all of ten minutes down the road and feeling this shit. When I say we were feeling this shit, I mean we were already on the verge of full-on tripping.

By the time we got back into Russellville, we were frying. I'm talkin' melting. We were about a mile away from Christian's pond, and I told Walter to pull over and let me out. I couldn't take it anymore. I was frying my fuckin balls off. I was all of twenty minutes into my trip. I decided I would walk the rest of the way. We were on a busy highway. Cars were flying past us and shit. There wasn't even a shoulder to pull over to, but I didn't give a fuck. I had to go. "Shane, we're almost there. Just hold on a second," Walter said laughing. I responded in a panic, "Dude, you better pull this car over and let me the fuck out." He pulled over, and I jumped out and started walking. "See ya in a minute," Christian said, laughing hysterically. It was complete chaos in that car, and I had to get the fuck out of there. I don't even know how Walter was keeping the fuckin car on the road. As I made my way to the pond, Christian, Donovan, and Walter couldn't stop laughing. Jacob was already making a path around the picnic bench. He was frying so hard that all he did was walk a circle around the picnic bench the entire night and chew on the tip of his hair. For six to eight hours he did that. He made so many damn laps around that picnic bench that he literally created a path that no longer had grass. That's how intense that acid was. The visuals were wonderful! Every tree I looked at was breathing—literally taking breaths. Every tree I leaned on or walked up to seemed as though the branches and leaves were forming a blanket around me to keep me safe. It was a great night and the first trip of many that summer.

Keep in mind, the more often you trip, the more you have to take each time you want to trip. For example, when we would trip twice a week, we took two hits the first time. We would have to take three to four hits the second time just to put us where we were before. Otherwise, you'd get off, but it would be more of a body high with a nice visual clarity. There would not necessarily be any tripping to speak of. Although, having a good body high with nice visual clarity sounds like the state we should be in at all times.

Anyway, me, Jacob, Christian, and Dane decided to tie another one on, but that time I was the one in the driver's seat.

I had to learn really quickly how to drive fucked up and still maintain. That was the only thing that bothered me. Once I got my license, I was pretty much the driver everywhere. It was cool, though. I got fucked up for free and usually got my gas tank filled.

The four of us each took three hits. We had just left Christian's house and were down the road at the gas station picking up a few items. We had already dropped the acid at this point. Remember me telling you how fast the acid with the ant on it kicked in? This was the same stuff, and its potency had not been lost. We were probably fifteen minutes in, and as we were getting ourselves situated to get into the car, sirens and lights came out of nowhere. I think we all had a small heart attack at that point because the once intense yet chaotic silence became a fuckin nightmare. We froze and quickly looked behind us to find an ambulance hitting its lights and sirens. We looked like we had just got caught stealing because the abrupt sound and vivid visual display stopped us like a deer in headlights. What seemed forever was all of about five seconds. We finally turned back to one another, laughing in relief, and Christian said, "We need to get the fuck out of here." The silent agreement showed as we quickly and frantically got in the car and bailed out. Dane decided to take us out to the middle of nowhere so we could trip in peace. Although, as we were going to our destination, I realized we needed gas. Whoops! Of all the times I needed gas, this was the worst time to actually need gas. That meant I had to get out and pump and go inside and pay. You see what I'm saying?

By that time, we were forty-five minutes to an hour into our trip, and with three hits in my system, I was fuckin lit. It was all I could do to get us where we already were. Hell, twenty minutes earlier we were driving down the cruising strip just to trip on all the lights. Well, that was all fine and fun for the rest of the guys in the car, but for me it was a fuckin nightmare. I told them we had to get the fuck out of there because we were gonna die if we didn't. Shit, all I could see was a blurry rainbow of colors.

So, there we were, on our way to the middle of nowhere, but before we could get to nowhere, we needed gas in the car. "We should have got gas when we were at the other gas station," Jacob said. "Sorry, but it didn't really cross my mind at the time," I said. They just looked at me, smiling. I knew it was up to me because if they were at any level close to where I already was—and trust me that they were—then I was the muthafucker getting out, pumping, and going in to pay. "I'm not going to be able to do this," I explained. "We have to get the fuck out of here," Dane said with a panicked look on his face. Meanwhile, Jacob and Christian just sat there, chaotically laughing. "Fuck! I'll do it," I said. Looking back at Jacob and Christian, I said, "Thanks for the help, fuckers!" "Here's five," Dane said, handing me a five-dollar bill. Pumping the gas wasn't the issue because we were the only ones pumping gas. This gas station was on the outskirts of town. The problem was going in to pay for it. I pumped the gas and began my walk into turmoil.

Keep in mind, back in those days you didn't have to pay for gas up front at most places. I'm sure as much as we pumped and jumped over the years, we contributed to changing that.

As I walked up to the store, it became even clearer that I had no business being around anyone that wasn't already in the same state of mind as me. I turned away with my hands covering my face and started walking back to the car. Christian and Jacob were dying laughing at that point. "Shane, you have to go in and pay for the gas. They're gonna think we're trying to steal it," Dane said, yelling from the car, even more panicked than before. There was no way out of the situation. He was right. "Fuck it," I said to myself. I turned around and walked inside the store. The lights from inside the store were too much to handle. I felt like I was still on the cruising strip we were driving down earlier because I was blind and in complete chaos from the acid running through me. It wouldn't have been so bad, but there was already someone at the counter talking with the clerk. These two were talking like there wasn't someone behind them frying his balls off on three hits of acid. They were in no hurry to end their conversation. Meanwhile, every time I brought my head up to look around, the entire store moved. Tracers were flying all over the place. It was fuckin with me to say the least. I just stood there until those fucks finally let me come up to the counter. They had finally stopped talking at some point because I remember the sound of silence. The guy talking to the clerk finally moved to the side, indicating that he was telling me to come up to the counter. None of which processed immediately. I was tripping so hard that I was just looking around trying not to be obvious that I was tripping. Too late! As I glanced up a little, I could see they were both looking at me, waiting on me to do whatever I needed to do. So, as I walked up to the counter to pay for the gas, they started talking again. Then I heard the clerk say, "Hey bud." I didn't say a fucking thing. With my head down, I laid my five dollars on the counter and quickly walked out. As I was walking out the door, I was covering my eyes, trying to readjust them and my mind from the unnecessary encounter that had just fucked my entire world up. Of course, all three of the guys were in the car having a great fuckin time watching me struggle. I'm sure what they were seeing as they were watching me was a trip in and of itself. For Christ's sake, I had been standing in there for what seemed to be many minutes, so I could imagine they were wondering what was taking so long. In all actuality, the whole experience was all of thirty seconds. Nonetheless, that was the most intense thirty seconds I had ever experienced. Anyway, we got the fuck out of there and wound up on some backroads where there was no traffic and just woods surrounding us.

At some point, Dane suggested we go to what he and Jacob called the snake pit. It was a location that Dane and Jacob had found a while back. They would go fishing there. "The snake pit?" Christian asked. "It's a place Jacob and I go fishing," Dane explained. "And it's called the snake pit why?" I asked. "Because it's infested with snakes," Jacob said. We all just started laughing hysterically. We stopped off at Jacob's place to pick up some frog gigs that we would soon be using on snakes. However, on the way to Jacob's, the police started following us. We were about a mile from Jacob's when the pig got on our tail. We quickly pulled into Jacob's driveway and turned the car off. That fuckin pig drove by us, went across the street at a stop sign, turned his car off, and parked. That fuckin guy was just going to sit across from us and watch us. Fuckin pig! We got out of the car and sat in Jacob's backyard. The cop's bitch ass sat over there for about ten minutes and then left. Cops were always harassing muthafuckers back then. It's still the same today. Worthless fucks!

With that being said, they knew who we were. We had already had a couple of run-ins with them earlier in the summer. Jacob and Dane went to jail both of those times. It was all alcohol related, but encounters we had with them, nonetheless. Fuck tha police!!

After that bitch muthafucker left, we waited a little bit longer and then headed out to the pit. We pulled up to our location and had to walk about fifty yards to get where we were going. The sun was up by that time. We were all still feeling the effects from the acid but definitely not tripping any longer. We just had that wired and exhausted feeling from tripping the past eight hours. Things still had a small but unique clarity and visual. We just didn't have the actual intensity and visuals from a full-on trip. That was good because as we were walking up to the pond that Jacob and Dane fished out of from time-to-time, Jacob almost stepped on a snake. "I guess that's why it's called the snake pit," I said to Jacob. Then, all of a sudden, the ground within a fifteen-yard radius started moving. Literally moving. There were fuckin snakes all around us. I mean everywhere! These weren't just garden snakes. These muthafuckers were cottonmouths. I was thinking to myself, "Holy Shit! Why in the fuck would they come out here to fish?"

I don't think I moved the first five minutes we were there. Christian didn't either. He was standing right next to me. Meanwhile, Jacob and Dane were by the pond looking for a snake to get with one of those frog gigs. Jacob hit his mark and pulled one up. That muthafucker was mad! It was moving around, fiercely trying to get the sharp metal point out of its back, mouth open and hissing. Mad muthafucker, boy! Dane ended up pulling one in as well. They both tried to get a couple more but were unsuccessful. Christian and I just stood back and let them do their thing. Neither of us were about to try that shit. We found a safe spot and stood there and just watched. That shit was a trip. After frying our balls off all night, there we were, surrounded by poisonous snakes. What the fuck?! Good times!

Later that summer, Walter and I were sent down south for a couple of days. I'm talking past Pine Bluff. That's where the prisons were and still are located. The parents thought it a good idea to send us to my aunt Alesya. She ran the nursing department at Tucker Prison at the time. It was the parents' attempt to scare us straight.

We had been fucking up—a lot. I was barely going to school, and when I did, it wasn't like I was paying attention or anything. And, we had stopped abiding by the midnight curfew. If we showed up at all, we would just wait a few minutes and then go back out.

The prison officials agreed to let Alesya bring us into the facility for a day. You've seen those *Scared Straight* shows, right? This situation was like that, but a little more hardcore. The only thing we weren't allowed to experience was actually being behind bars with the inmates. That would have been illegal and, not to mention, unsafe. The inmates had one rule. They were not allowed to touch us. Everything else was fair game. We got down to my aunt's house around dinner time. She took us to get some grub. When we got back, we hung out for a while and went to bed.

A little bit about this aunt: You don't fuck with her. She doesn't take any shit. With that being said, she's cool as fuck. Laid back. I love her! She didn't give a fuck about us smoking weed. She just wanted to help my parents and us with preventative maintenance. Meaning, my parents didn't want us to get to the point where it was too late and we wound up dead or in prison.

We woke up the next morning early. It was five o'clock in the morning. At that point, the only time I had ever seen 5:00 a.m. was when I was still out partying. My aunt lived about ten minutes away from the prison. As we were walking up with my aunt to enter the prison, she said, "This is where we part ways." Walter and I just stood there confused. "Someone will come get you guys shortly and bring you in," my aunt said. So, there we were, outside of Tucker Prison standing by the gate and guard shack to get into the prison, and it's pitch black. Well, maybe not pitch black at that point. We could actually see the sun starting to come up. What we didn't know about were the mosquitos. My aunt thought it would be funny, good opener for us to experience the mosquitos. There wasn't anything funny about that shit. We got ate the fuck up! I mean ate up. The mosquitos down there were fucking horrible. Imagine being put in a room full of mosquitos and left there for almost two hours. I'm not talking about a few mosquitos. I'm talking about a room full of fucking mosquitos. That's what it was like waiting outside of the prison. By the time someone came to escort us in, Walter and I were already pissed. We'd had enough.

The guy who came to escort us was called The Warden. He was the guy in charge of all the guards and inmates. Whatever he said was law, and that was that. As we were walking in, we passed the barber shop and infirmary. The barber shop was run by inmates, and everyone, including guards, would get their hair cut there. My aunt worked in the infirmary, and the first thing we saw as we were walking past was a guy strapped to the table on his stomach under suicide watch. The inmate had tried killing himself because he couldn't protect himself from being raped. Therefore, he had to stay strapped to the bed until the doctors—there were only two doctors and a few nurses—said it was okay to release him. That's fucked up! Trying to kill yourself because you can't stop from getting raped? Fuckin horrible! We got to an area where we began to walk down a long and wide hallway. It was one of the areas where the barracks were. They weren't cells. There were barracks on both sides of the hallway, full of inmates. The Warden immediately started treating us like inmates. "Walk on the right side of the line against the wall and shut up," he said, forcibly. There must have been fifty to a hundred people in each barrack. Maybe more. As we approached where the barracks began, all the inmates were inside talking and doing whatever they do when they're locked up. They were pretty assertive and loud. By the time we got to the barracks and the inmates saw it was The Warden walking us down the hall, everyone stopped talking. I mean they shut the fuck up. None of the inmates were allowed to speak when The Warden was passing by. I looked on both sides, and no one was saying a fuckin thing. That's pretty hardcore when you have to shut the fuck up because The Warden is walking down the hall. The inmates were staring hard at me and Walter. They already knew Walter and I were coming that day. Across from a set of barracks was a guard sitting behind a podium. Next to the guard was a door that led down a short hall to The Warden's office. "You come with me," The Warden said to Walter. "You wait here," he said to me. The Warden took Walter to his office to talk, and I was stuck standing in the hall by this guard sitting behind his podium while the inmates proceeded to fuck with me. As soon as The Warden took Walter to his office the inmates went back to talking, yelling, and being rowdy. They were having a good time with me. Some were asking questions about what I was wearing and if that was the style. I was just wearing jeans and a tie-dyed t-shirt. They weren't the most popular or trendy clothes. Some of the inmates were asking me to turn around so they could see my ass. See what I'm saying? Most were just yelling and cussing at me, telling me how pretty I was, that I was gonna be a bitch when I got in, that I was gonna get my ass kicked when I got in, and all kinds of ghetto-ass prison shit. Most of the time I was just smiling, laughing, and shaking my head in disbelief. It was chaos. It was like being in a zoo, and I was the prey. It was a bunch of people acting like animals, thugs, bullies, and whatever other negative term one can think of to describe these people. I call a tomato a tomato. I don't call it a fuckin banana. Understand?

At one point, I was getting tired of the harassment and chaos and asked the guard a few feet away if there was somewhere else I could wait. That was a mistake. "Get away from me, and go stand by the wall like The Warden said, and shut the fuck up," the guard said. I looked at him like he had lost his fuckin mind. "You'll leave when The Warden says you'll leave," the guard said. All I could think of was that if we were in a different situation, that muthafucker would have been defending himself because those were fighting words as far as I was concerned. After I calmed down, I realized the guard was right; he was playing the role he was supposed to play. I wasn't there to be protected. I was there because I was fuckin up and needed to be shown how things were going to be if I ended up in prison. The Warden and the guards weren't there to be kind to us but to show us and teach us that prison life is fucked up, that we would be struggling every day to stay alive. I realized really quickly where I never wanted to end up. Fuck that place! Shortly after that, an inmate walked up to me. He was sent over to talk with me. "You Miss Alesya's nephew, right?" the inmate asked. "Yeah," I replied. "You think they playin' with you when they tell you to turn around?" he asked. "You think they playin' with you when they say you gonna be a bitch or that you gonna have to fight?" he asked. "They ain't playin' with you. This shit is real, man," the inmate said. I'd had enough at that point. "I don't give a fuck," I said in a smart-ass tone. "Oh, you don't give a fuck?" the inmate asked. "That's right," I quickly responded. "I don't give a fuck because I'm never gonna end up in this fuckin place," I said, angrily. "Oh yeah?" he asked laughing. "We gonna be waitin' on you, boy," the inmate said. "We gonna be waitin' on you. You a smart ass," the inmate said. I saw the guard give him the walk away nod out of the corner of my eye. As the inmate was walking away, he was mumbling something. I'm sure it had something to do with how lucky I was that I was a guest, otherwise I would have already been fighting and getting my ass kicked. I'm sure he wasn't used to a civilian talking to him like that, and had I really been being processed, my day would have consisted of defending myself. All the things you hear about prison are true. You're just another muthafucker in prison. You ain't special, and you sure as fuck have no one in your corner—short of joining a gang or some shit. Luckily, about five or ten minutes after that, Walter came out of The Warden's office and told me to go in. I sat there listening to The Warden tell me how I needed to get my life together and how that kind of life wasn't the road I wanted to go down. He would ask me questions about where I saw myself in a few years and what I wanted to do with my life. He was actually a pleasant guy. He didn't act like he did when we first met him. Of course, in front of others he had to be a hard ass. And, like I said earlier, he wasn't giving his time to coddle us. He was there to teach us a lesson, to try and talk some sense into us. Then, all of a sudden, he said something about my long hair. Everything was going fine up to that point.

You gotta understand something. The only thing that I thought I ever had going for me as far as looks was my hair. I know it seems retarded (That's right! I said it!), but my hair was and is badass. I'm only confident in saying that because over the years, whether it was said by guys or girls, I was always told how badass my hair was. I didn't pay much attention at first, but after a while I realized those people were absolutely right. My hair was badass! No matter how I wore or styled my hair, it worked for me.

The Warden asked why I had long hair. I couldn't believe he went there. What did that matter? "Why do I have long hair?" I asked, "I don't know. Why do you have short hair?" Before he could answer, I asked, "What the hell does that have to do with anything?" "You know what?" he said, "Alesya said it was Walter who was the stubborn one and that Walter was the one who needed the most realization, but after talking with him and you, I think it's you. I think you're the one whose gonna end up in here before your brother. You have a stubborn, smart-ass streak in you," he explained. "You don't want to listen, and you want to argue and do your own thing, and that's what got everyone out there locked up in here. I have no doubt that if you keep up the attitude you have now, I'll be seeing you in a few years. We're done here. Let's go," he said, "I wanna show you guys some other things."

He was absolutely right. I did continue to do my own thing and live the way I wanted, and it cost me. We'll get to that later. Oh, Walter cut his hair when we got home the next day. Little bitch!

So, the next place he took us was out to the fields. Actually, I think they referred to it as the farm, which was appropriate because they grew crops out there. The inmates were put to work during the day. Maybe not all of them, but a lot of them were. Walter and I were standing to the side as the guards were roll calling and assigning tasks to the inmates. Most of the guards were on horses, so, as the inmates are out in the field, the guards could keep a good watch on them to quickly recover them if someone ran off. After roll call and the tasks were assigned, we went over to a shop that was out in the field. At that point, The Warden went on with his duties, and one of the guards was assigned to me and Walter. This one inmate went up to the guard with a bag in his hand. The inmate said to the guard, "Here ya go." The guard responded, "I'll get that grill for ya." The guard showed us what was in the bag. It was what looked to be about a pound of weed. We just looked at each other like, "What the fuck?!" The guard just smiled. He said something about favors working both ways. I don't know what the guard did with that shit afterwards. I guess they smoked it. Who knows? From that situation, we moved on to where the trustees lived, which was in a house built by the inmates on the prison grounds past the farm area. The trustees actually lived in this house and wore regular clothes. There were three or four of them. Maybe five. If I remember correctly, they were all lifers. It was a nice house considering they were in prison. The trustees did a lot of work with and for the guards. One of the trustees had his arm bandaged up. He explained to us that it was his turn to help train the dogs. That meant running out past the prison grounds as if one was trying to escape, hiding and doing whatever it took to try evading the dogs. Needless to say, the inmate didn't win that game. The dogs wouldn't normally attack unless given the command, but one of the dogs was in training and ended up attacking the inmate. The guard just smiled and said, "We broke the dog of that." The inmate just kind of grinned. I was thinking to myself, "I guess it beats living in a cell and sharing a shower with a bunch of convicts."

Just a side note on those dogs. They were vicious. They were bloodhounds, and they were mean. Hell, when we walked up to the pins where the dogs were kept, they were barking and going nuts. The guard just taunted them by kicking at the gate and laughing. I've seen a lot of mean ass dogs in my time, and these bloodhounds were at the top of the list for being mean and vicious.

What seemed like days had only been a few hours. They took us back to the main barracks where we had started and just left us there for a couple more hours. Inmates would randomly walk up to us and talk for a bit and then move on. They all knew who we were and knew my aunt was responsible for us being there. Inmates would mention her often as they talked to us. I actually didn't realize it until that day, but the inmates didn't fuck with my aunt. In fact, they respected her and were nice to her. Of course, she and her crew were the ones who brought prescriptions to the inmates. If an inmate fucked with my aunt or any of her people, guess what that inmate wouldn't receive. So, the inmates were kind and showed respect to her. After the nightmare was over, which was about five or six hours later, my aunt came out to escort us back out and take us to her place where the parents would pick us back up. My aunt knew I was pissed. "I'm sure you're angry at me right now, but it was important for you to see those things," she said. "I love you and don't want to see you in here," she said. At the time, it didn't matter what she said to me. I felt betrayed. The last person I ever thought would do something like that was my aunt. I didn't stay pissed at her for too long. I knew she was absolutely right. Like I said earlier, Walter cut his hair the next day and acted as if he was gonna get his shit together. I just went on about my business like it never happened. We continued our summer as we had started it, frying our balls off. Oh, in other news, I sold my Power Sonic drum set because I was going to invest in a new set. I had a couple hundred dollars saved already and was going to add that to what I got for the drum set, which was about $300. When I told my parents what I had done, they weren't even mad at me. In fact, dad said he was proud of me and would go in half with me on a new set. That was so awesome! I was really blessed. My second drum set was a seven-piece Pearl Export. It was black.

By the time school had started in the fall of '92, things had got aggressive. About two weeks into my junior year, me, Donovan, Connor, and a guy named Vaugn went to Blackwell to get some liquor. Connor was back from Texas. No one was twenty-one yet, so we had to get someone to buy our liquor. Usually, Connor or Donovan was able to buy, but the liquor store had been getting complaints about selling to minors, so they had started carding anyone who looked too young. Unfortunately, the person Vaugn had asked to buy our liquor was an undercover ABC agent—Alcoholic Beverage Control. They were really cracking down on people like us. We got on the interstate, and not ten minutes later we were being pulled over. We were pulled over at Atkins. What is it with Atkins? They didn't take us to jail but took all the alcohol we had and wrote tickets to all of us. Donovan just paid his ticket off. He still had money left from the accident. Connor, me, and Vaugn had to do four Saturdays of community service, picking up trash in Atkins. It wasn't too bad. All we did was walk backroads and neighborhoods picking up trash and smoking weed. Well, Vaugn and I were smoking. Connor didn't. I tried to hide that situation from the parents, but there was nothing for it. They got suspicious the second Saturday I got up at 7:00 a.m., which never happened. I told them I was recording music the first Saturday, but they weren't buying it the second Saturday. After they asked what was really going on, I told them what was up. They actually said they were proud of me for acting like an adult and handling my business. They were happy that I chose community service over the fine, which they would have paid because I didn't have any money, and they were happy I chose community service because my insurance rates would have gone up, which they would have been paying for as well. I was relieved that they weren't pissed at me. They were upset with me for buying alcohol but were prouder of the fact I took the initiative to take care of my mistake. That was the last time I tried to hide anything from them.

The first time was a year earlier when the maid had found my bag of weed on my dresser. I guess I had forgotten to put it up. I came home from school that day to find a note on the bag asking if my parents knew about it. Needless to say, when they got home, they had a talk with me and Walter. I just told them it was my first time and that I was experimenting. Bless their hearts. They bought it. Anyway, it was brutal honesty from that point on. And, oh, it was brutal.

By the time September of '92 rolled around, Walter was sent to rehab his senior year. At the time, I thought that shit was funny. Plus, Walter was an all-time asshole at that point, and I was glad to see that I wouldn't have to put up with him for a while.

Walter, Donovan, and I were at our house when, all of a sudden, a sheriff's deputy showed up. Mom and dad came walking up, telling Walter they think it's time for him to get some help and that he's being sent off to rehab. Walter didn't even get mad. It was like he was caught with his hands in the cookie jar. He just put his head down and said okay. I had forgotten that we had about a pound of homegrown weed stashed away in Walter's closet. When the deputy pulled that out of the closet, Donovan and I just looked at each other and decided it was time to get the fuck out of there and let Walter handle this one on his own. At that very moment, Donovan's parents called the house. They were back in state for a while from working. Donovan got on the phone, and I could hear his mom yelling and screaming at him to get his ass home. Turned out, my parents and his parents got together to try and stop us in our tracks from going down the wrong road. I thought that was what the whole prison thing was supposed to do, but the parents saw we were still fucking up and the whole prison, *Scared Straight* thing didn't work. The fear in Donovan's eyes quickly showed me that the day was going downhill quickly. "They found our stash of ditch-weed and they're pissed," Donovan said. "What the fuck?" I asked. "Dude, let me go with you," I frantically said. "Dude, you can't. I'm in trouble and have to deal with this shit," Donovan said panicking. He was right. What the fuck was I thinking? I wasn't. I just knew I didn't want to be left at the house with the parents and that cop. Donovan saw that look on my face and said, "C'mon, muthafucker." I hopped in his truck, and we got the fuck out of there. Trust me that at that moment, Donovan's house was much better than my house, even if Donovan had to deal with his parents finding the ditch-weed we had bagged up and were selling. Donovan's relationship with his parents was one that they would yell at him all day, but it's not like they could ground him or stop him from doing whatever the fuck he wanted. I'd rather wait in his bedroom, listening to the yelling and screaming over there versus dealing with a cop and my parents. For some reason, I couldn't drive. I don't remember why I couldn't bail out in my car, but it was a no-go at the moment. I think dad and I were putting new struts in. Anyway, I didn't have access to the car, so I bailed out with Donovan. That was a mistake. When we got to Donovan's, his parents were fuckin mad. They were yelling and cussing at him and me. I just sat there with my head down and let Donovan take care of everything. Hell, it didn't matter because fifteen minutes after we got there, my parents pulled up. They were there to pick my ass up and take me back to the house. They were there to help scold me and Donovan as well. Donovan and I explained to them that what they found wasn't really weed. It was literally ditch weed, which had nothing to do with marijuana. We had just been picking some shit out of the ditches that looked like weed to the untrained eye and selling it to dumb muthafuckers who didn't know any better. I think we had sold all of fifty dollars' worth, but it was fifty dollars we didn't have, and we thought the shit was funny. Both sets of parents seemed a little calmer, but confused on what we just told them, which was the actual truth. One of the parents asked what would happen if someone got sick on what we had been selling them. I don't remember what the answer was, but we just started laughing and then agreed with them that we shouldn't have been doing that.

Actually, we threw out everything we had and never fucked with doing that again. It was wrong, and we knew it. Just dumb kids, I guess.

Anyway, I rode back home with the parents that night. I asked where Walter was, and they said he was being sent to a rehab in Conway. The facility was called Charter. The parents said he was going to be there until things got better and that this was a time for me, Roman, and even themselves to live without having to deal with Walter. It didn't matter to me because Walter wasn't even living at the house at that point. We just happened to be at the parent's house when all this went down.

During the time Walter was gone, it was business as usual. We were getting fucked up and doing fucked up shit. I was in my junior year in high school and rarely showed up. When I was there, I wasn't actually there. Ya know what I mean? Let me illustrate.

I was sitting in a history class one day, sleeping off the night before, and the teacher decided to call on me for an answer. I have no idea what she asked. The girl sitting behind me woke me up by tapping on my shoulder. I barely lifted my head to grumpily ask what she wanted. It was then that I heard the teacher ask, "Do you know the answer, Shane?" "What?" I asked, in a hateful manner, as if she had no right talking to me and should have raised her hand to speak. "I have no idea what you're talking about," I responded, half asleep as I put my head back down to continue my slumber. I guess she continued with what she was saying because the next thing I know she's calling my name again and asking if I know the answer. "Bitch, I said I don't know the answer," I said, angrily. "What the fuck? Why don't you leave me alone?" I asked. "I'm minding my own business, trying to sleep," I explained, quite rationally. As I was saying those things, I realized I was being extremely aggressive and thought that it might be a good time for me to take my leave. The girl sitting behind me just rubbed my shoulder as if she was letting me know that things were going to be alright. So, I got my things together at my desk and was heading out when the teacher finally told me to get out. I couldn't believe it took her that long to tell me to get out. I didn't even get in trouble for that from the school. I just went home the rest of the day.

I recall another situation not long after. Liam and I had a class together. I don't even remember what class it was, but I do remember that the normal teacher was out for an entire week. We gave that substitute teacher hell! One day in class, Liam showed up with some glow sticks. I don't remember where he got them or why he had them. Nonetheless, we put them to good use. All of a sudden, Liam got up out of his seat, walked over to the light switch, and turned the lights off. He broke one of the sticks open and threw the liquid that was inside all over the wall in the back of the room. He didn't give a fuck! The wall looked awesome as it was glowing in all its glory. We were both laughing hysterically. In fact, the entire class was laughing except the teacher. Liam quickly gave me a glow stick, and I proceeded to also crack it and throw it all over the wall. The wall was really glowing at that point. The substitute teacher just calmly said, "Knock it off, guys." We settled down for a few minutes until Liam decided to turn the lights off again and throw more of that liquid fun all over the wall again. Needless to say, we gave that poor sub a run for their money. We just didn't give a fuck! And guess what, we didn't get reprimanded for that behavior either.

Although I didn't realize it at the time, but the school was counting up the infractions and the days until I was eighteen. Then, they were going to let me go. Ya see what I'm saying?

I was so done with school at that point. Although, it turned out none of that mattered anyway because two weeks after Walter came back from his thirty-day stint in rehab, it was my turn.

Around October of that year, we were gearing up to attend what we thought at the time was the concert of our lives: the Ozzy Osbourne *No More Tours* tour. The tour name was a play off his album, No More Tears. Yes! Ozzy Osbourne! The Godfather of Metal. I had only been to two other shows at that point, which were AC/DC and Metallica. My third concert was to be Ozzy Osbourne. That's badass! The day of the show, it was Liam, Christian, Donovan, and I that were going to ride down to Little Rock together to see the show. I would be driving. Dane and Jacob didn't make it for some reason. The school had been put on notice about how big the concert was because they said anyone caught skipping and leaving early would get detention or suspension. Oh, no! Detention or suspension? Well, let me just stop everything and rearrange my day so I won't get in trouble. I didn't give a fuck, and neither did Liam or Christian. In fact, Christian didn't even go to school that day. Liam and I, of course, left early and went to pick up Donovan. We then headed over to get Christian from his house. As we were getting on the interstate, we noticed a car on the side of the onramp. This person started waving their arm out of the car window to signal or grab our attention. As we got closer to the vehicle, I realized it was my mom. I pulled over to the side and parked in front of her.

I didn't know what the fuck was going on. My first thought was that something bad had happened. Then, I wondered how the hell my mom knew how to find me and why she would have thought to sit on the onramp to wait for me. She knew I was going to the concert, but how did she know when I was leaving or that I hadn't already left? Turned out, the school called her to let her know that I had left school early. It was like the school knew what my plans were. Although, I guess it wasn't hard to figure out. They knew my ass was going to that concert and that I would probably be leaving school early or not show up at all.

As I was walking up to my mom's car, she was getting out to approach me. "What's up?" I asked. "Is everything ok?" "You're gonna have to find another ride to the concert," my mom said. "You left school early, so you're not taking this car," she angrily explained. At that point, she got into my car and took the keys out. "You guys are gonna have to find another ride to the show," Mom said to everyone in the car. "Get out of the car," she said. "I need to lock it." "What the fuck, mom?" I rudely shouted. "I leave school early and you're gonna take the car, so we can't go to the show?" I asked. "Yep," she said. "Well, what the fuck are we gonna do?" I asked. "You just gonna leave us on the side of the interstate?" I asked with embarrassment. "Yep," Mom said. And she got in her car and drove off down the interstate. And that was it. She left our asses standing on the onramp, wondering what the fuck we were going to do. Christian and Donovan were laughing, but Liam and I were still wondering how the fuck we were going to get to the show.

My mom had every right to do what she did. That wasn't my car. I didn't pay for it. I didn't own it. Mom and dad owned it. I just had the privilege of being able to drive it. Both mom and dad were fed up with my shit at that point. Their rules and threats didn't work. So, I guess that was their moment of glory, punishment, and finally stopping me in my tracks. I deserved it. Although, I did get the car back the next day.

We walked our asses off the onramp to the gas station that was about fifty yards away. Donovan called Walter to come and get him and take him to his house so he could grab his car. That pissed Walter off because he was about to hit the interstate to make his way down to the concert as well. Luckily, we caught him before he left his house. Walter came to the gas station and picked Donovan up to take him to his car. "The parents got your ass, Shane," Walter said laughing. "Fuck you, dude," I said. We waited about twenty or thirty minutes for Donovan to come back for us. We were going to the show! We had a minor setback, but we were going to the show. Now, we were going to the show in style—not comfort, but style. Ya see, Donovan bought an R/T Twin Turbo Dodge Stealth with the money he got from the accident. It was a fast sports car, and, as you know, sports cars don't really have backseats. They do, but they might as well not be there because there's absolutely no room for anyone to sit short of a child. It didn't matter. We were just happy to be going to the show at that point. I, Donovan, Liam, and Christian were on our way to Barton Coliseum in Little Rock to see one of the best shows of our lives. Everything was right!

By the time we got there, Motorhead was in the middle of their set. I was never a big Motorhead fan, so I was good with it. Although, I definitely wanted to see Alice in Chains. They had just put out the album *Dirt*. During the Motorhead set, we decided to fire one up. As soon as we lit that thing up and started passing it around, an arm with a badge appears in the middle of our circle. I look to my left and, sure as shit, there's two fuckin pigs standing there. "Put it out," one of the officers said. One of us put it out on the floor, stepped on it, and put it back in a cigarette pack. They walked off and left us alone, and we continued on. But it was a trip.

I don't know why, but it seemed like Liam and I were the only Alice in Chains fans there. As soon as they hit the stage, we fired another one up. At some point during their performance the audience started chanting "Ozzy! Ozzy!" I'm sure we weren't the only AIC fans there, but I think some in the crowd were just caught up in the moment with excitement that Ozzy was up next. Nonetheless, the crowd was chanting "Ozzy" during some of AIC's set, and it pissed the band off. I don't blame them. It was disrespectful.

Arkansas fans didn't know any better back then. Liam and I were looking around as the chanting continued. I could tell he was thinking and asking himself the same thing I was: "why was the crowd doing that?" They just didn't understand who was in front of them. Arkansas fans were still stuck in the '80's. They just didn't know how to process the new era of music that was being created. Grunge and nu metal were the music that took the world by storm for the rest of the nineties and early aughts. It was the new sound that Liam and I were looking for.

Finally—during one of the "Ozzy" chants—the lead singer of AIC, Layne Staley, said, "Throw some fuckin' weed on stage, we'll get off," —or something like that. At that point multiple joints went flying in the air onto the stage. Layne went to picking them up and continued with the set. Seeing Alice in Chains was amazing that night! Unfortunately, because of that incident, AIC would never return to Arkansas to play another show. Jerry Cantrell, the guitarist of AIC, returned a couple times during his later solo career years, but Arkansas would never see AIC again. As of this writing, AIC has never come back to Arkansas. Anyway, the next day I went out and bought *Dirt*.

Alice in Chains has been my favorite band of all time from that point on. They've gotten me through so much shit over the years. I only saw AIC one other time, which was 2008, in Tulsa, at Cain's Ballroom. By then, of course, Layne had tragically passed.

A couple weeks after all that, in mid-October, I woke up one morning and did my normal routine. When I got in the car to leave for school, it wouldn't start. I tried turning it again, and nothing. I went back inside to tell the parents that the car wouldn't start. That should have given me a clue at that point because the parents were always gone to work by the time I left for school. "Hey y'all, the car won't start," I explained. "We need to talk," Dad said. "I've taken a part out of the car, so it won't start," Dad explained. "Shane, we've decided it's in your best interest to go to rehab," Mom said. "Rehab?" I asked, "Where Walter just came from?" "We're not sending you to the same place," Mom said. "Walter seemed to respond well to the treatment, and we think it'll be good for you," she said. And wouldn't you know it? A goddamn sheriff's deputy pulled into the driveway at that moment. I knew at that point that the parents were dead serious. The parents let the deputy in, and he asked if everything was ready. I immediately ran out the door and started for the woods. I heard the parents yelling for me to come back, to not be scared and all that. Fuck that! I was getting the fuck out of there. But where was I going? I was in shorts and flip flops, running towards the woods. How far would I actually get? The deputy quickly caught up to me in his car, and before I disappeared into the woods, I heard the deputy say, "We can do this the easy way or the hard way." After getting all of fifty yards away before the cop caught up to me, I thought it best to go the easy way. I was taken to the detention center and processed. My parents showed up to take me to rehab. They were asked if they wanted an escort since I decided to run. My parents declined. I got into the backseat, they locked the doors, and we hit the interstate. Shit is not so funny now. Just a month and a half earlier I was laughing my ass off watching Walter get taken away. Now, I'm on my way to a facility. I was in tears and full of hate and anger towards my parents, especially my mom. After an hour or so, we arrived at rehab in Little Rock. It was a facility called Rivendell. As I was being processed, my parents were allowed to sit with me. It didn't matter because we weren't talking anyway. Well, I wasn't talking. The parents were trying to talk to me, but I just kept telling them to fuck off and that I hated them. I had never felt so betrayed. I couldn't believe that I was being forced to go to rehab. I wasn't even on hard drugs. I was just drinking, smoking weed, and taking acid. What the fuck was wrong with these people? I didn't understand.

However, as the years progressed, I realized why the parents sent me. It wasn't just the drugs they were worried about but my overall behavior and attitude. I was headed nowhere fast. I did need help.

By the time my month and a half were up, I realized how lucky I was to have had that intervention. A pause. A pause that was definitely needed. My time in rehab showed how important communication was in everyday life. I learned that talking can help with the anger, hate, and frustration I was experiencing on a daily basis and how being intoxicated all the time could add to the already teenage angst I had and blah, blah, blah. Get the fuck out of here! You wanna know what I walked away with from rehab? The only thing I walked away with from rehab was the first part of what I said: communication is vital. I really did learn the importance of clear communication and how much can be accomplished. Other than that, I learned that the counselors and teachers in those facilities are just as fucked up as the people being treated. Shady and corrupt muthafuckers with one agenda: society's agenda. Conformity. You must act a certain way to be a part of society. Become part of the machine. Fuck that! I was old enough to know that I didn't want to be a part of society the way it was then (nor the way it is now). Clones! They can't think for themselves. It's the kind of place run by people who voice opinions that could keep a muthafucker in that kind of facility for a long time. For instance, the English teacher that I had in rehab put in his notes that he thought I had mental retardation. What the fuck? He wasn't a doctor or any type of therapist. He was literally just there to teach English to the minors who were locked up and still in school. Fuck that guy! That was one of the things that was mentioned to me on my way out of that fuckin place. Had I not been turning eighteen, and had my parents' insurance continued to cover the therapy, they could have kept me longer based off that muthafuck's remarks. Fuck that bitch, muthafucker! Anyway, like I said, the intervention was a much-needed pause. A pause that would help me see and think about the things I needed to maintain— while intoxicated.

The first night I was out, I had people knocking on my bedroom window wanting me to come out and play. I didn't answer. I didn't even look out the window to see who it was. I just ignored the tapping. I was actually wondering how anyone knew I was home. It was probably from Walter, who, during my stint in rehab, had moved out of the parent's house.

Keep in mind, it had been a month and a half since my friends had heard from me or seen me. After Liam, Christian, and Donovan hadn't heard from me for two days, Liam drove to my house to see what was up, and the parents told him where I was and that if everything went well, I'd be back within thirty days. That pissed Liam off. He immediately drove to Donovan's and Christian's to tell them what was up. One day I was there. The next day I was gone. Anyway, the facility was going to have to let me out by December 2, because I would turn eighteen, and the facility was for minors. Of course, the adult facility was at the same location, but the parents' insurance would no longer cover it, so they had to let my ass out. It was closer to forty-five days when I finally got out.

When I got to school the next day, Liam was thrilled to see me, and I him. After school, we went to Christian's house and smoked a fatty. Christian was also glad to see me, and so was his mom. Christian asked what had happened, and I told him how it all went down. Christian and Liam then told me what all had happened while I was gone. It was hardcore fun that wasn't good—but was good. Make sense? We all went to Donovan's later that evening. Donovan was happy to see me as well. The love was pouring out from the three of them. It felt good. I explained everything that had happened to Donovan. He also confirmed the debauchery they had gotten into while I was gone. We went over to Jacob's and Dane's later that evening as well. I remember Dane coming right out to me and shaking my hand, laughing, saying, "Welcome back, jail bird." I explained once again what had happened. Of course, Jacob and Dane also mentioned the fun situations they had been getting into and were curious to know if I had heard about these situations. I confirmed. I became very excited and curious to partake. What were the next situations to be?

The first weekend back, everyone threw a welcome-home party for me. We had it at Theresa's mom's house. Her mom was gone for the weekend. It was Theresa, me, Liam, Christian, Dane, and Jacob. We obviously got drunker than shit. In fact, by the end of the night, I had passed out on the front lawn. Dane picked me up, carried me inside, and put me on the couch.

On a side note: a week before I went to rehab, Dane had fronted Christian and me a quarter of some badass hydro bud. We had to pay $35 for it but weren't going to have the money until later that week when we got paid from our jobs. Unfortunately, I got shipped to rehab before I was able to pay my part. When I got back from rehab, Dane told me that Walter had covered the bill. Anyway, Dane was obviously cool about the whole situation, and Walter had actually stepped up to cover me, which was surprising. Things felt back to normal.

It didn't take long to get back into the swing of things. By January of '93, I was up to no good again. I was back to smoking, drinking, and partying all the time.

By February of '93, Donovan and I stopped playing music together. Donovan started to temporarily settle down. (Trust me, Donovan wasn't done livin' it up yet.) Since Donovan wasn't really interested in playing music anymore, I put the word out that I was looking for a full-time band. Music was too important to me to just stop. Anyway, that's when I met a girl named Susan—a couple of weeks before I left school. She introduced me to some guys who were looking for a drummer. We'll circle back to that shortly.

Donovan had started dating the woman he would marry (and is still married to this day), so they were hanging out a lot. We still hung out with Donovan, but not as much in '93 as we had been the previous years. That left me, Liam, Christian, Jacob, and Dane to our own devices. I was also living with Christian by this time. Two months out of rehab and the parents were done with my shit. I was eighteen anyway, so they kicked me out.

By the middle of February of '93, my life took a turn. At that point I was pretty much done with school. Although, I really don't remember a time until college that I wasn't always done with school.

I showed up to my first class that morning and was called to the office shortly after. I hadn't even seen Liam that morning yet. I walked into the office and up to the secretary's desk. There was a sheet of paper on her desk. All she asked was, "You ready to go?" Then she handed me a pen. "What's this?" I asked. "This is a drop out form," the secretary said. "You can sign it or come back to eleventh grade," she said. "You're eighteen now and an adult, so decide what you want to do," she explained. "Shit, I'm out this muthafucker," I said. I signed it and walked out. That was it. I was done with high school. Fuck it! I wasn't there half the time anyway, and when I was, it's not like I was participating or learning anything. I was so relieved to be done with that fuckin place. I immediately went to Christian's (home for me at that point) to celebrate with a fat one. When I walked in, I had a huge smile on my face. Christian already knew what was up. "You done?" he asked. "Hell yeah," I said. Grinning, he said, "You probably shouldn't have done that. You should have stuck it out." I quickly explained, "They told me I was gonna have to repeat the eleventh grade, and I'm not repeating another grade," I said in a panic. "They were gonna make you repeat?" he asked. "Yeah!" I said. "Damn," Christian said, "that's fucked up." "I know," I said in agreement. "Mom's gonna be mad at you," Christian stated. "Why?" I asked. "Because she looks at you and Liam as her kids, and since I dropped out, she was hoping the two of you would make it," Christian explained. I felt like a failure at that point. I didn't even give a fuck what my parents were going to say about the situation. I did care about how Cheryl would feel and what she would think about the situation. She let me move in with the understanding that I wouldn't drop out of school. She told Liam the same thing. For some reason, at the time, I didn't think making it another year and a half would be a hard task to accomplish. That was a retarded thought. It just goes to show where my head was. Apparently, after everything I had done and been through that year, I was still under the illusion that I was going to pass the eleventh grade. I was a fool to think that. Like I said, my head just wasn't in school. Period. Christian went on to explain that Cheryl was also going to be upset because she didn't want my parents to think my dropping out had anything to do with Christian or living with him and his mom. That made me nervous as well. I wasn't nervous that my parents would think it had something to do with Christian or his mom because they would have known better. They would have known it was all my doing. I was nervous because I didn't want Cheryl to think that my parents believed it was because of her or her son. I knew I would have some explaining to do when Cheryl got home from running errands. I dreaded telling her.

When Cheryl got home, Christian went and sat on the couch, and I was in the kitchen. Christian knew what was about to happen. When Cheryl walked in with groceries in her hand, she immediately asked why I was home. Half smiling, I said, "I dropped out of school today." I'll never forget how upset she was. She started hitting and cussing me and asking why. She was crying. I was no longer smiling. As I was trying to block her hits, I was trying to explain to her that they were going to make me repeat the eleventh grade. "That's because you assholes never showed up and when you did you were fuckin up!" Cheryl yelled. "I'm so mad at you," she said. "Where is Liam?" she asked, "Did he drop out, too?" "I don't know," I said in shame. "I guess he's at school. I haven't seen him today," I said. "Both of you get out of my sight," Cheryl said. "I don't want to see any of you right now," she explained in disgust. I looked over at Christian, and he was grinning as he was getting up from the couch. It was a grin like he was thinking to himself, "I told you. I knew what was going to happen."

He was right. Cheryl was right in her response and actions as well. I let her down, and I let myself down. That was Cheryl's point. She didn't want to see any of us do what we were doing to ourselves. We were fuckin up, and it ate her up to watch it. Of all the people that I didn't want to let down, Cheryl was at the top of that list. I wasn't even worried about my parents. I'm sure they had been expecting it by that point. However, I had let the woman down that took me in as her own. I was very ashamed of myself. I was selfish.

Later that night, I went to the parents' house to let them know what was up. It was just as I had expected. They didn't blame Cheryl for anything. They already knew I was fuckin up and that it was my fault that it had come to that. They were disappointed and looked at me with horrible sadness. They weren't even mad. Needless to say, that made me feel like a failure all over again. Wait, I was a failure. I fucked everything off. It turned out that I did care what the parents thought about me. Obviously, that day wasn't a highlight in my life. Everyone that cared for me I had let down. The parents looked at me, and dad asked, "Now what?" "I wanna get my GED," I stated. "Can y'all help me?" I asked.

Of course, they would help me. My parents were full of love. They just wanted me to get my shit together and stop fuckin up. It was the same way Cheryl felt about me as I'm sure she felt with her own son Christian. Yeah, the parents had kicked me out, but it was well deserved. They had no other option but to show tough love. By the way, I didn't get my GED until a couple of years later. Anyway, that chapter, that situation of my life, was closed for good.

4 THE ART OF NEEDLEPOINT

A couple of weeks later, the shit hit the fan. It was March. My life took yet another turn. It was a turn that I had not expected. It was a turn that would change my life forever. Remember me telling you about the crew getting into things that had never been done previously while I was in rehab? The thing that everyone had tried when I was in rehab and had not done since, was methamphetamine. AKA: meth, dope, the shit.

Walter, Donovan, Jacob, Christian, and Liam had all tried meth one night at Donovan's when I was in rehab. They all shot up, meaning they used intravenously. Walter's and Donovan's experiences were not good ones. Walter never did it again. Donovan never shot up again, but snorted lots and lots of dope over the years. Also, I'll refer to meth from here on out as dope. That's how we all referred to meth and how it was referred to on the streets. Since that night at Donovan's, no one had done any dope until Liam, Dane, and I did it.

I'll never forget that day. We were at a place we called the keyhole, in Russellville. It was an area off Highway 124 that had been cleared out for a housing development. It sat there cleared out for quite some time, so we would use it every now and then as a meeting place to hang out for a bit, to drink and smoke out. There was only one way in or out of the keyhole. Once you drove in, it opened to a big field in the shape of a circle, which is why it got the name keyhole. That was the location where my life changed. Liam had picked Dane up and then came and got me. I was at the parents' house that day. They had already done a big shot and were good and tore up. They looked different than I had seen them look before. They looked fucked up, but it was a different look. Eyes were dilated, jaws were grinding, and there was lots of conversation. Conversation was a normal thing, but this was conversation from being wired and amped up.

If you've done dope before, you know what I'm referring to. When you're tore up, your high is on a different level. Everything is going a hundred miles per hour. Your thoughts, your eyes, everything is moving with an infinite madness. You feel wonderful! Everything is good! You're happy! The high puts you in a world of GO, with euphoria like you have never experienced. I was soon to be on that same level.

"You wanna get fucked up?" Dane asked. "Hell yeah!" I said with excitement. "Whatcha' got?" I asked. At that moment, I looked over at Liam, and all I saw was his pupils and him smiling, nodding his head in approval for what I was about to get fucked up on. "I got some dope," Dane said, almost in question form. "Let's go!" I said with excitement. "Let's go to the keyhole," Dane said.

We pulled into the keyhole and parked facing the entrance as we always did. Dane pulled a spoon out with a pack of rigs. Rigs are how we referred to needles and syringes. He pulled out the dope, poured some into the spoon, took the cap off the bottle of water, and poured some of it into the cap. Dane then got a new rig out of the bag they just bought, uncapped it, and then drew some water back into it. Then, he shot that water into the spoon.

At that point, I was as excited as I had ever been about getting fucked up. I was also scared and nervous about the whole situation. I was about to let someone stick a needle in my arm, something I never thought I would do. I never thought I would shoot up—for two reasons. The first reason: the stigma that came along with being someone who shot up, which was being a scumbag and a junkie. The second reason: I was terrified of needles. When I was a young kid at the doctor's office and had to get a shot, for some reason I would start shaking and sweating. I'm not sure why I developed a fear of needles, but I did. I think it was from this one time when I was nine or ten, my mom took me to the doctor to get a couple of shots. I don't remember why I was getting the shots, but I imagine it was part of the vaccinations one gets as a child. It took two nurses and a doctor to hold me down so they could give me those shots. I was terrified. I remember crying and screaming. It was horrible.

As Dane was getting the shot together, mixing it up, I asked Liam what it was like. He said it was unlike anything he had ever done. "You're about to get high," Dane said, smiling. Liam started laughing and backed Dane's statement up with, "You're about to get FUUUUCKED UP!" That time, I wasn't scared of the needle. But what was to come next? What was the situation I had put myself in? All I could get out of those two fucks was how fucked up I was about to be and that we were gonna have fun. As Dane finished up the mixing, Liam grabbed a cigarette and tore a piece of the filter off and then handed me the cigarette. "You're gonna need that in a minute," Dane said, grinning. Liam could see the confusion in my eyes. "There ain't nothing wrong with that cigarette," Liam stated. "We need a filter to put in this, so any cut or impurities aren't sucked into the rig," Dane said. "Oh, okay," I said with curiosity. Dane rolled the piece of cigarette filter into a small ball and put it in the spoon. He grabbed the rig and with the plunger pushed all the way down, he started drawing back the dope into the rig.

I know this part might not seem like much, but it was fuckin fascinating to watch that liquid go into the tool that would soon change everything from that point on. I thought I was excited when I dropped acid the first time. Shit! Take that feeling and multiply it by a hundred, and that was where I was at.

As Dane drew the dope into the rig, he would stop and then force all the dope into one spot in the rig by doing a hard-downward motion with his arm so that all the dope in the rig would go to where the plunger was. Then he pushed the plunger forward towards the needle to grab any dope that was stuck to the side. Then, he would continue drawing the dope out of the spoon. He did that a couple times until all that was left in the spoon was a light film of the stuff which didn't break down, the cut impurities and a shriveled-up piece of filter. He rinsed the needle off in the bottle of water used to break the dope down and then looked at me and smiled. He asked, "You ready?" At that moment, I was more ready than I had been for anything in a long time. I was ready to take my drug use to the next level. "How much is in there?" I asked. "Twenty units," Dane said.

We used 1cc insulin syringes, which meant you could fit one hundred units into the syringe.

"I'm not gonna die or anything, will I?" I asked, as if anyone could for sure guarantee my life, or as if it actually mattered. Dane and Liam both laughed. "You'll be fine," Dane said. "I did the same amount earlier," Liam said. "Give me your arm," Dane said. I stuck out my right arm. He inserted the needle into my middle vein. I had virgin arms, and my veins were nice and thick. He poked my vein with precise accuracy and drew back blood. Then, he pushed the poison slowly into my arm. Poke! Draw! Push! Then, I lost my mind!

As the dope coursed its way through my vein, I immediately started rushing. Dane pulled the needle out, and as he did, I felt the dope travel through my entire body. My body was experiencing the same thing my mind was experiencing. "Hold your arm up," Dane said. As I put my arm up, my eyes went blurry for a couple of seconds, and the euphoric rush got more intense. "Let me out!" I forcefully stated. Liam let me out of the backseat, and I stumbled away from the car. Dane told me to put my arm down.

Breathtaking! Magnificent! Astonishing! Overwhelming! Beautiful! Erotic! Those are just a few of the words that describe the feeling I was having—but not fully. Think about what having an orgasm for the first time felt like, or even any time after that, and then try to multiply that feeling times ten; then you might have some sort of idea of what I'm talking about. I leaned over and put my hands on my knees because the rush and high were so intense. I even felt a little nauseous for a few seconds, but it quickly went away. Still bent over and smiling, as I was getting my shit together from the intense high, I turned my head to the car and saw Liam smiling. He knew what I was feeling. Dane was sitting there wide eyed with worry. "You ok?" he asked with concern. I sat up smiling and started walking back to the car. I just giggled and replied, "Oh hell yeah!" Dane started laughing, "Well c'mon. We gotta get out of here," he said.

I was supposed to work that evening, but due to the new condition I was in, I didn't make it. Instead, the three of us met up with a couple of other people at a motel and proceeded to get fucked up. Actually, we met up with this girl named Hazel, who was a cool person, and this guy named Eddie, who was a dealer. This was my—and Liam's—first time getting fucked up on dope. We each did another shot while we were at the motel and just sat there and smiled the rest of the night. Liam and I ended up leaving the motel around sundown for the simple fact that things got awkward, not to mention boring. We went to my house and hung out until we crashed. By the time we got up the next day and went over to Christian's house to tell him about our previous exploits, Christian had talked with Dane and Jacob—Jacob had hooked up with Dane and Eddie sometime after we had left—and told us that Eddie had convinced Dane that we were sitting there with our dicks out, literally jacking off. Liam and I just looked at each other puzzled and confused. We both looked at Christian like, "Really?" I explained to Christian, "That's the most ridiculous shit I've ever heard in my life." Liam responded, "No shit!"

Christian just laughed, saying that he knew it was bullshit and had told Dane and Jacob that he thought it was bullshit as well. Nonetheless, that was the situation that Dane believed after being up for a few days. Actually, Dane knew it wasn't true, but that didn't matter because Eddie said it was true. And when the tweaked out and jealous dope man says it's true, it's true, and you go with it; especially while you're staying up for days getting fucked up on a powerful drug that you've just started doing. There is an adjustment period when you first start doing dope. You have to learn the drug and how it effects your mind and body so you know how to recognize "the monster" when it shows up.

You see, the monster is a little different for everyone. It can take many forms. For example, it could be the tweaky, been-up-for-days monster where you damn near believe anything and everyone is a cop and that they're out to get you. Or it could be the "shadow monster." The shadow monster fucks with you after a few days because you are literally seeing shadows and impressions of movements everywhere you look. Or the monster may take shape in the form of complete and utter social breakdown, when you might hide in the bushes or even the national forest for a few days just to make sure everything is kosher. Or the monster may take any combination of the previous mentioned. Make sense? That's why it's extremely important to know where that line is so you can continue to maintain. Anyway, I don't blame Dane or Jacob. I knew it was the dope. Trust me, I will have many shortcomings like that as this story continues.

About two weeks later, Dane and Jacob came back around. Dane apologized for the situation. He said he had gotten caught up and tweaked out. Dane told us that, apparently, Liam and I had fucked up Eddie's plans for him and Dane to fuck Hazel that night. And Eddie was pissed that Hazel was talking mostly to me and Liam, which was probably the only time Liam and I said anything. Therefore, Eddie talks a bunch of shit and makes things seem what they are not. Like I said earlier, jealous. Eddie may have had good dope and weed, but so did others. After a short time, Dane stopped fuckin with Eddie. Eddie got strange and weirded out by all the dope he had been doing. Plus, he was a shady piece of shit anyway.

About a year or two later, Eddie was murdered in Texas. He had been given a syringe full of what he thought was dope but turned out to be something else.

The point is, Dane started getting dope from a couple different people, and from that point on, we were getting fucked up. It wasn't just us getting fucked up. It seemed like the entire town of Russellville was getting fucked up. Everyone we came across was getting tore up. I'm not kidding. We knew of teachers, nuclear plant employees, distribution center and warehouse workers in management positions—and everyone in between—getting spun out. It was even rumored that a couple judges and police officers were using as well. I won't mention any names, but they know who the fuck they are. Meth, it seemed, had made its way all over Pope County. In fact, it made its way all over Arkansas. That ain't no shit. Complete infection.

Keep in mind, as I'm talking about dope, it's not like the shit today. These days, it's mostly crystal meth or ice. Today's dope is much different than the dope we were doing. We were doing what was referred to as crank. Now, I'm no chemist. I'm not exactly sure how it's made today or what changes it from the shit we were doing back then to the shit being done today, but trust me, it was different. For example, some of the shit back in the early days was made with P2P, or phenylacetone. You'd know it if you ever did P2P dope. It's clean and not as hard on the body. It's good shit! Trust me! Eventually, the making of meth moved to using pseudoephedrine. Cooked properly, that dope is just as good. Trust me! Pseudoephedrine was mostly the kind of dope we were doing back then. Good cooks still use pseudoephedrine or P2P today, but muthafuckers are also using shit like anhydrous ammonia and lithium, among other things, to make dope.

Anyway, my point is, the dope we were doing back then was the finest dope around. There's a reason why local residents referred to the Pope County area as Dope County. I'll tell you this as well, I would have taken the fuckin Pepsi Challenge with anyone else in the state or the nation, including Cali, when it came to the quality of dope we were doing. There were many times we had to cut the dope to weaken it, just so we could sell it to people without worrying that someone was going to overdose. I shit you not. That's how good the dope was. Hell, we even had to start off slow at times and build our tolerance up because we were also a little nervous about overdosing our damn selves. How would we know? Simple, we would be told by the dealers to make sure and start slow or cut the shit before selling it. If the dealers were telling you to take it easy at first, then you better take it easy. Am I making sense? Do you understand the quality of dope I'm talking about?

A couple days after hooking back up with Dane, we decided to go fishing one night. I can't remember what time it was, but it was late. It was me, Christian, Dane, Jacob, and Kelly. We had all just left Jacob's place after everyone but Kelly had done a shot of dope. (Kelly didn't start shooting—or slamming as it's called—until later. He was doing lines.) Needless to say, we were nice and fucked up. We had already been up a day.

The destination was Atkins. We ended up on some backroad, on what used to be a functioning bridge, and started fishing. I was fishing as well. I couldn't believe it. There I was, in the middle of the night, somewhere in Atkins on a bridge, tore the fuck up, and fishing. Actually, five tore up muthafuckers were fishing. Fuckin hilarious situation! After a while, Jacob decided that it was time to do another shot. That would be all fine and dandy except that we had no supplies, no rigs, no spoon, and no fresh water. Well, for some reason, Jacob had decided to bring his rig and a little dope. The rest of us left everything at his place. Keep in mind that before we left for our fishing adventure, we stopped at the gas station to pick up some beverages. When I say beverages, I mean soda. Not a damn person one had any water. "Did anyone bring any water?" Jacob asked. I think we all started giggling because we knew the answer was going to be no. "Why don't you just wait til' we get back?" Dane asked. "No shit, bro," I enforced. "Shit, we ain't got no spoon or water, Jacob," I explained. "I'm just gonna use this creek water," Jacob said. All of us immediately scoffed at him as if he were nuts. Everyone unanimously thought that was a bad idea. "That'll make ya sick, Jacob," Christian said. Kelly quickly followed up, "Yeah, you don't wanna' do that, Jacob."

You could tell that Jacob was getting frustrated. He was already high as fuck, but that didn't matter. He wanted to be higher, and nothing was going to stop that. So, Jacob decided, "Fuck it." He took the cap off his soda, poured some dope in the cap, and proceeded to dip the needle of his rig into his soda, Orange Crush specifically, and drew some of that yummy, orange goodness into his rig and then carefully broke his dope down with said drink. Obviously, as we did with the creek water, the group voiced their concern. It just didn't matter. Jacob was going to do another bump, and that was all there was to it. "Jacob!" I shouted. "You can't use that, bro," I stated with a concerned voice. "Carbonation? Air Bubbles? Does any of that mean anything to you?" I asked with a final attempt. Jacob just giggled, "It'll be alright." He did his thing, and he was right. He was fine. Afterwards, we didn't fish much longer because after all that, the rest of us were ready to do another one. I don't even think it took another ten minutes and we were packed up and headed back to Jacob's place. You already know what happened when we got there.

The following week, we were up to no good again. This time, it was me, Liam, Christian, Jacob, and Dane. We were at Jacob's place again doing what junkies do. We had been up for a couple of days already when the next situation came up. We were to go to Fayetteville. Dane needed to get rid of some dope, plus his daughter was up there, so it was an opportunity to see her as well.

We had all just been doing what we always do when we got tore up, which was kick it at Jacob's, Christian's (mainly the pond), drive around town all night doing junkie shit, or end up in the mountains. The past couple days we had just been kicking it between Christian's place and Jacob's place.

We really loved being at Jacob's place at that time because he lived right next to a church, and the church had a pretty nice basketball court, which we loved to utilize during the wee hours of the night. We would play basketball for fuckin hours. Although, there was a Salvation Army right by Christian's place that was once a church; it also had a basketball court, but playing at night wasn't as good due to lighting. Therefore, we did most of our balling at Jacob's. Good times!

We packed up in my car and headed out. It was always me driving. If it wasn't me, it was Liam. Before we were to hit the road, we needed to stop off at Christian's for some reason. As we pulled onto Christian's road, Dane noticed someone ducking behind a tree across from Christian's grandma. I didn't see a fuckin thing. Of course, I was so fucked up that I could barely see anyway. The next thing I know, Dane is yelling, "Stop!" Not knowing what the fuck was going on, and only that I heard the tone in Dane's voice, I stopped. I don't even think I came to a complete stop, and Dane was out of the car, moving quickly to where this person was hiding behind the tree. As Dane approached the tree, I noticed the person back up from behind it. By that point, the rest of us were out of the car. "You been the one taking shit from his grandma?" Dane asked. Before the guy answered, Dane slapped the shit out of him. I couldn't believe it, but both Jacob and Christian at the same time said, "That's enough." Dane was ready to punish that muthafucker. Ya see, Christian's grandma had been having shit come up missing the past couple of weeks, which Christian talked about in one of our many junked-out conversations. When Dane saw that muthafucker, he knew immediately who it was. "Get the fuck outta here, and don't ever come back!" Dane aggressively stated. The guy quickly walked away. As we were getting back into the car, we all started laughing. We weren't laughing because we thought slapping that mutha-fuck was funny, but because the asshole who was stealing from Christian's family was not only caught red handed, but because we all knew that muthafucker would never come back around. That entire situation of shit coming up missing from Christian's grandma's house was over with a situation that took all of thirty seconds.

We hit the road close to 1:00 a.m. We chose to take the long route, which meant travelling what's called the Pig Trail. It wasn't that I-49 (I-540 back then) wasn't open yet, it was just because we were tore the fuck up with a shit load of dope on us. We figured the Pig Trail was the safest route, even though it was the longest, most treacherous route. It was the safest route in the sense that there would be less traffic on the Pig Trail since I-49 was finally open. Less traffic meant less chance of seeing the police. It was the most treacherous because the Pig Trail was three hours of steep, curvy, mountainous road. Even though we no longer had to worry about the traffic, with five tore up muthafuckers in the car, it was definitely still treacherous. And it also meant being on the road longer with a bunch of dope. Nonetheless, that's the route we decided on.

Ya see, in order to get to Fayetteville—before I-49 into Northwest Arkansas was created—from the direction we were coming, besides Highway 71, which would have been no better than I-49 for our situation, meant taking the Pig Trail. And on the Pig Trail, not only did you have to worry about the road, but you had to deal with massive amounts of traffic, including 18-wheelers.

We drove for about an hour on I-40 before we had to get off the interstate to get on the Pig Trail. Right before we got off the interstate, Dane told me to pull over right quick. Next thing I know, he's got two huge lines fixed up on a pamphlet he found in the back seat. "Here!" Dane said. "Do those right quick," he stated. Christian and I looked at each other and laughed. Neither one of us had ever snorted a line. When we did dope, it came from a spoon. We weren't used to doing lines, much less the fat fuckin lines he had just told us to snort. Although, what is a person supposed to do when they're on the side of the interstate with a bunch of dope? We both fiercely snorted our lines. I went first. Christian went right after me. "Alright!" Dane said. "Let's get outta here!" After snorting that fuckin mountain of a line, I proceeded to pull back on the interstate. As Dane started preparing lines for Liam, Jacob, and himself, Christian and I were doing what we could to get our shit together as the dope was quickly moving its way through our bodies. Amazingly, it didn't burn. That dope was so clean. I gave myself one more strong snort to force whatever was left in my nose to my brain and the back of my throat. As soon as I did, I felt an even faster rush starting, and my body was warm and tingling. The drip was also making its way down the back of my throat. My eyes were wide open to say the least. I felt so fuckin good after doing that line. It was almost like slamming for the first time in the sense that I was getting off in a way that I had not yet experienced. As everyone else finished doing their lines, we covertly made our way up the Pig Trail in the blacker-than-black night. For three hours, besides one stop at a gas station along the way, not much was said. If everyone else was feeling like I was, then it was a quick three-hour trip for the simple fact of how fucked up we were. Based off the lack of any sort of real or rational conversation during those three hours, I'd say we were all making our way down the mental highway at the same speed.

A sense of relief was the vibe as we pulled into Fayetteville. Things started feeling a little less dark and heavy. Conversation and laughter began to fill the car once again. It was almost as if we hadn't been in the car the past three hours, travelling on curvy and hilly roads, tore the fuck up. I don't remember our exact location, but we entered a set of apartments somewhere near downtown Fayetteville. As soon as we walked in, Dane put out some dope and told us to take care of ourselves. He went to the bedroom with his ol' lady. Jacob or Christian mixed up a bunch in a spoon, and we all took however much we wanted. I was still comfortable with twenty units. Actually, that's pretty much where all of us were at, give or take five to ten units. Depending on the mix, it can make a difference.

Like I said earlier, we used 1cc insulin syringes. Now, as you'll see later, I eventually began doing bigger doses. Although, what you have to understand is that it's not necessarily about the quantity, as in the number of units one would do. Rather, it's all about the mix. The mix, my friend. The mix meaning the ratio, the amount of water to the amount of dope. The less water you put on good dope, the better the ride is going to be. Otherwise, you could risk diluting the dope too much and end up doing more water than dope. We liked things on the thick side. It's all about thick thirties or thin tens.

As Jacob was doing his shot, I noticed tears falling from his eyes. I looked at Christian and saw that he also noticed the same thing. Christian asked with concern, "You alright, Jacob?" "Damn, brother, no doubt," I said, "You ok, man?" Jacob just sort of giggled nervously, and as he was pulling the needle out of his arm, he replied, "Yeah." That's it. Nothing else was said. We just continued with what we were doing, which was getting tore up. I remember that he teared up a couple more times during the next day or so. I would ask to make sure he was alright. He just responded the same way he did the first time. After two or three times, I never saw him do that again. To this day I don't reckon I know what was bothering him. I thought about it a few times over the years and would always ask myself the same round of questions. Was he upset about the fact that he was doing dope? Was he upset over the fact that he had a needle in his arm? Was it because he felt like a junkie or a failure? Had he been hitting the same spot too many times and was physically in pain? Was it all the above?

I don't know. I do know this, though: I could answer yes to all the above questions. Yes, I've been upset over the fact that I was doing dope. Yes, I've been upset and ashamed over having a needle in my arm. Yes, over the years I've felt like a junkie and a failure. Yes, I've physically put myself in pain on one level or another doing dope. Although, in the beginning, I didn't feel that way at all. In fact, it was exciting for me. It took a few years before I was to feel some kind of way about it. I did accept right away that I was a junkie. We were only a month in, but that didn't matter. We were shooting up like we had been doing it for years. It was just part of the natural succession into delusion. Moving on.

A few days later, I finally met up with the guys who were to consist of my new band. Susan met up with me so I could follow her to the place where I would be trying out. Of course, I had Liam and Christian with me. Liam had a truck and helped me move my drums from Donovan's place, which was a little awkward. Nevertheless, I had to move on musically, and I knew it wasn't going to be with Donovan. We pulled up to a huge double-wide trailer. I, Liam, and Christian started unloading my drums. I met Brian first. He lived at the trailer and was the bass player of the band. Brian and I hit it off quickly. Kenley was his roommate and was a guitarist in the band. As I was setting up, another guy with the band, the main guitarist, walked in. His name was Devin. Devin was soon to be the only guitarist. The other guitarist, Kenley, was a lazy alcoholic and would soon be kicked out of the band. Finally, Burton, the vocalist, showed up. Everyone else started getting set up and ready. When it was time to start playing, Brian looked at me and asked, "What do ya know?" I responded nervously, "Well, Ozzy, Metallica, Guns N' Roses—" But before I could continue, Brian asked, "You know 'Crazy Train'?" "Hell, yeah!" I replied excitedly. "But I only know the live version, from the Randy Rhoads' Tribute album," I explained. Everyone just started grinning and kind of giggling. "It's the same song for everyone else," Brian said. "It's just that your part is a little harder," he said laughing. "Yeah, but it's a much better version," I said grinning. "Awesome!" Devin said. "You ready?" he asked. "Yep!" I replied. "Count us off," Devin said. I did a four count, and we started the song. By the time we were done playing the song, everyone was smiling. Christian and Liam were smiling and nodding in approval, and so was the band. "Well," Brian said, "that about does it right there." We played many other songs and had a wonderful time. I did it! I was in a new band. A complete band. It wasn't just me playing with a guitarist. I was playing with two guitarists, a bass player, and a singer. It was awesome! Oh, and Devin? He was the best guitarist I had ever heard up to that point. I was so excited!

Later that evening I met one other person. His name was Tyler. Tyler and Brian were best friends. Tyler also lived at the trailer and played guitar. Let me tell you something about Tyler. He was *the* guitarist. Over the years when I had heard his name mentioned, I would usually also hear Eddie Van Halen's name mentioned. Do you understand what I'm saying? Shit, I didn't even understand the full extent of this man's ability to play guitar—at least not yet. Something else I didn't know yet, was that Brian and Tyler were planning on moving to California at the beginning of '94 to start playing music. They just needed a drummer who could keep up with what they were playing. When Brian heard me play—and then Tyler heard me play later that same night—the scheming on a plan to get me to join the two of them in a move to California was in the works. We'll circle back to that again shortly.

At some point in early April, I decided to have a party at my parents' house. They were out of town for some reason. I didn't know it at the time, but it was to be a pretty epic party. Actually, it was supposed to be a "get together" among close friends. Somehow a bunch of muthafuckers showed up. Robert was even there that night, which was awesome. Walter's bitch ass showed up. He even poured a mixed drink on some bitch's head. He did it in the parents' living room. Like he didn't know better. He didn't give a fuck. He wasn't living there; I was the one that would have to explain the huge whiskey stain on the fuckin carpet. Thanks, asshole! Needless to say, the majority of the night I was taking care of the inside of the house. Don't get me wrong, I was drinking. I was drinking steadily. I was just keeping an eye on the inside because of what Walter had done. Plus, I had noticed that the get together kept growing. Not to mention, muthafuckers were in and out of the house constantly. I was already getting a little stressed. I won't lie either. I smoked a couple of cigarettes in the kitchen just to help calm my nerves. Alright, alright. Yes, I smoked a couple of joints first, but ya gotta understand that this was my parents' house. It was a nice, big house. I definitely shouldn't have had a bunch of rowdy muthafuckers over there. Although, like I said, it wasn't the initial intent. Trust me, it wasn't the first get together I had ever had at my parent's house. It was just the one that turned into a monster.

"Hey, man, the cops are outside," Christian said grinning. Christian wasn't grinning in the sense that he thought that part was funny. He was grinning in the sense that he also knew that the so-called get together had also grown beyond the initial intent, and now the cops were outside. Don't get me wrong, Christian had been helping me maintain the inside of the house throughout the evening as well. Because he was helping me, knowing I was already a stressed-out, nervous wreck, he also knew what my reaction to the cops being outside of my parent's house would be. My response?

"Are you fuckin shitting me?" I asked very nervously. "County," Christian said. When I walked outside to confront the situation, I realized why the cops were there. There were at least thirty muthafuckers outside drinking, smoking, listening to music, and having a good ol' time.

Keep in mind, there wasn't one muthafucker at that get together that was of age. Another thing to keep in mind is the location. My parents lived in a nice neighborhood. It wasn't Skyline nice, which is where the real rich muthafuckers lived, but it was a very nice neighborhood. I don't think there was a house in that neighborhood under $200k. In fact, most of them were probably well above that. Back in the early '90s, that was pretty good. As far as location, the cops had never had a reason to show up in that neighborhood until my parents moved in with their thug kids. I can for sure tell you that because the neighborhood was a brand-new development. Lots of the people that lived there were people that also had to transfer from Little Rock, as my parents did, to work at the nuclear plant. No other kids were throwing parties in that neighborhood. Just us. Unfortunately, my parent's house was the only spot that had ever had the cops show up: once when Walter went to rehab, once when I went to rehab, and now the current situation I'm addressing. Do you see the picture I've painted for you? Do you understand what I'm saying?

When I walked up to the cop, he already seemed to know I was the one he needed to talk to. I guess he could tell by the way everyone was watching me as I approached him. Compared to what was previously happening outside the house at that point, the silence was deafening. "You the one who lives here?" the Deputy asked. "Yeah," I responded in a low voice. "The neighbors keep calling and complaining about the noise," he said. "Do ya mind keeping it down a little?" he asked. "Yeah sure," I said, "no problem. Sorry about that." "No problem," the deputy said. "Y'all have a good night," he said as he was walking away. I couldn't believe what had just happened. Did this county law-dog just ask a bunch of underage kids if we could "keep it down a little" and then drive away? He sure fuckin did. It was amazing! I think everyone else was just as amazed—and at the same time grateful—that they didn't go to jail. Trust me, he could have taken every muthafucker there to jail. Hilarious!

"Hey!" I exclaimed. "It's about time everyone goes to the house," I said firmly. That meant if you weren't part of the immediate circle, get the fuck out. About 10 minutes later the party was cleared out. The only ones left were me, Christian, Robert, Walter, and some bitch. I don't even remember who the fuck it was. I'm sure it had been someone Walter was planning on fucking but just didn't work out for him that night. "I'm out," Robert said laughing. "Y'all have a good one," he said. "Alright, man. We'll see you later, bro," I said.

Walter asked if we wanted to ride with him to take that girl home, and then he would bring me and Christian back to the parent's house. For some reason, we agreed to ride with him. Christian and I did some quick picking up around the house. I locked everything down, and we bailed out.

After we dropped that girl off at her house, for some damn reason Christian said, "Let's ride on top of the car." Walter didn't seem to think it was a bad idea. I too thought that riding on top of the car would be a good idea. You know: nice, fresh summer air blowing in our faces. Obviously, we were drunk as fuck. Anyway, we got on top of the car and laid on our stomachs. Christian was on the driver side, and I was on the passenger side. "Y'all hold on," Walter said laughing.

There we were, going down backroads on top of Walter's car after dropping this girl off at her house. We were having a great time! Did I mention we were drunk? During our trip, Walter thought it was a good idea to drive by the police station while we were riding on top of his car. He obviously didn't put much thought into the route he was taking. With that being said, none of us had much rational thought in that moment. As we're going by the police station, the cops were apparently in the middle of a shift change or something because there were a lot of them standing out back as we drove by. All Christian and I could do was wave. I'm not even sure the cops could comprehend what they were seeing. As we passed by the station, you could tell that all of them had stopped talking and just started watching as we drove by. I imagined a record-scratch moment of silence when they saw us go by. They must have been thinking, "What the fuck?" I'm sure it wasn't the most bizarre thing they ever saw, but I'm sure they were wondering why we did what we did.

We made it about a quarter mile before Walter stopped to let us back in, but by that time it was too late. As we were getting off the top of the car, we were surrounded by cops. I don't remember anything after that except pulling into the detention center. We obviously went to jail. Although Walter didn't. I'm not sure how the fuck he got out of going to jail, but they let him go. I'm assuming he got a ticket or something and then went home. Walter was living on his own by then or with a roommate. I can't exactly remember. Anyway, there Christian and I were, in the drunk tank for public intoxication, which was immediately dropped. We were "adults" but underage kids having a good time. The cops knew it. At the same time, they couldn't just let us walk away. So, they took us to jail for a few hours. My parents were out of town, so there was no one I could call to bail me out. Christian's mom showed up and got him out and then came back a couple hours later and bailed me out. She's such a sweet lady. I knew she didn't have the money to do what she did. When my parents returned, I had to tell them what happened so they could pay Christian's mom back. That was my first experience in jail, but it wasn't the last.

A breath of fresh air showed up a few days later. Phillip came back for a short time. I finally got to meet the guy. I had heard so much about him. Well, I'll tell you this, he is one of the kindest and coolest people I have ever met. Connor is the only other person I could say that about. Like Connor, Phillip would do anything for a friend. I'll tell you this as well, Phillip was and still is a muthafucker you don't fuck with. Trust me.

Liam, Christian, Phillip, and I ended up going to a party one night. We had heard about it from some old high school buddies. It was a college party at the Dardanelle Armory. Liam drove. We had already been drinking before we showed up. When we got to the party we indulged even more. After a while we left, but for some reason came back. We probably went to go smoke one, but I can't remember. We were walking up to the entrance in a staggered, single-file line. Liam was in front, Christian was behind Liam, Phillip was behind Christian, and I was last. Just as Liam made it back into the armory, some jackass said something foul to Christian, which I didn't hear. But Phillip heard it, and that was all it took. The next thing I know, Phillip let his jacket slide off the back of his arms. Then, going over Christian's shoulder, Phillip punched the guy in his bitch face, knocking that guy the fuck out. I'd never seen anything like it. One punch and that muthafucker dropped his beer and collapsed to the ground. By the time that guy hit the ground, Phillip had already hit the guy's buddy who he thought was gonna defend his friend, but he got his ass knocked the fuck out as well. I couldn't believe what I just saw. It happened so fast that I don't think Christian had a chance to respond to the guy who said something to him before Phillip came over his shoulder with the fuckin punishment. Anyway, by the time Phillip KO'd the second guy, it was on.

Some big boy screamed and immediately attacked Phillip. Then the rest of the crew showed up. They sprinted towards me and Christian. Phillip was in the parking lot fighting the other guy at this time, which is where me and Christian had moved to. As the five or six muthafuckers moved towards Christian and me, Christian picked up one of the beer bottles that just so happened to be laying there in the parking lot. I picked up one as well, and there we stood, back-to-back. We were ready to get it on. As those college fucks surrounded us, Christian yelled, "C'mon muthafuckers!" I couldn't believe what was about to go down. "That's right, muthafuckers!" I screamed as my adrenaline was pumping. "Let's go!" I yelled. I swear, it was like what you see in the movies. I couldn't fuckin believe it. Keep in mind, from the time Liam walked through the armory doors to the moment Christian and I stood back-to-back took about thirty seconds to unfold. Meanwhile, Liam realized something was going on because he told us later that someone had yelled, "fight in the parking lot." So, according to Liam, that's when he ran back outside, only to see his three brothers were the ones fighting. That must have sucked to walk back out and see that. Hell, one second, it's a party and the next second: what the fuck?! Liam started running to his truck to get a machete. All three of us were pretty close to Liam's truck. By the time Liam got to it, Christian's and my situation had changed. It turns out that when you surround two drunk muthafuckers, holding beer bottles, standing back-to-back and telling them to "bring it," well—it seemed they had a change of heart. They decided it best to leave us the fuck alone. Plus, Liam pulled out a fuckin machete. So there's that. As the crowd around us dispersed and Christian and Liam made sure no one else was gonna come up on us, I looked over and saw Phillip still fighting this muthafucker. Only this time the guy was on top of Phillip hitting him. I'll never forget the look on Phillip's face as he was on his back defending himself against that guy's hits when, out of the corner of his eye, he looked over at me like, "get this muthafucker off me." I don't know why it took so long for me to respond.

Everything was happening so fast. It broke my heart to see Phillip down like that. I quickly ran over and pushed the guy off. "Get the fuck off him!" I screamed. We both headed over to the truck where Liam and Christian were and got the fuck out of there. Holy Shit! That was a trip. I didn't expect the night to end like that. Of course, I'm not sure any of us expected that shit. That was crazy shit. We actually ended up having to go back to the armory because Phillip had left his jacket there. Although, by the time we went back, the party at the armory was over and the only people left were those cleaning up. We were told the next day that we had been fighting football players from the university in Russellville, Arkansas Tech University. I don't know if that was true, but I'm sure none of the people that night forgot about that situation.

A few weeks later Phillip went with me to practice. I'm not sure where Liam and Christian were. There were a bunch of muthafuckers over at the practice pad that night. It reminded me of being at Donovan's place. Before we started jamming, Kenley (the alcoholic rhythm guitarist I mentioned earlier) was handing out cocaine like it was free. Although, the cocaine was so bad that I could see why it was free. Phillip and I helped ourselves to whatever was allowed. After that, the band jammed for a while. About an hour later we were finishing up. There was a guy who showed up with some bitch. I don't remember her name, but the guy's name was Mitch. I didn't know him, but I think Phillip did. Everyone else seemed to know who he was. Apparently, he was the guy with the yayo.

Mitch's coke was okay. I guess he stepped on it before he gave it to Kenley. Or Kenley stepped on it before he let everyone do some. Either way, this guy had some alright coke. At some point, he invited us over to the house of the chick who came with him to our practice pad. Phillip and I decided to go. We got over to the chick's house, and Mitch broke out some coke for all of us. Well, as we were doing our lines, he was breaking up some coke in a spoon. I thought that was pretty interesting for the simple fact I had never shot coke. "Y'all wanna do some like this?" Mitch asked. Phillip replied, "No." I replied, "Hell, yeah! You got an extra rig?" "No," Mitch replied, "but you can use this one when I'm done." "Hell naw, I ain't usin' that rig!" I replied with an are-you-fuckin-crazy tone of voice. "I'll just do these lines," I said.

This muthafucker finishes drawing back the cocaine out of the spoon and doesn't even bother trying to get the air out of the rig, much less the air bubbles that he had acquired while drawing the shit back into his rig.

Look, we always considered ourselves responsible junkies. We were taught to make sure and do things the most correct way possible. Besides Jacob doing that shit with the Orange Crush, we were pretty responsible junkies. We knew to make sure and force the dope into one spot, to push the air out and make sure there were no bubbles. Now, I know that may not matter to most of you, but if you are gonna be shooting up, you might as well be as responsible and safe as you can. Although, when you're a junkie, all rules eventually go out the window.

He stuck that needle in his arm with no concern. He probably had thirty or forty units of actual yayo in his rig, but because of the air bubbles that leave gaps within the rig, it looked as though he had about fifty or sixty units. I was like, "God damn! You ain't gonna try to get any of those air bubbles out before you do that?" "It'll be alright," he replied. "Dude!" I exclaimed. "You're gonna blow your fuckin heart up," I said. "Fuck that!" I stated.

Now, picture this if you will. First: this muthafucker got that needle in his arm with a rig full of air bubbles. Second: he started digging in his arm like he was blind as fuck and digging for gold. He must have spent a good sixty seconds looking for a goddamn vein. Do ya see what I'm sayin' to ya? Look, if you can't find a vein within the first fifteen seconds, then you need to call it quits for the night and try again later. You know what I'm sayin'?

Finally, once he found a vein, he couldn't even inject himself. Check this shit out: he had either mixed it so thick that it made it impossible to push the plunger in without bending it, or there was too much air, or the rig was that old. Turned out that the rig was that old. "Dude!" I hastily stated. "You're gonna fuckin die. Stop," I forcibly shouted. "It's ok," he said. "It's just a really old rig," he explained. I looked at Phillip, and we just shook our heads. He finally managed to clear the rig. As soon as he was done, he laid the rig down on the dining room table we were sitting at and stepped outside on the front porch. I sure am glad Phillip was there that night. We left shortly after.

Phillip would end up only staying for about a month before going back to Texas. I was sad to see him go back. Although, Texas was his home. Nonetheless, we got a lot accomplished during the time he was there. I would see him again, though.

A few days later, Christian, Liam, and I were in Liam's truck driving through the university campus for some reason. I think we were taking a shortcut to get back home because we had just picked up some weed. Right as we pulled up to a stop sign, about to leave university property, we're hit with blue lights. It was campus police. "Fuck!" Liam said. I just remember Christian turning to me and asking, "You got the weed crotched, right?" "Yeah," I said nervously. Christian sighed, "Fuck," he said. "Aaahh!" Liam grumbled in frustration. I knew right then that we were going to jail. There was nothing for it. It's not like I could have stashed the weed somewhere else. Too much movement would look suspicious, not to mention that I was riding bitch (in the middle).

We were riding in Liam's "damn doe green truck". That's what we always called it. I'm not exactly sure where the term was coined, but, nonetheless, that's what we called his truck. Anyway, it was a green, two-tone '72 Chevy with a long wheelbase. It actually had bullet holes in the hood. I'm not sure how they got there, but we didn't do it. The truck ran really well. You could only sit three people comfortably, and that night I got bitch.

I was getting pretty worried at that point. The campus cop came up to the driver window and immediately said, "I smell marijuana!" I'm sure he did, but I knew it wasn't from the bag in my pocket. It was from the weed we had been smoking earlier that day. He told Liam to get out of the car and for me and Christian to sit there and not move. "I'm callin' in city PD," he explained.

A minute or two later, Russellville's finest showed up. One of the cops came to the passenger side and told Christian to get out. I sat there sweating for two or three minutes. I heard Christian getting mouthy with the cops. I'm not sure if that's what his plan was, to act as a distraction, but whatever his plan was, I guess it entailed going to jail because that's exactly what happened. I heard them handcuff him and tell him that he was going to jail for disorderly conduct. While all that was happening, another cop came and told me to get out of the truck. Oh, and Liam? Liam had already been put in the back of one of the cop cars while the truck began to get searched. While Liam's truck was being searched, I was being searched. I was shaking. I was shaking so bad that I thought I was going to collapse. I knew the cop could feel me shaking. I was scared as shit. That was my first time ridin' dirty, being pulled over, and then searched. I just figured I was gonna end up in the back of one of those cars. The cop even made me open the front of my pants so he could see if I had weed located in my crotch area. Luckily, they didn't make me pull my pants down along with my boxers because then they would have found the bag of weed that was sitting under my balls, and then I would have gone to jail. But that didn't happen. He took a quick peek, didn't see anything, and then started his interrogation. You know the basic questions: Where is the pot? Do you have anything on you? Shit like that.

In the meantime, the campus cop was searching Liam's truck. At that moment, I was thinking that Liam and I just might get out of the situation. Christian seemed to be the only one going to jail. Alas, that was to be furthest from the truth. Do you remember that machete? Yeah, it was still in the truck, located behind the seat. Although, that's not all. He also had pieces of a bong behind the seat as well. I'm pretty sure Liam knew that they would find the machete, but I don't know if he remembered that he had parts to a bong in his truck. Or maybe he did know. Either way, he was on his way to jail. At that point, Liam was pulled back out of the car and placed in handcuffs. He was arrested for instrument of a crime and possession of an illegal weapon. By that time, the cop who arrested Christian had already left with him, and they were on their way to the detention center. As one of the officers was finishing up with Liam, my interrogator finally decided that it was enough for one night and basically told me I was on my own. As the cop walked away and got back in his car, Liam was being driven off to jail. His truck was to be impounded. My brothers were taken to jail, and I was literally left on the side of the road—with a big fat sack still under my balls. I immediately ran across the street to a pizza place and called Cheryl on a pay phone. She came and got me, and I explained what had happened. We were home for about thirty minutes when Christian finally called to let his mom know he was processed and ready to go. Before she hung up, she handed the phone to me and said he wanted to holler at me right quick. "Hey," I said. "You still got that?" Christian asked. "Hell, yeah!" I replied. He started giggling. "Well, get one ready," he said. I started laughing and told him it would be ready when he got home. Obviously, we smoked a couple of fatties when he got home. In fact, guess who showed up a couple hours later? Liam! It was awesome. I started laughing my ass off when he showed up. I couldn't fuckin believe it. Nothing was going to stop us from getting high that night.

By that time, Tyler and Brian had already told me of their plan. They had decided they wanted me to move to California with them. They brought me to the side one night after practice and told me they had actually been scheming on a plan to get me to leave Russellville and go with them to California. I was shocked. I had no idea they thought I was that good or that they had plans on moving to California. As it turned out, they did think I was that good, and they wanted me to go with them. I was honored. I couldn't believe it. Naturally, I accepted the offer. Things seemed like they were coming together for me musically.

I had always dreamed of being in a competent band and maybe, someday, making it big. Sign a record deal! Make hit records! Play live shows all over! Oh, so naïve I was. Such a silly goose.

I was thrilled. This was a huge step. In March, Tyler had been accepted into Musicians Institute. The goal was that we move to California and, while Tyler was doing his thing in school, to write music, play local shows, and try to get some recognition. I immediately moved my drums back over to my parents' house because we were going to start practicing over there. However, Brian and I did help the band we were in with recording an album. We went to Fayetteville and recorded at a studio there. After that, Frustrated Cruelty was the main focus, which is what we named the band. We were an official three piece, which was and still is rare in the industry for rock bands, comparatively speaking. Some of the great three-piece bands that quickly come to mind are Rush, ZZ Top, Nirvana, and The Police.

Tyler had already been writing tons of music. When the three of us got together for the first time, it was magic. Liam and Christian were there. I could tell by the expressions on their faces that they were hearing the same thing I was hearing, absolute awesomeness. It was like we had been playing together for years. Each one of us knew what the other one was about to do. It was unlike anything I had ever experienced. Donovan and I were tight, but this was something on a whole new level. Tyler's writing was second to none, and so was his playing. Everything I had always heard about Tyler was true. This guy was fuckin unbelievable. Had he lived in the digital age we live in today, he would be one of the greats. Understand? I've never seen anyone else play like Tyler except, of course, the greats such as Eddie Van Halen, Nuno Bettencourt, Steve Vai, etc. Do you understand what I'm saying to you?

We were writing music quickly together. We felt like everything we were writing was ahead of its time. Had we lived in the digital age we live in today, I dare say I might not even be writing this. Anyway, musically, things were blossoming. On top of the originals we were creating, we were playing covers from bands I had not previously covered. For example, Red Hot Chili Peppers, Van Halen, Extreme, and Alice in Chains. The only thing Donovan and I ever played was Metallica, Guns N' Roses, and some Ozzy. And we sure as fuck never wrote any originals. Ever. I was so happy to have a band.

To celebrate our new union together, Tyler and Brian wanted to trip— on Robitussin DM. I had never done it before. Have you ever experienced tripping on Robitussin DM? I wouldn't advise it. It's nothing like acid. In fact, it's horrible. All motor skills are pretty much destroyed. It's like you're drunk, but you're not. It's hard to explain. It's like tripping and drinking at the same time, but in a different realm or universe. It was also very intense. I think we were only fucked up for about two or three hours. That was the first time I was ready to come down, but it wouldn't be the last.

It was June. Things were speeding up quickly. Literally. We were getting fucked up constantly. We would have friends that didn't get down like that, who would see us after a week-long binge, and they would look concerned. Indeed, they should have been. Dane, Christian, Jacob, Liam and I were going hard at it. It was business as usual that summer. We didn't stop for nothin'. I had to do as much debauchery as possible before stopping for the outage at the nuclear plant. One afternoon Christian and I were at his house. We had just gotten some badass, white rock dope. You could smell that shit through the baggy. We were in Christian's bedroom, and he was mixing up our shots.

At the time, I still couldn't hit myself. I could hit someone else, but I couldn't hit myself. In other words, I couldn't put the needle in my arm, pull back the plunger to make sure I'm in the vein, and push it in. Mainly, I couldn't yet do it because every time I would pull the plunger back, I'd lose my grip or spot on my arm. Basically, I'd risk missing my vein. Missing the vein is bad. One: it hurts terribly. Two: it'll create knots in your arm. And three: you've just wasted your dope, which I reckon out of all those things is the worst scenario. However, I eventually found a way around that problem, which I'll get to later.

Christian mixed both shots thick. Ya see, that was the thing about Christian. Whether he was mixing up a shot or poking your arm, you were about to get fucked up. I mean, you would get fucked up anyway, but if Christian was mixing or poking, it was going to be a thick mix and a fast push of the plunger. The thicker the shot meant less water, which meant a more concentrated dose because there was less water diluting it. As far as the quick push of the plunger—well, we just got off watching each other get off. Anyway, like I said, the shots were thick as fuck. On top of that, Christian decided to give us thirty units a piece. I didn't realize at the time that he had mixed that much up. I saw the rig before it went into my arm. "Is that thirty?" I asked. "Yep!" Christian happily replied. Nothing else was said after that. Just in case he wasn't able to hit me properly after he did his shot, he went ahead and hit me first. By the time I lifted my arm up, it was over with. There was no need to lift my arm because I was already needing to bend over and hold on to the wall. "Holy shit, dude!" I silently whispered. "God damn!" Christian said excitedly. He proceeded to hit himself. While he was doing that, I kept getting higher. My vision was blurred, and I thought I was going to throw up. At that point, Christian finished up and quickly realized what I was experiencing. "Dude, I need to go outside," I quickly explained. From what I could tell after hearing Christian cough, he was about to lose his shit as well. We rushed out of the room, struggling down the hallway to get out the front door. I rushed over to the back of my car, and using that for balance I gagged a couple of times and just kicked it there until I got my shit together—for example, my vision. Christian was hunched over by a tree trying to get his shit together as well. I knew when he coughed that he was in for a ride. I heard him gag and spit a couple times, so I knew he was nauseous. After a few minutes, we were both good. Neither of us threw up. Though, let me just tell you, I was high as fuck! I had not been as high in one moment as I was at that time. After I got most of my vision back and no longer felt like I was going to throw up, I felt so fucking good! No! No! I felt absolutely amazing. I was higher than I had ever been. I remember rushing for about an hour. Although, the next few minutes were to be a goddamn nightmare, so that might have played a small part as well. Ya see, Christian decided to take JJ off the chain. Let me explain who JJ was. JJ was a beautiful pit-bull that Christian had acquired a few months earlier. Make no mistake, JJ was a killer. However, to humans (for the most part) he was one of the sweetest dogs you'd ever meet. He just loved to love. For other animals, though, he didn't have a lot of patience. Keep in mind, I'm only saying this to illustrate how carelessly high we were. Also, JJ was to become the father to several generations of pit bulls. Christian was determined to breed a docile bloodline instead of the normal aggressive pit bulls we were used to in our area.

So, there we were, enjoying our carefree, high-as-fuck summer evening, when, all of a sudden, a disastrous situation took place. I had just lit a cigarette. I was standing there enjoying my amazing high, watching Christian interact with JJ, when Christian unhooked him. I don't even think it took two seconds for JJ to bolt off. It caused

Christian to kind of fall off balance because he had been kneeling while he was loving on JJ. By the time I knew what the fuck was happening, JJ had the cat in his mouth. Christian was yelling at JJ to stop as he was running towards the dog, but it was too late. With one bite and twist of the head, the cat went in two different directions. As I was processing what just happened, Cheryl, Christian's mom, came running outside to see what all the ruckus was about. Christian yanked JJ up and was yelling, cussing, and hitting him as he took him back to his chain. Cheryl was in tears and was mad as fuck. That was the family cat. It was old, which explained how JJ successfully got to the cat. I felt like a piece of shit. I was sick to my stomach. I threw my cigarette to the ground. I was sad about what happened to the cat. Christian was also. But mainly, we felt bad about how Cheryl felt. In fact, I felt worse for her than I did the cat. Christian felt the same. After Cheryl told us to get the fuck out of there, we stopped at the gas station so Christian could call and apologize. It was a fucked-up situation. We stayed up for a few days after that.

Although, that whole summer wasn't filled with debauchery. Well, it was, but we did other things as well. We may have been fucked up most of the time, but we did other things, nonetheless. For example, we'd get fucked up and go play basketball. Or we'd go play video games at the bowling alley or at this place called Shotgun Sam's. Dane and Jacob loved playing pinball. Christian, Liam, and I preferred the video games. Dane usually paid for everything: soft drinks and quarters to play the games. At times we had our own money, but most of the time Dane paid for our shit, which was usually because either me or Liam were driving night after night and sometimes for several days at a time. Anyway, the point is that we loved playing basketball and being at the arcade. In fact, it was at Shotgun Sam's one night that Liam and I found a game called Samurai Showdown. We fell in love with that game. Although, that version had already been out a while. By the end of that summer Samurai Showdown 2 was already out, which was even more badass than the first version. Liam and I would go to Shotgun Sam's as much as possible to play that game. We had a blast! None of what I just told you was necessarily important. I guess I just wanted to illustrate that we weren't completely ate up—yet. We still had an innocence about us. Do you understand? If you don't now, you will soon.

Oh, on another sidenote: I just have to express another thing that happened to me that summer. One night, Brian and Tyler introduced me to a band called White Zombie. Their second album, La Sexorcisto: Devil Music Vol. 1, had already been out just over a year. I couldn't believe what I was listening to. Brian let me borrow the CD, and the next day I immediately went over to Christian's house to let him hear what I had just discovered. He put the CD in and turned the volume up, which, on Christian's stereo, didn't have to be up that loud to shake the house. I told him to play the song "Welcome to Planet Motherfucker/Psychoholic Slag." As the song got going, he just looked at me, smiled, and turned the volume up even more. It sounded so fuckin good! Christian's mom was outside mowing the yard and came banging on the window, telling him to turn it down. If we weren't listening to Alice in Chains, we were listening to White Zombie and, of course, the mighty Pantera.

On the music side, things were changing also. We had to change direction. California was really no longer a feasible option. Tyler had been accepted into MI but had no money to pay for it and, for some reason, didn't qualify for a scholarship. Therefore, we didn't think it was a good idea and decided that Dallas was the best place to go. We wouldn't be as far away from home going to Dallas, and we wouldn't be going to a part of the country we had never seen before. Dallas, however, we were familiar with, and we knew that the music scene there was good. So, Dallas was to be the next destination. We'll see about that.

At that time, it was a matter of getting jobs so we could save money for the move. Brian's dad had a contact for us, so we could get jobs for the next outage at the nuclear plant. But that wouldn't start until the fall, around September. Nonetheless, we had to get our names on the list for laborers because there would only be so many hired. We submitted our names and were approved. In the meantime, Tyler and Brian got summer jobs at Hickey Pool. Tyler was a lifeguard, and Brian worked concession. I did absolutely nothing except practice my drums for hours each day in a hot ass garage. To be honest, that's all that mattered to me at the time. I knew that once the outage started, all I would be doing was working. Back then, outages took about two to three months to complete, and that was working seven days a week doing twelve-hour shifts. The money was good, but there would really be no time for anything else. Therefore, all I did was practice my drums every day for three or four hours. I shit you not. By the time I was done practicing, there would be a small pond of sweaty dedication underneath me. Then, later in the evenings, after Brian and Tyler got off work, we would practice anywhere between two and four hours. I had never before been so dedicated to something, not even before I was playing with Brian and Tyler, when I was just playing with Donovan at night instead of doing homework and studying like I was supposed to be doing. Besides doing drugs, music was the only thing that mattered to me. Not to brag, but I was good at it. After all, music was the first true love of my life. Music would remain a central focus of my life for many years to come.

On a side note: I had been working. I was a cook at an Italian restaurant the past year and a half, but I was finally let go for not showing up. I know, big surprise, right? I had called in two or three times. Ok, probably three or four times. Plus, a stay in rehab. Yes, the owner had let me keep my job while I was in rehab. He was a cool guy. When he let me go, there was no anger or anything. In fact, he was a little sad. He told me that he wanted me to become his apprentice, to teach me Italian cuisine. I was honored that he said that. He looked at me, grinning, and said, "I guess there are just other things you're wanting to do right now." He wished me luck, and I went on my way. I learned a lot while I was there. I still use some of the foundational techniques he showed me when I'm cooking an Italian dish at home. Good stuff!

It was September, and plans had changed again. Tyler, considering that no one had made any money and that Brian didn't get a job at the nuclear plant like we had, suggested Tulsa. He had lived there before, so he knew the area and the music scene. Livin' on Tulsa time seemed fine with me. So, it was settled. We would be Tulsa bound by January of '94. Like I said, Tyler and I were gearing up to start working at the nuclear plant. Brian, however, didn't pass his drug test, so he wasn't able to get in. I could only imagine how awkward that conversation must have been for him with his parents, considering his dad was the one to hook us up with the job contact in the first place. Whoopsie-daisy! Oh well. Brian ended up getting a job at a gas station, so it was all good.

Let me tell you about working at the nuclear plant. It was awesome! I know what you're thinking: How the fuck did a junkie get a job at a nuclear plant? Well, I stopped shooting up and smoking weed thirty days before I had to take a drug test. I was determined not to fuck up that opportunity. I had a goal. It was about doing the music thing and starting what was hopefully to be an awesome career in music. At least, that was the intention. Anyway, just getting into the nuclear plant meant not only drug testing but also passing a five-year FBI background check as well as mental evaluations and tests. Make no mistake about it, when working at a nuclear plant, you are entering what they refer to as a secured area. The only thing that really made me nervous was the mental evaluations. I wasn't worried because I was a psycho or anything, but for the fact that, in addition to rehab, I had been in and out of therapy over the years. The therapy was nothing too serious. It would usually just cover the typical teenage angst behavior: hate, anger, and the occasional wanting-to-die thoughts. You know, just the normal teenage shit. Anyway, after passing the drug test, FBI background check, and mental evaluation—including an extra therapy session I had to take—I was approved for security clearance. I know what you are thinking, and you're right. What the fuck?! Well, have you ever watched *The Simpsons*? The depiction of a bunch of idiots and burnouts running a nuclear plant is not too far from the truth—at least when it comes to the contractors they bring in during outages. The laborers, carpenters, electricians, pipe fitters, and welders, for example, are not all that way, but I've known some muthafuckers working out there that had no business being there. You think I'm bad? I'm a goddamn saint compared to some of those fuckers. For example, there were people out there who were very antigovernment. Yet they passed the mental evaluations. There were people out there who were involved in militia. Yet they passed a five-year FBI background check. Then there were a bunch of muthafuckers like me, full time junkies with part time jobs. Needless to say, you had an array of folks working outages.

Just getting behind the security fence everyday was a task. It was like trying to get to your gate at the airport in today's world. You had to use your badge just to get into the security checkpoint. Then you had to go through a scanner for weapons. Next, you would have to put any personal belongings into an X-ray machine. Then you would be manually scanned by a guard one more time to make sure that you had no weapons. Then you would come out the other side, into the secured area. Finally, you would make a quarter mile trek to the breakroom. Keep in mind that the security at these places included armed guards walking around. When I say armed guards, I mean armed. The guys weren't just carrying handguns. They also carried assault rifles and tactical shotguns. A secured area consisted of a more military-style security.

Tyler was working the day shift, from 7:00 a.m. to 7:00 p.m. I was working the night shift, from 7:00 p.m. to 7:00 a.m. Tyler was immediately assigned to a carpenter's assistant position, which for laborers is the best position to have. You're still doing laborer work, but you're doing it with a crew of carpenters, which was badass. As a laborer with the carpenters, you got paid an extra 50¢, plus you got more time in the reactor, the turbine building, and other really neat places you wouldn't see as a normal laborer.

About a week into my normal laborer position, I got assigned to a carpenter's crew, which was awesome because the first few days I was at the outage, I had spent all my twelve-hour shifts sweeping the carpenter's warehouse. The carpenter's warehouse was where the wood was stored and where they had a couple of different saws. The main job of the carpenters at that nuclear plant was to build scaffolds so that others could do their jobs. That place wouldn't function without carpenters.

I knew nothing about carpentry. But the crew I worked with was great. They taught me a lot. And they looked after me. They showed me the dos and don'ts. For example, how to navigate the secured area, where it was safe to go and where it wasn't, how to navigate and pace myself while in the reactor area, and many other things. I stayed busy with those guys, but there was a lot of "hurry up and wait." For instance, we would be told to hurry up and go over to such and such location to build a scaffold for the electricians, but when we got there, we couldn't start for some reason, and we would wait hours sometimes before starting a job. There were other times when we were slow. Our foreman would tell us to go and hide. So, we would go and hide. Literally. Our crew would either go together or split up across the plant to secret places that most didn't know about. What would we do? Well, we would talk or sleep. We'd show up for dinner, and if it was still slow, we'd pick a new hidden spot and wouldn't show up again until it was time to go home. I know. It was a trip! You wouldn't think it would be like that at a nuclear plant, but it was at times. Although, I stayed busy with those guys for the most part.

If you've never been inside a nuclear reactor building before, let me just say that it's hot work. Obviously, you're dressed in a radiation suit. Each person wears a dosimeter, a radiation pen. The dosimeter keeps track of a person's radiation exposure. They are programmed to the area one is working in. For example, you're always working in an area where you can't exceed a certain amount of exposure. When you get close to exceeding that exposure rate, the dosimeter sounds an alarm, which is basically telling you to get the fuck out of the reactor building. You could be working in a low radiation area inside the reactor area your entire shift and never exceed your exposure amount. On the flip side, you could be in an area for all of five minutes and your alarm starts sounding. In those cases, you probably should only be working in that spot for about three minutes before it's time to go. However, there are many in-between scenarios as well. Everything depends on the area and how much time you have. Although, in some cases, things just get fucked up, which I will illustrate shortly.

I remember one night not long after I had been with the crew. We were in the reactor building doing some work. We were building a scaffold at the very top level. The scaffold had to be built on the other side of the safety rails and had to go down a little. Keep in mind that on the other side of the safety rails was at least a hundred-foot drop to the bottom. Needless to say, this was a very dangerous scaffold the crew had to assemble. As things got started, one of the guys in our crew decided to go on the other side of the rail without having his safety harness attached. As soon as he jumped over the rail, he went to move to his right and lost his grip. The only thing that saved his life was the hand of another crew member grabbing hold of him as he began to fall to his death. He was taken for a medical evaluation just to make sure.

There was a big safety evaluation as well. Safety at nuclear plants is a very big deal. Something like that doesn't just go away. We were all questioned about the incident. That guy was eventually let go.

Closer to the end of the outage, our crew had another crazy experience. Before going into the reactor area, we had to have a briefing, because we were going into what was called a "hot area." Working in a hot area meant that, due to a high exposure risk from radiation and hot particles, we could only be in that specific area for about ten to fifteen minutes before we would have to bail out. Usually those jobs were done quickly, so there would be nothing to worry about. However, this situation turned out a little different. After our briefing, we had our dosimeters calibrated accordingly and got dressed in our radiation suits. Once we were in the reactor building, it took a few minutes to get to our location. According to the map we were given, we had to go behind a locked gate to get to the area where we were supposed to work.

In a reactor building, locked gates usually indicate a high radiation area. A crew had to be pre-approved to go behind a locked gate, with everyone's name documented as to who was going to be in that room. We could all go through a locked gate at one time. In contrast, if you were going behind what was called a security door, each person would have to scan their badge and go through the door one at a time. Each person had three seconds or so to get through the door. Sometimes it took several minutes to get through a door because of the supplies. Each time one of us would go through the door, we would wait on the next person until the whole crew was through before we moved on. That's just how things were done. But, if someone at any time while going through the security door fucked up the process, they would see armed guards within seconds telling them to get their hands up. I know because I experienced that one night.

Once we all got behind the gate, we proceeded to make our way around the corner to the worksite. When we got around the corner, what was supposed to open up into a room opened up to nothing. Literally. It was a fuckin dead end. Within the locked gate room that we were already in, there were a couple of other locked gates going into other rooms, which meant even higher radiation, and there was some sort of small digital component area and some transformers. While we were trying to figure out where the fuck we were, suddenly a transformer exploded and, for some reason, the room started flooding. Our dosimeters immediately started going off, which meant we were getting crapped up (radiation exposure).

I don't know if you've ever experienced a transformer exploding, but along with a loud *pop*, there's a small light show of sparks, with bluish-white electrical bolts and a small amount of smoke. Now, pair that jolting effect of a transformer exploding in a room next to you with the fact that you're in a nuclear reactor building; the room is flooding, the device that tells you that you have reached maximum radiation exposure is screaming at you, and all of that is happening within sixty seconds of entering what is considered a hot area—and you have yourself a situation. "Get out!" I heard someone yelling. "Run!" "Get the fuck out of here!" I heard echoing amongst the crew. By the time we ran out of the room, the water was up to our shins but had started subsiding and slowing down while nearby drains swallowed the water as it gushed out. By that time, HPs (health physics) were on site yelling at us to get the fuck out of there as well as trying to maintain the flooding and transformer situation. When we finally got out of the area, we had all met or exceeded our radiation exposure for that job. Half of us spent the rest of the night getting "un-crapped," and most of us lost our clothes. Getting clean entailed just that, getting clean. Well, it also entailed time, which meant waiting. Sometimes washing yourself and your clothes would take care of it. Sometimes just waiting for the radiation to diminish or decay does the trick. That type of exposure goes away relatively quickly after cleaning and waiting it out. I've also seen certain parts of people's pants or shirts cut off, and then they come back clean once those parts were cut off. Any other night, we would have been dressed in scrubs already, but when we had started our shift that night, they had temporarily run out of scrubs. Although, the HP folks had a healthy stash of them when we were in there. I went home in scrubs that night. Luckily, I got to keep my boots.

It was November. The outage was over. The band was back to practicing, and I, of course, picked up where I left off two months earlier with Liam, Christian, Jacob, and Dane. Tyler and I had seen each other every now and then at work, usually when he was working late. I hadn't seen Brian at all. We hadn't been practicing because after working seven days a week, twelve hours a day, you usually just want to relax for a little bit before going to sleep. Nonetheless, we were back at it. Finally! I had saved quite a lot of money the two months I worked that outage. I had saved about $5,000. Plus, after the outage was over, I got to collect unemployment. It was only a couple hundred dollars a week, but that was plenty. I had no bills. Musically, we picked up where we left off. We were practicing two to three hours a day. Things really seemed like they were coming together as far as the music and the move to Tulsa. It was so awesome.

Another thing that was awesome: in late November, Arkansas was blessed with another great show. Pearl Jam! Brian, Tyler, and I attended the show. It was fabulous! They had just released *VS* a month or so earlier. Can you believe it? They opened up with *"Release"*. It was so fucking epic! All I saw were jaws dropped to the floor. Mouths were open as if people were waiting for manna to drop from the heavens. Well, that's exactly what it sounded like when they opened up with Release. It sounded like Heaven.

A couple of days later it was Thanksgiving. My parents would always go to Minnesota for Thanksgiving to see my dad's sister. So, me and the boys would have Thanksgiving at my parents' house. Our turkey days would usually consist of a lot of beer, weed, and—most of the time—deer chili. Although, that Thanksgiving we hadn't planned anything except for the beer and weed. That changed when I had Kelly and Christian stay the night with me. That morning we had decided we were going to go deer hunting to try and fix the issue of not having anything for Thanksgiving. On top of that, we decided to go deer hunting in my parents' neighborhood. They lived on a mountain surrounded by woods. Even better was a tiny spot down the road that didn't have houses around it. It was down in a huge valley where we would go when we were younger to get safely fucked up. We woke up Thanksgiving morning, smoked a fatty, and went down the road to that valley. I had a .22. Needless to say, I wasn't deer hunting so much as I was sitting around smoking weed and watching squirrels. Kelly and Christian went together to do the real hunting. They headed up on a ridge about 200 yards away from where I was going to be. So, there I was, the first time ever "hunting," sitting by a tree, smoking a joint. I look up, and all of a sudden there is a buck trotting towards me without a care in the world. He got maybe ten feet from me before he finally noticed me and stopped dead in his tracks. We must have stared at each other for at least five seconds before he ran off. He was quite beautiful. About an hour later, I hear a gunshot in the nearby distance. I started back to the house. Wouldn't ya know it? Turned out that Mr. Great White Hunter and Fisherman himself, Kelly, showed up about forty-five minutes later. He had shot the same buck I had seen earlier. We had deer chili for Thanksgiving.

December quickly showed up and we had plans, yet again, to go see a badass show. This time in Dallas, to see White Zombie at a club called The Bomb Factory. And the show was on my birthday. I gave myself a great birthday present. We had some girl that Tyler was fucking drive us. It was her, Tyler, Brian, me, and Liam. Actually, there was another girl with us too, but she didn't even have a ticket and was just along for the ride. The concert was wild! Brian, Tyler, and that girl went close to the front, while Liam and I stood in the back. We wanted to smoke weed and were already paranoid, so we thought a dark corner in the back was the best bet. Besides, the place wasn't that big, and we could see everything just fine. It was a great show!

As we were leaving, the chick that drove us got turned around and ended up running a red light. Yes, we got pulled over. There were six of us in the car. Three in the front seat. Three in the back seat. Somehow, I ended up sitting shotgun on the way home. When the blue lights hit us, I thought for sure I was going to jail. Keep in mind that we just left a White Zombie concert and there is a car of four long-haired guys with two girls, and I'm sure we smelled like weed. Of course, I did have an ounce on me at the time. I don't know why I decided to bring that much, but I did. So, that was another reason I thought I was going to jail. There were two cops. One approached the driver side, and one approached my side. While the one cop is fuckin with the driver, the other cop asks me to lift my jacket up off my legs so he could make sure I wasn't hiding anything. Totally forgetting where I had put my weed, which happened to be sticking out of the inside pocket of my leather jacket, I lifted my jacket up off my legs to assure the cop that I wasn't hiding anything dangerous. Thankfully, when I lifted my jacket up, the front of it didn't swing open or that would have turned into a whole different situation. The cop said thanks and just stood there in silence the rest of the time until his partner was done with our driver, which was a quick ID check. Then we were able to leave. As we're driving off, I'm looking around for my weed and realized where it was. My heart sunk thinking about how things could have turned out just then. I immediately rolled a couple of joints to help calm my nerves and celebrate the rest of the evening. I only had a half-ounce left by the time we got back home. Good times!

Tyler, Christian, and I drove to Tulsa the following week to find a place to live. Yep! Christian was moving with me. It was exciting. Liam had plans to come after he graduated high school. It took Tyler and me going down a second time before we found a place. We had found our band house. Tyler and I put the deposit and first month's rent down, got our utilities set up, and headed back to Russellville to let Brian know we got a place and to start prepping to move. Robert was also leaving about the same time we were, except he was going to North Carolina. It was time to leave Russellville.

5   LIVIN' ON TULSA TIME

January 1, 1994, was when we left for Tulsa. I was nineteen. Mom and dad helped me move my stuff and get settled in. Christian had just bought a car from Liam and drove it packed with everything he owned. What he couldn't fit in his car my parents took in the trailer, hauling my drums and whatever else I had. Tyler's mom and stepdad helped him move. Brian, however, didn't leave at the same time we did. He was still saving some more money. I had saved enough money to give myself a cushion, but we all immediately started looking for work. In the meantime, Tyler and I started writing more music. When I wasn't looking for work or playing music, Christian and I went back to Russellville a couple of times to get weed because we still hadn't found a hookup in Tulsa. By the time February came, no one had found a job, and Brian still wasn't in Tulsa. Tyler and I drove to Russellville one night. We walked into the house of the girl that Tyler had been fucking before we left for Tulsa, went back to the bedroom where Brian was sleeping—because he was fucking that other girl's cousin—turned on the lights, and yelled at Brian to wake the fuck up and get his ass to Tulsa. He woke up confused but smiling. "I'm leaving next week," he said still half asleep. Tyler and I immediately started busting his balls like, "Yeah right, muthafucker!" "No, really," he said, "I'm serious. I'll be down next week."

The next week rolled around, and he showed up with his dad helping him move. We were glad to finally see him. So, we decided to have a little party, just the four of us. The drink of choice that night was a half-gallon of Jim Beam along with some beer that we had brought from Arkansas because you couldn't get six-point beer (6% alcohol) in Tulsa at the time. Their shit was three-point beer. Ya might as well drink water. Ya know what I mean? Anyway, Jim Beam was Tyler's favorite whiskey. It's my favorite whiskey as well. So, we were quickly getting pretty drunk. After a while, we started listening to some Dre, as in Dr. Dre.

The Chronic had dropped in late '92, so we spent a lot of '93 listening to that album. Then Doggystyle dropped in late '93. So, by the time we arrived in Tulsa, we were all over that shit as well. And yes, we loved that music! And yes, I still keep up with all that great kind of music. Rap and hip hop have always been—and always will be—a huge part of my life. I remember as a kid listening to greats such as The Fat Boys, who I actually saw in concert, Run-D.M.C., Beastie Boys, NWA, and LL Cool J. I remember the first time I listened to NWA's album Straight Outta Compton. I was thirteen, living in Little Rock. I was waiting in the car while my mom went inside the grocery store. I only had the tape because my mom bought it for me after I talked with her about a new group I was wanting to check out. Had she known what the content was, she would have never agreed to it. Anyway, there I was, in the car listening to what helped evolve my musical vocabulary. I was blown away! I had never before heard such rawness. And even being a white, thirteen-year-old boy living in Little Rock, I understood what they were talking about. I was never blown away by another album again until about a year later when I first heard And Justice for All by Metallica. Holy shit!

Well, with drunkenness comes drunken behavior. We were all a little caught up in the moment. We had all made it to T-Town, as Tyler used to call it. We were southern boys havin' a good time in the city. And we were away from the dope. That was a good thing. I had acquired a 9mm from a friend before leaving for Tulsa because I wanted to make sure I had some sort of protection. And, of course, it fed my immature ego of having a profile of some sort of gangsta. Although, that behavior had started way before Tulsa was even in the picture. We were already fuckin' with guns and carrying them around. The 9mm was like the third gun we had been through in '93. Not to mention, Donovan gave us a sawed-off shotgun earlier in '93 that his grandfather used to carry around. So, we had been carrying that muthafucker around with us already. We were southern boys livin' in a small town, yes. But we weren't fuckin around.

Anyway, we're all drinkin', smokin', singin', and havin' a good ol' time, when someone started talking about the gun. So, I went to my bedroom and got it out. We started fuckin' around with it. Now, I'm not really sure what brought us to the next moment, but, for some reason, Tyler and Christian thought it was a good idea to tackle me while it was loaded, chambered, and cocked. Why did they decide to tackle me? I don't know. It wasn't aggressive or anything. It was just a playful tackle amongst brothers who had been drinking. Furthermore, why was the gun loaded with one in the chamber and cocked? Well, I can't answer any of those things. But what I can tell you is what happened during the tackle. "Dude!" I yelled. "What tha fuck are y'all doing?" I asked in a drunken haste. "The gun is loaded!" I yelled as they were giving me pretend hits while I was on the ground. "It's loaded and cocked! Quit!" I said, laughing.

All of it happened within seconds. Somehow, my finger ended up on the trigger and the gun was pointed into my stomach. That's just the way it happened to end up after the tackle and while I was moving around, telling them to get off me. As they started getting up, the gun went off. *POP!* With fear and confusion on their faces, Tyler and Christian jumped way back. I think everyone at the same time either said, "Fuck" or "What the Fuck!?" All the laughter in the room had stopped. I could only imagine that they thought I had just been shot. At the same time, I was wondering if I had just shot someone. I had no idea where that fuckin' bullet went. Well, luckily it was no longer pressed into my stomach when the shot went off. But it was, however, pointed towards the direction where Brian was standing, which we didn't figure out right away. We found the bullet hole on the upper part of the wall where Brian was standing. The bullet entered closer to the ceiling, but in Brian's direction, nonetheless. I put the gun up for the rest of the night.

Tyler got a job at a restoration service the following week, and two weeks after that, both Brian and I got jobs at a steakhouse. I was a grill cook, and Brian was a kitchen cook. Things were actually coming together. Unfortunately, Christian had already had enough and had gone home. He left JJ with us. He would be back.

Within four months of being in Tulsa, Tyler was already booking us shows. And we finally met some new people and got weed connections from working at the steakhouse. The first person we met was a wonderful girl named Bethany. We met Bethany at a dance club that Tyler had taken us to one night. Bethany is still a part of our lives today. The second person we met was a guy named Colton. He was working at the same steakhouse. Colton had the weed hookup. He then introduced us to a couple of brothers by the name of James and Mikey. Bethany, Colton, James, and Mikey quickly became part of our pack. We all became really tight. Liam, Kelly, and Christian would make periodic trips up to Tulsa to hang out, and when they met the four of them, they immediately liked them. They were part of the family.

A quick sidenote. April of '94 lost a pioneer in music. Kurt Cobain, from Nirvana, took his life. Nirvana was a revolutionary band that helped bring music into a new era. His passing hit the music industry and fans with a sudden punch to the gut. I just think it is important to note.

As time progressed, so did the debauchery and chaos. I had met a girl from the steakhouse I was working at and, by that summer, had already moved out of the band house and into an apartment with her. Brian and Tyler were mad. And they had every right to be. Mikey took my place at the band house. I had started losing focus of what I was in Tulsa to do. I was supposed to be focused on the music. I was focused. Somewhat. I was also focused on runnin' the streets and doing as much partying as possible. Well, so be it.

About a week before the Fourth of July, I was hooking up some smoke from another guy I had met at work. Not Colton. Colton's weed was good. But it was $40 a quarter, and we weren't used to paying those kinds of prices. So, the other guy, Jarvee, could get it at the prices we were more familiar with. Although, the difference in the quality of weed was very significant. Colton could get us chronic, or what is referred to today as kush. Jarvee could get us Mexican, or brick weed. I know, I know. But, when you're young and livin' off Ramen, you do what ya gotta do.

A quick sidenote about Jarvee. Jarvee was a cool guy. He worked the buffet at the steakhouse. Apparently, Jarvee had just gotten out of prison for runnin' drugs and being involved in a shootout with the police. That's what he told us. With what we had experienced since we had met him, it seemed feasible. Not long after we met Jarvee, he introduced us to crack. He wouldn't even charge us for it. We'd just be hangin' out, and he'd bust some out. Cool! I'll smoke crack for free. Well, have you ever smoked crack? Let me tell ya something about crack, it's more worthless than cocaine. Meaning the high is not long at all. Hell, at least with cocaine you can stay high for a little bit. But not with crack. Oh, you get high. You get high as fuck. It's just too quick of a high for me. It leaves you wanting more and more, which I guess is where the addiction can come in. But fuck that! If I'm gonna be addicted to something, it's gonna be something I can at least get off of for a good amount of time. Ya know what I mean? Fuck crack! Yeah, ok. Fuck crack! We'll see about that.

Anyway, I was meeting up with Jarvee to get an ounce. Unfortunately, I brought my girlfriend with me that day, and she had been drinking. And when she drank, she was one of those annoying, insane drunks. We followed Jarvee to the north side of Tulsa. We pulled up to his buddy's house. As we were getting out, my girlfriend decided to grab my 9mm, which I always kept under the passenger seat, and tuck it in her waist behind her back. I didn't realize she had even grabbed the fuckin' gun until we were already going inside. I asked her what the fuck she was doing, and she just giggled as we were going inside the house. We get in there, and Jarvee introduced me to everyone. As we're taking our seats to start our business, that bitch decided she was gonna do some gangsta shit—like take the gun out and put it on the living room table. I couldn't believe what she just did. I was in the wrong environment for something like that to have taken place. There's a time and place for that type of behavior, and that situation wasn't it. "Bitch!" I said hatefully, "What the fuck is wrong with you? You don't just come up in someone's house you don't know and do that kind of thing." Jarvee quickly moved between me and her and said, "No! No! No! Shane," Jarvee laughed, "it's cool." I quickly looked over to Jarvee's friend and apologized. By that point, he had already pulled his gun out and laid it on the table and stated, "Oh, that's how ya like to do business. We can do that." "It's all good," he continued. Then another guy sitting on a recliner pulled his gun out and put it in his lap, and then another guy came around the corner with a fuckin shotgun and leaned it up against the wall. "You fuckin bitch!" I said to my girlfriend. I turned to Jarvee and his friend and again apologized and told them that wasn't how I did business and explained the foolish behavior of a soon-to-be dead bitch. Believe it or not, they all just started laughing. They were actually pretty cool about the whole situation. I was glad I left there in one piece.

It was July 4, 1994. I started the day having to work. But it was so dead that they sent me home by noon. I hooked up with the Tulsa crew, and we began drinking. For some reason, James suggested we go out to his parents' house, which was out in the country, to shoot some guns. Sounded like a good idea at the time. So, that's what we did. We went out there and shot guns for a while. Afterwards, we went to a Fourth of July firework show off the river. When the show was over, we all parted ways. My girlfriend and I started heading in the direction of a Village Inn. But right before we got there, someone decided to pull out in front of me at a major intersection, and I t-boned their ass.

Back then, we weren't wearing seat belts. It totaled my car, but everyone in both vehicles were fine. My girlfriend ended up in the passenger floorboard, but she was fine. The cops and paramedics showed up, and I was immediately given a sobriety test. I passed with flying colors. Meanwhile, my girlfriend is talking with the paramedics, and they end up taking her to the hospital just to make sure everything is alright. I think she just wanted an ambulance ride because, besides a bruised knee, she was fine. But she must have said something to them to make them think she needed to pay a visit to the emergency room, so that's what happened. My car was totaled, so the paramedics let me ride with my girlfriend to the hospital. You know, because why not? Loved ones need to be with those close to them during a traumatic situation. So, I hitched a ride to the hospital. The problem, however, with the entire situation was simple. One: I had just left a 9mm under the passenger seat of my car. At least, that's where I thought it still was. Apparently, during impact, the gun ended up in the floorboard, which my girlfriend had been on top of at one point. I could have sworn I checked the floorboard, but things were so chaotic after the accident that I could have easily overlooked the black gun on the black floorboard of my car—which leads us to number two: I didn't realize that the gun was in the floorboard. Three: I didn't think the police were going to go through my car. After all, it wasn't my fault that I was in that situation. Why would they need to look around in my car? They should have been looking around in the other muthafucker's car. Not mine. Alas, that wasn't what happened, which leads us to my fourth problem: By the time my girlfriend was being discharged from the hospital, the cop who was originally at the scene greeted us as we were walking out of the emergency room because it turned out that fourth problem of mine was the whip cream. The gun came back stolen, which I knew it had been. The fact that it was a stolen gun was pretty serious. What I didn't know, which became my fifth and final problem: When the cop approached and asked if I knew that I had a stolen gun in my possession, my idiot reply was, "Yes." That the charge would be even more serious was the cherry on top. What the fuck?! "Yeah," the cop said. "I'm gonna have to take ya to jail," he stated. Turned out that it had been stolen from a cop somewhere in Arkansas. I have to give the cop credit, though. He let me smoke a cigarette before he took me to jail, and he even let me ride up front with him. On the way to the jail, he told me to, in the future, never admit that I know something is stolen. Thank you. I'll definitely keep that in mind during my criminal career. Luckily, the Fourth of July that year landed on a Monday, so I didn't have to wait through the weekend. Although, because it was a felony offense, my bail was set higher than normal. But my girlfriend had just gone through a DUI, so she called her DUI lawyer, and he agreed to bail me out and put me on a payment plan. I was able to get out the next day. I appreciated that.

My parents got me a lawyer. I was suddenly facing five years in prison. My lawyer told me the only thing I had going for me was that it was my first offense as an adult and the fact that I was nineteen years old. The next few months were torturous, a mental hell. I was constantly wondering for the next three months if I was going to prison. All I could do was play as much music as I could until my court date in October. But that wasn't really the only thing I could do. I could also keep getting fucked up. And that's exactly what I did. I spent the next few months getting as fucked up as I could. But I still wasn't doing dope. Of course, I hadn't been looking for it either. At some point after the gun situation, I lost my job at the steakhouse.

Fuck it! My girlfriend started stripping and was bringing in plenty of money. Her doing that allowed me to focus on music and drugs. Indeed. Orange sunshine was the acid going around the summer of '94. We came across some of it in August of that year. At least, that's what we were told it was. I don't know if it really was orange sunshine acid, but that shit was dy-no-mite! Colton and I took two hits each and did a day trip. It was my first day trip and unlike any trip I had ever taken. We were fucked up for hours. We started at the band house and, at some point, ended up at a Captain D's. From there, Colton drove us around until nightfall while we were tripping and listening to music. Alice in Chains was what we mostly listened to that night, especially *Jar of Flies*. Anyway, I don't know how the fuck Colton did it. But he did. By the end of that night, we were buying some weed and smoking out of a six-foot pipe, which was pretty cool. And then we ended the night playing pool.

By the way, have you ever smoked opium? Well, my friend, it is the shit! I had gotten the hook-up through Colton. We were buying tootsie roll-sized chunks of that shit at a time. In fact, every time we got some, they were always packaged in tootsie roll wrappers. If ever given the opportunity, I highly recommend smoking opium.

I'll wrap up that first summer like this: it was intoxicatingly dark. The only time I felt I had no worries was when Bethany would let me and Brian borrow her car; we would open the sunroof, put some Snoop on, specifically starting with the last song on the first album, "G'z up, Hoes Down," fire up a fatty, and just ride for a while. I felt like things were going to be okay during those moments.

Most people wouldn't know about the song "G'z up, Hoes Down" from the album Doggystyle. Only a limited supply was distributed due to some dispute over the sampling of Isaac Hayes' song "The Look of Love." Therefore, unless you were quick about picking up the first copies of Doggystyle, you wouldn't have that song because it was redistributed without that track.

It was late October and two nights before my court date over the gun charge. We were recording a couple of songs. Tyler had acquired a four-track recorder from someone, and we thought it would be nice to have a demo put together so we could start branching out as far as the shows we played. Of course, Tyler and Brian didn't know what my future was going to be, and they needed something for someone to listen to in case I would no longer be around. For some reason, Bethany had brought a video camera that night; I guess to document the recording process. Anyway, I had spent the prior night cutting myself. I wasn't trying to die. I was trying to release the stress, anxiety, and mental pain from wondering if I had ruined my life over a fucking stolen handgun. Things couldn't have been worse. A few days before my court date, I had managed to find a job washing dishes. My first day on the job was the day before my court date. I could tell the judge that I had a job. But it turned out that on the day of court, my name wasn't even on the docket. Can you believe that shit? My lawyer walked up to the judge, gave him my name, and the judge said, "Well, I don't see his name on the list. Dismissed." I couldn't fuckin' believe it. Dismissed! I guess my lawyer made a deal with the prosecution or called in a favor or something. I'm not sure what the fuck it was, but I didn't give a fuck. I was not going to prison! Awesome! However, before my lawyer and I parted ways, he told me that I was going to have what they call a master file. Basically, a master file means that I was charged with something pretty serious, but that the charges had been dropped; and as long as I didn't get into any more trouble, they wouldn't open that file and decide to prosecute me. It also meant that any time I would have my name run, it would come up showing that I had a master file, but I couldn't be questioned about it. Pretty crazy shit. That was fine. I was free! As I was leaving the courthouse, my lawyer shook my hand, looked at me, and said, "Don't get into any more trouble." "I won't," I replied. I went home, grabbed my weed, and then hauled ass to the band house. I woke everyone up, yelling and screaming that I was free. Brian and Tyler slowly came out of their bedrooms, eyes still half shut, congratulating me. We smoked a bunch of weed and then played music. And no, I never went back to wash dishes. It was a great day!

Walter's dumbass showed up in November. And Heath was with him. Walter was about to get married to some girl he met from Tulsa. We all went out and ate some pizza. I'm bringing this up for two reasons. One: Walter was around again, here and there in 1995. Once he finally got married, he wasn't around as much. Plus, I think he went back to

Northwest Arkansas—specifically Fayetteville—to continue college. He'll show up again later for the last mutha-fuckin' time. The second reason I'm bringing this up is Heath. After the night that he showed up in Tulsa with Walter, I had seen him only a handful of times throughout the years. He was in and out of trouble over the years, and when I would see him, he would just keep it very formal, as if he didn't want to catch up or get into memories and all that. The last time I saw Heath was by accident when I was walking my dog. He drove around the corner and noticed me. He stopped to ask me about Malachi, which was my fifth-generation bloodline (JJ) pit bull. We talked for a few minutes, told each other it was good to see one another, and that was it. That was in early 2006. Unfortunately, Heath decided to take his life in 2008. I was sad to hear of that.

December quickly rolled around, and so did the holidays. I had managed to get another job as a grill cook for the same steakhouse that I had originally worked for but at a different location, which was awesome because it was closer to where I lived. And I finally had a car. I was to start the new job at the beginning of the year, January of '96. Brian transferred to the steakhouse I had just been hired at as well, so that was cool. The three of us went back to Russellville for Christmas. Brian and Tyler only stayed in Russellville a few days. I was there just over a week. As soon as I got back into Russellville, I called Donovan, and he came and got me. Holy Shit! Donovan was a tore up muthafucker. Everyone was. Hell, Liam was lying on Donovan's couch, passed out. I tried waking him up, but he was dead to the world. In fact, the whole week I was there, that was the only time I got to see Liam because he eventually left Donovan's, went home, and slept. I wouldn't see him again until he moved to Tulsa, which would be soon. Donovan told me everything that had been going on the past year I had been gone. Turned out that everyone had been tore up for most of the year. Dope had become just as common as weed. It seemed as though everyone was on it. Well, I didn't go to sleep the entire time I was visiting, I'll tell ya that for damn sure. Christian wasn't there when I showed up at Donovan's, so we went there next. It was good to see him. Although, he was a tore up muthafucker, too. I could see why. The dope I was doing since I had been back, which was only a few hours, was wonderful dope. While we were at Christian's place, I met someone; someone who was to become a brother. His name was Anthony. He was sitting in Christian's living room, tore up, watching TV. He didn't say much. We'll see more of him shortly. Of course, even though I had just done one a couple hours before coming to see him, Christian demanded I do one with him. So, I did. We did. Good god, that one fucked me up even more than the first one. Hell, it had been a year since I had done any dope. Yet there I was, having done two nice shots within a four-hour time period. Yeah, I was wired. I was beyond wired. I was high as fuck. I spent the next few days hanging out with Christian and Donovan. I barely even visited with mom and dad when I was there, so I was kinda feeling like a piece of shit about that. To be honest, I thought the little bit of fun that I had in December was going to be it. I didn't know that by February of '95 things were going to take a huge turn.

The shit I had seen a couple of months earlier when I was visiting Russellville made it clear to me that the 3:00 a.m. house call I was about to receive was, at that moment, the beginning of a ride that I was fully prepared to participate in. James and I had just picked my girlfriend up from work. We had only been home about twenty minutes before I heard a knock on the door. Holy Shit! It was Liam, his brother Hawkin, and Anthony, the guy I had met a couple of months earlier at Christian's place when I was visiting Russellville. I couldn't believe my eyes. It was a very unexpected visit. But it was completely awesome!

"What the fuck is up, bro!" I said smiling as I hugged him. "What's up, muthafucker!" Liam said grinning. He introduced his brother, Hawkin, whom I'd never actually met. "What's up, man!" I said, greeting him. "How's it goin'!" Hawkin replied. I could definitely see the resemblance. He was just an older and taller version of Liam. And, of course, Anthony. "What's up, bro!" Anthony said. "Hey, man! Good to see you again, bro," I said while shaking his hand. Liam had met James and the girl I was dating in previous trips to Tulsa. But he introduced Anthony and Hawkin to the two of them. He then went on to explain to me that he was moving to Tulsa. The night just kept getting better. But wait. What was I noticing? Were these extremely tore-up people with dilated, black holes for eyes? Indeed! "Y'all wanna get fucked up?" Liam asked. "Hell yeah, I wanna get fucked up," I excitedly replied. "What are y'all talkin' bout gettin' fucked up?" James asked. "Dope, muthafucker!" I said laughing. I turned to Liam for him to produce what I was talking about to James, but Anthony and Hawkin both pulled out 8-balls. My excitement was beyond excitement. "Bro! I don't have any rigs," I said panicking. Of course, Liam pulled out a bag of fresh rigs. I immediately had to take a shit. So, that's what I did. Meanwhile, Liam started fixing mine up.

In case you're wondering, having to take a shit right before doing a bump is the first true sign of being a junkie. Ya see, it takes only a short time of doing a lot of dope before you start feeling like that. It's the exciting anticipation of knowing you're about to do one, because you know the way it's going to make you feel. Do you understand? Your heart starts racing. Your mouth gets dry, and your gut starts to move around. Before you know it, you are already high over the joy of what you're about to feel. Ya see what I'm sayin'? Junkie!

By the time I was done in the bathroom, Liam was in the middle of stirring the dope in the spoon. It was thick and clear. There was nothing in the spoon after he drew it all back into the rig. Nothing left in the spoon meant it was clean dope. It wasn't cut. Oh, and yes, Liam liked to mix them thick as well. "Ya ready?" Liam asked. I saw James and my girlfriend smiling, as if they couldn't believe what was going down. They looked unsure. "Fuck yeah, I'm ready," I replied. It was thirty units of pure magic. I was already tasting it before Liam was done pushing it in. I felt so good! It felt good to be that high again! Hawkin and Anthony giggled when I looked over at them. Liam was over there just shaking his head in agreement, smiling. Apparently, I looked as high as I felt. The next thing I know, I hear James ask if he could do one, followed up with a quick "Me, too?" from my girlfriend. Everyone started giggling. I was still enjoying my high. My russsssshhhh! Liam replied, "Hawkin, you fix one up for James, and I'll fix hers up." Now, that was to be my girlfriend's first time doing one. James? I wasn't sure. He claimed he had shot up once years earlier. However, I was always a little skeptical. Nonetheless, none of that was about to matter.

Hawkin was in the bathroom fixing James' up, and Liam was in the kitchen fixing my girlfriend's. Hawkin was done first, which was exciting because I couldn't wait to see James get off. He and Colton had definitely been my partners in crime the past year. I told Hawkin to only mix twenty units for James. I didn't want the muthafucker flopping on us. But that didn't matter, because that's exactly what happened. Hawkin pushed that twenty units into James' arm and barely got the needle out of his arm before James' knees started buckling. As he started to fall back, Hawkin and I held on to him and were both asking him if he was alright. All of a sudden James said, "I'm about to piss and shit myself." We started to get out of the bathroom as quick as possible when he suddenly decided he was going to go outside and do that. Well, the biggest problem with that was that my girlfriend and I lived in an apartment complex. We had no yard for him to do that in. His only option would have been the sidewalk, the parking lot, or the small amount of grass that ran across the front of the apartments. He chose the latter. Luckily, Anthony was already out there pissing on account we were all in the bathroom. So, he was able to help out James. Meanwhile, back inside the apartment, we were laughing our asses off. That was some hilarious shit. Except, little did we know, the same thing was about to happen to my girlfriend, minus the piss and shit. Liam hit her, and by the time he got the needle out of her arm, she started to fall to the ground. Liam and I caught her before she hit the ground. We leaned her up against the wall and started yelling at her to wake up. After three to five seconds, she opened her eyes up. We're all like, "What the fuck?" We began asking her if she was alright and if she knew where she was and all that shit. For the first few minutes, she couldn't keep her eyes open. We kept having to wake her up. But after five or ten minutes, she seemed fine. She was alert and wide-eyed. The only thing we could come up with was that she had overamped. Basically, an overdose of some kind. I had to go to work later that morning, so Anthony, Liam, and Hawkin stayed with my girlfriend to make sure she was alright. When I got home from work, we all did some more—even the girlfriend. Anthony and Hawkin stayed for two weeks and then went back to Russellville. They spent the first week staying fucked up, and they spent the second week cleaning up because they were going to go to truck driving school together. But that never happened. No worries. Hawkin would end up moving to Tulsa for a while. And Anthony? Well, let's just say that we'll see him again.

The first month or two that Liam was living in Tulsa came with little to no sleep. We remained fucked up. By March of '95, I had acquired a dope connection through my weed man. I had been getting Russellville prices as far as weed. Then my weed man saw the dope potential, so there was that. Plus, Colton had acquired a dope connection. Between the two of us, we kept ourselves pretty fucked up. Consistently. Brian and Tyler, of course, let Liam move in with them. And Liam got a job at the steakhouse where Brian and I worked. He became the bread maker. Plus, we all worked days. Therefore, besides Tyler having to work nights here and there at a Mexican restaurant (he lost his job at the restoration business), we were able to practice during decent hours and then have time to party or play shows without much of a problem. Although, I don't think playing music or partying was ever much of a problem for the simple fact that that is what we did: played music and got fucked up.

Speaking of music, I had been turned on to a new group called Bone Thugs-N-Harmony. The first song I heard was "Thuggish Ruggish Bone." Mind blown! I immediately went out and bought their album *Creepin on ah Come Up*, which was actually my favorite song on the album. The EP had come out back in '94, but I had just heard about it. Liam and I used to roll to that album a lot when he first moved to Tulsa. Also, about that same time, I was turned on to a band called Nine Inch Nails. I heard the single "Closer" from *The Downward Spiral*, which had come out in '94, either on the radio or MTV. But that was all I was familiar with until Bethany let me hear both albums in full. I listened to *Pretty Hate Machine* first and wasn't sure how to receive them. Then I heard *The Downward Spiral* all the way through, and I really didn't know what to think. For me, both albums were completely different. Both albums hit two different spectrums that I was not familiar with on that level: electronic/techno and industrial mixed with rock, pop, and metal undertones. Incredible! After a couple more listens, I was absolutely hooked. Thanks, Bethany!

As time quickly sped past us, so did rational thought. Or maybe it was more along the lines of just not giving a fuck. Either way, we were completely out of control by March. One night, Liam, Hawkin, and I decided to try and rob a muthafucker. Actually, it was me who had talked them into helping me. Ya see, there was this fucker who was selling weed for what I thought was entirely too much money. He was selling quarters for sixty dollars of the same quality of weed Colton was getting for forty. I know what you're thinking. Today, that's a pretty damn good deal. But back then? I felt it a little extreme. So, I decided we were gonna teach this fuckin' asshole a lesson about overcharging people for weed. After slamming a couple grams of cocaine, we decided it would be a good idea to get dressed up in disguises and travel in the heavy snow for a 211. I have no idea where we got the coke from. I don't remember which one of us got it. I just remember having it.

That was the first time I shot coke. Let me tell ya something about coke. First: it's not the same high as dope. Second: it doesn't last long at all. A person can go through an 8-ball with no problem in one night. I don't give a fuck how good the coke is. I'll take the fuckin' Pepsi Challenge with the coke I've done over the years, and it just don't matter. The high is good, but entirely too quick, even when ya shoot it. Now, when ya shoot coke—watch out. Good cocaine, after slamming it, will allow you to hear your blood flowing, or rushing, or spinning, or something. It ain't like any other high I reckon. Cocaine is a night-on-the-town drug. You can go to sleep fairly quickly, and you can easily eat while on it. But it's fun!

After we were done getting ready in our disguises, which consisted of scarves covering our faces, a St. Patrick's Day, green top hat that I was wearing, a face-covering that Hawkin was wearing, and whatever other psychotic shit we decided to wear—we grabbed a machete (no, not the same one from earlier), Hawkin's 9mm, and headed towards our destination. The snow was heavy that year, and we were already travelling pretty fuckin' slow. It was way too slow to try and rob a muthafucker, put it that way. But, nonetheless, in all our genius decision making, we were on our way to do just that. As we approached the destination, we thought it best to park in the parking lot across from our victim's apartment complex. Sure, the parking lot we decided to park in contained a business that was open. Of course, that business was a restaurant. And, sure, it was the steakhouse I worked at. But fuck it. Ya see, our deluded thought process was that if the shit went down and we had to make some sort of ninja-like escape, that it would be best that we run to the car—that way we wouldn't get stuck in the snow trying to escape. We figured that we could make better time on foot if we had to. I know. Don't ask. Anyway, as we were walking up to the apartment that would change our lives forever, we were silent. It was the kind of silence that you might not expect when about to commit a felony, but silent we were. On top of that, it was snowing. Do you know the silence of snow falling and collecting on the ground? It can almost be a deafening sound. Do you know what I mean? Beautiful, but deafening. In fact, the only sound I remember was our footsteps approaching a new level. Had it come to this? Was I so fucked up that I was about to rob a person for their weed? Who was I? What had I become?

When we got to the door, we all looked at each other one more time and grinned. Hawkin knocked. He knocked hard. It was the kind of knock that meant business. There would be no mistaking that kind of knock. Ya see, the plan was to rush him once he opened the door. Then, we'd go straight for the kitchen, which is where we were told he kept his shit. Hawkin knocked again. My heart was racing. On top of being high, I was experiencing yet another high. One that I'm not sure I could explain. I guess ya just had to be there. Finally, we knocked again. Yes, I mean all three of us. It was apparent he wasn't home. Or he just didn't answer the door. Either way, I'm grateful nothing happened. Had he answered that door, I'm not sure what would have happened. I guess the same kind of thing would happen that always happens: a muthafucker would have gotten beat up a little and robbed. Or a muthafucker or muthafuckers would have been shot. Or a bunch of muthafuckers would have ended up in prison. Or a bunch of muthafuckers would have ended up dead. Fuck that! I mean it. Fuck that shit! I was and am thankful that shit didn't go down.

Here's another example of being junked the fuck out or just not giving a fuck: working. Yes, we showed up. It's not like we were performing rocket science. It was a fuckin' steakhouse for Christ's sake. So, fuck it! We were getting so fucked up that we would bring rigs full of dope already prepared and watch each other's work area while the other one was in the bathroom shooting up. We were also selling weed out of that steakhouse. The restaurant employees had no illusions about where they could go to get whatever they wanted. So, when an employee needed some weed, they would come to me and Liam. And

Liam would deliver it so eloquently. Ya see, every meal would come with rolls. And since Liam was in charge of making the rolls and I was in charge of cooking the meals those rolls came with, what better way to deliver a product than within the roll itself from my kitchen? Fuckin' genius! I love that man! "Here ya go," Liam would say, "I made these rolls special for ya." The waiters or waitresses would pick up their special rolls and do their thing. We would either pick up the money after the shift or they would just bring the money back in a roll basket and ask for more rolls. Great system, and no one missed a beat. Although, after a while, we were missing the beat. As we got further down the rabbit hole of meth, it started showing. It started showing physically and mentally. For fuck's sake, our arms looked like a goddamn battlefield. Not to mention, trying to say complete sentences to folks at work became a task. One of our managers used to bust our balls by always telling us that we were in a drug induced stupor. He would laugh, but there was also truth to his comments in that he knew. He knew it wasn't just weed we were smoking. Another guy who was working there just flat out walked up to me one day and said, "You need to get off that needle." I guess it was at that point that I figured I ought to take a break for a while. Besides, it was just a matter of time before I would lose my job in that muthafucker again.

In April, everything was everything. It was business as usual. We were at work one day and the steakhouse was giving away pins. On the pins was the phrase "I'm Drug Free". When they got to me and Liam, of course, we refused them. The district manager said, "Well, at least you're honest." There wasn't anything for it. We were well into our path of self-destruction. But then something else happened. There was more destruction. Except this time the destruction was not self-inflicted. It happened while we were getting the restaurant ready to open for the day. I noticed my boss running through the kitchen and out to the dining room. I was at the grill area and had a huge open view into the dining room because that was where the servers would come to pick up their orders. When my boss got to the back of the dining room, he started turning on the TVs that were hanging on the wall. There was news broadcasting on each television. I still wasn't sure what was going on, so, based off the odd behavior I was witnessing from the boss, I walked out to the dining room to see what the hell the problem was. The problem was some asshole decided to blow up a federal building in Oklahoma City. The explosion killed 168 people, including nineteen children. There were several hundred more people injured. The Oklahoma City bombing was deemed "the deadliest act of homegrown terrorism in U.S. history," according to the FBI.

In May I received yet another 3:00 a.m. visit. The knock on the door was subtle, but ferociously aggressive at the same time. It was the kind of knock that is constantly there and doesn't go away. Ever! It was like a constant drip from a kitchen sink. The knock had entered my sleep like an annoying alarm clock. It finally stopped echoing as I started waking up. But unlike an alarm clock that you can roll over and stop, that knock would acquire much more of my attention. As I stared at the door, still half asleep, I already knew who it was. The knock was very familiar. I can't remember if I was excited or reserved about the situation. Nonetheless, I knew what was about to happen. I guess I was excited. But I was also scared. Both feelings clashed throughout my brain. I was even shaking a little as I got up to answer the door. I opened the door. "What's up!" Christian stated. "What's up, brother!" I replied. Obviously, he was tore up. What came next? You know what came next. He brought the fuckin' shit with him. I know. I know. I keep saying that, right? It's because it's true. You wouldn't think the dope would continue to just get better. But it did! Christian broke out some rocks that looked like macadamia nuts. I shit you not. I remember specifically saying to him, "Holy shit, dude! They look like macadamia nuts."
I could literally buy a jar of macadamia nuts, put them side by side, and you would have never been able to tell the difference. This time, however, Christian and the dope weren't even the big surprise. Can you believe it? As soon as we got done doing a couple of thick shots, Christian told me that Robert and Anthony were with him. I couldn't fuckin believe it. "What?" I asked. "Yeah," he replied. "They're all over at Debbie's," he continued. Debbie was Brian's old girlfriend. She had come to Tulsa about the same time as Liam and got an apartment right next to mine. Needless to say, Brian didn't care for that at all. She was in Tulsa about a year before she bailed out. Anyway, Robert and Anthony were there! I went right over there and hugged Robert and Anthony. That was a great night. Christian and

Anthony left a couple of days later, but Robert ended up staying and living in Tulsa at the band house for a while. It was awesome!

It was already June of '95. Things were breaking down. My relationship with Tyler and Brian was getting bad. Musically, we were on top of our game. The shit we were writing and playing was second to none. Hell, we even had people coming to our shows asking for autographs. People were wearing Frustrated Cruelty t-shirts. Here's the kicker: we didn't make those shirts. Those folks spent their own money. But that didn't matter. We were losing touch. I especially was losing touch. We barely hung out anymore. Usually it was just Liam, Colton, James, and me. When practice or a show was over, the four of us were out and doing whatever the fuck we were doing, which was usually dope. Although, we would dabble in the occasional acid. You know! Christian and Kelly came to Tulsa in June of '95. It was crazy because Tyler and I had just learned the first four songs of White Zombie's *La Sexorcisto: Devil Music Vol 1*.

Yes, Astro Creep 2000 was already out, but I had always wanted to play those first four songs for fun, so Tyler learned them one night within about an hour and we played them. That night was the only time we played those four songs. As far as cover songs went, we usually didn't play them. However, Mikey had recently turned us on to a band called Tool. We were a little late in the game because their second album, Undertow, had already been out for two years by the time we heard them. Nonetheless, I fell in love. Hard! I had never liked a band as much as Alice in Chains until I listened to Tool. We learned "Crawl Away" and started playing that. We didn't add it to our set list or anything. We just started playing it because it was fun to play, and it was badass. Then I listened to Opiate. Good shit! That summer was when I had also heard Rage Against the Machine for the first time. I don't know how the fuck neither of those bands came on my radar until '95, but that's what happened. Better late than never, I guess. The first song I heard from Rage was "Killing in the Name Of"—while I was watching a stripper at a club do her thing. I was blown away because their first album had come out back in '92. Where the fuck had I been when all that great music was coming out? Oh, that's right, I was consumed by debauchery and hedonism. Oh, and that needle thing. That was a muthafucker too. I'm sorry, I digress.

Anyway, Christian and Kelly came up because they had some good dope. Colton had some good acid, so we were going to do some trading. We were all at the band house. I don't remember the kind of acid we had, but I remember the dope. It was red. It was so red that when we broke it down and drew it back in a rig, it already looked like blood. Luckily, we were professionals. Speaking of being professional, James had a girl there with him that night. Look, I'm not judging her. She was amongst fellow junkies. But that girl's poor arms were so fucked up that it took a while to find a vein. She had used her veins so much that her skin was basically scar tissue. It took me several attempts before I was able to successfully get a vein. I'm glad I gave her a healthy dose because I wasn't going to try and hit her again. After I finally got done hitting this bitch, I walked into the living room. Liam had just finished one after I specifically told him not to do one until he came down. What was I wanting him to come down from first? Acid! We were always told to never mix chemicals like that. Well, he figured out why. I don't think he said anything for about eight hours. Any time someone would ask him a question or talk to him, he would just have this blank stare like nothing was registering. He wasn't flopping around on the ground. He was standing up walking around. The best thing to do was to just let him go through the process and keep an eye on him. By the time sunrise hit, he was speaking again. Crazy, muthafucker!

By the middle of August, we were all going to the long-awaited Megadeth concert. I was excited to see those guys. Plus, it was the first concert I had been to in almost two years. It was time. I was excited. Liam, Robert, and I rode together. But, after we got in the amphitheater, we pretty much wandered in our own directions for some reason. That was the first concert I actually spent the majority of by myself. Strange. One of the opening acts that night was a band called Korn. Let me tell ya, I hadn't heard music like that before. It was badass! I remember looking around at the crowd when Korn was playing, and there were a lot of people standing there with their mouths open. Wow! Great fuckin' show! Although, I think Megadeth ended early that night, which sucked. People kept jumping into the water that was between the fans and the stage. It had flooded. So, where the pit was supposed to be was just water. The members of the band kept warning folks to stop doing that, or they would have to stop. People kept jumping in anyway. Oh well. I walked away that night knowing that I had found yet another great band. Finding Tool, RATM, and Korn in 1995 showed me that music was changing and that Frustrated Cruelty was already behind the times. Not long after the Megadeth show, Robert left Tulsa and moved back to Russellville. His stay there would be short lived.

Fall rolled around, and we continued life as usual. James, Liam, and I had been hard at it for a couple of nights when we picked my girlfriend up from the strip club. She informed us that we needed to go to this guy's house she had met earlier that night. Apparently, he had some dope. Off we went. When we got to this guy's house, turned out that we weren't the only ones he had invited. It seemed as though we had arrived at some sort of late night gathering. It was a little awkward when we walked in because it was pretty quiet in there. It was as if everyone had been waiting on us to arrive. The guy that invited everybody told us all to relax, and he would be right back. About a minute later this fuckin' guy came out with a rock the size of a goddamn softball. I shit you not! I had never seen a rock that big in my life. We all just started laughing because what else can you do in that situation? This guy had a rock the fuckin' size of Texas. I think I also heard echoes of "holy shit!" and "god damn!" when the guy first took out the rock. He took out a razor blade and just started shaving dope off the rock for everyone. Gee, I wonder what happened next?

One night, not long after that, Liam, James, and I had been out drinking pretty heavy. I had failed to pick my girlfriend up from work, so she had to get a ride from someone. James and I dropped off Liam at the band house, and we went to my apartment. I already knew I was going to get an ear full. But what I didn't expect to get was a fryer full of hot oil thrown on me. I can't even remember the exchange of words that took place, but, all of a sudden, she decided to throw a fryer full of oil on me. Thankfully, it had only been heating up for a couple of minutes, so it wasn't scalding hot. But it was hot enough for the dog we had to attack her and for me to grab her by her throat and put her head into the wall. By the time that little situation was over with, James was freaking out, making sure I was alright and was getting my shit together to get the fuck out of there. That was it. That was the final straw. Our relationship was toxic from the beginning, and nothing we had done since ever helped it. Fuck that shit! I was out. I moved back to the band house, and she moved back to Florida with her mom. Christian had also moved back by October and was living with me, Liam, Brian, and Tyler at the band house. Mikey had moved out by then. Christian had gotten a job at the steakhouse. He worked the buffet bar on the night shift. It was good to have him back. And wouldn't ya know it? Walter's dumbass started showing back up again around November. But this time he wasn't coming down for social calls. He needed something, and that something was weed. And he knew who the muthafucker was that could get the weed for him at affordable prices. Me! He was living in Fayetteville at the time, going to school. And the weed up there was expensive. So, I started hooking him up. He would get a quarter-pound to a half-pound at a time. Once the student, now the master. Interesting! It was December, and that meant that it was my birthday. I don't usually make a big deal about my birthday. But since I turned twenty-one in December of '95, I thought I would mention it. Again, not because there was a lot going on or anything. I was twenty-one. Big deal! I had already spent the past couple of years playing in bars and clubs because I was playing music. And when you're in the band, you get free alcohol. So, I was already familiar with bars and clubs. It wasn't anything that I looked forward to. I ended up passed out and throwing up in front of the very same apartment complex we were going to rob ten months earlier. We knew some people from the steakhouse who lived there. I have no idea why we ended up there at one point. Maybe we had gone to the steakhouse for some reason, which, if you remember, sat right across from that apartment complex. Anyway, thankfully, I had my brothers with me: Liam and Christian. And that was that. That was my twenty-first birthday. I was passed out in the back seat of my car the rest of the night while Christian drove and Liam navigated. Good times!

Later that month, Walter came back to Tulsa again. Christian and I met him somewhere to get the money for a quarter-pound. He would wait while we went and picked up the weed. At that time, I had to go out to Broken Arrow to get my smoke. Broken Arrow is about fifteen minutes outside of Tulsa. On the way to get the smoke, Christian looked over at me from the passenger seat grinning, and he said, "Ya know, we don't have to go get him weed." I looked back at him and smiled. I already knew what he was alluding too. "You know what, dude—fuck that muthafucker!" I said passionately. "It'll put more money in our pockets," Christian continued. "Hell yeah!" I replied excitedly. Instead of hitting the interstate to go to Broken Arrow, we hit the mall to go get some new music. Christian bought the new Ozzy Osbourne album, *Ozzmosis,* and I bought the new Alice in Chains. The self-titled album. A couple hours later, I called Walter to let him know that "I had been fucked." There was no conversation from him about it. He knew what we had done, and there wasn't a mutha-fuckin' thing he could do about it. That was long awaited and long overdue. Christian knew it. I knew it. And Walter mutha-fuckin' damn well knew it. I saw him one time after that, years later at mom and dad's in Russellville. We didn't say much. He tried telling me that all the shit we had done over the years didn't mean shit. Of course, it didn't mean shit to him. He's an ain't-shit-muthafucker. He didn't and probably still doesn't understand the meaning of brotherhood or fellowship. Fuck him!

After a short break, January of '96 wasn't looking much better. As far as the band went, we were all but split up. Liam, Christian, and I had gone to Florida in December to pick my ex-girlfriend up and bring her back to Tulsa. She was stripping again, so there was plenty of money. By the middle of January, Liam and Christian had moved back home. I didn't blame Liam and Christian a bit for leaving. Between the dope, losing jobs, and scrounging for food, it was a pretty bad time. Liam had lost his job back in November, and Christian had lost his in December. James, Colton, my girlfriend (again), and I pretty much stayed up the entire month of January. Junkies? Probably. Nothing mattered anymore. Things sucked. Bad! It got to the point where I would have to do a shot of dope just to get my head right—just so things would make sense. That's fucked up, my friend. If a muthafucker has to do a shot of dope just to get his thought process in order, that muthafucker needs help. Hell, it got to the point that I could do a shot, eat, and still go to bed at the end of the day. Shit got so bad at the end—I even got a DUI in February. Believe it or not, I actually remember that night. Brian, Tyler, James, Colton, and I were at this bar we would often frequent together. It was a popular college bar where you could get cheap drinks. We closed the muthafucker down. I was shitfaced. I had no business driving. I ended up getting about a mile down the road and got pulled over doing sixty in a forty-five. When the cop approached the car, he started asking me if I knew how fast I was going, but then he answered his own question when he started laughing and said, "Naw, I don't guess you do know how fast you were going." He told me to get out of the car and asked how much I had been drinking. I replied, "A lot." He proceeded to give me a field sobriety test, at which time I tried explaining to him that there was no need for all of that because I wouldn't pass. He laughed again and said it would be a quick and simple test. Guess what? I failed. When I blew a .3 the cop was amazed that I was still awake and talking. And as he was saying that, I felt myself blacking out. Just minutes earlier I had been driving down the road with no worries. I felt great! When I got to jail, they processed me as quickly as possible on account that I kept throwing up everywhere. My girlfriend bailed me out.

I found out the next day that Brian and Tyler were getting a new place and that everyone had to be out of the band house by the end of April. A couple of weeks after the DUI, I lost my job. At the beginning of March, my girlfriend and I moved back out of the band house and into an apartment that Colton was renting but not staying at. Colton got me a job at the iron foundry he was working at. It was long hours but good money. I only worked there until April. Then I quit. By that time my girlfriend and I had moved into an apartment with one of her stripper friends. But none of that really mattered because, by the end of April, my girlfriend and I broke up, and so did the band. I ended up staying a couple of more weeks with Colton. And then, with nothing left but the twenty dollars Colton gave me—in shame and defeat—I went home.

6   THE RETURN

I had been in Tulsa just short of two and a half years, and I came back with a few pair of clothes and my drums loaded in the car. Obviously, I wasn't supposed to be driving because I still didn't have a license from the DUI. But I needed a restart, and the only way that was going to happen was to get back home. Besides, I had fucked everything off in Tulsa and didn't really have any ground left to stand on. I did it to myself. I had been consumed with infection that had diluted any and all rationale thoughts. I knew two things when I got back to Russellville in May of '96. One: I knew I had fucked a good thing up. If I were to ever be in a band again that was serious about music, I would never again be the person I was in Tulsa—that I would always stay focused on the music, no matter how fucked up I got. Did you see what happened there? Did you notice that? I made it clear to myself that I was a junkie but that I would never again let that fact get in the way of music. I sure as fuck never promised myself that I would stop doing dope, just that I wouldn't let it get in the way. Wow! Can you say *junkie*? And the second thing I knew: when I got back to Russellville, I would stay current with the music scene. I would do as much as I could to know about the music and the artists themselves. In fact, it would become almost obsessive compulsive. Not in a psychotic way but in a very curious and even scholarly way. I had to come to terms with the fact that I was no longer playing music and that I may never again have the opportunity to play music on a level of musicianship that I was playing with Brian and Tyler in Frustrated Cruelty. I mean, for fuck's sake, I was back in Russellville. It's not like there was a plethora of musicians to choose from. At least not that I was aware of. Shit, I was lucky when I found Brian and Tyler. I wasn't holding my breath for something awesome to ever develop again. Plus, I guess I was trying to make up for what I had lost—or rather what I had fucked up. The only evidence I had left of FC was some live video footage. Luckily, I had that. But I had to prove to myself and my peers that I was more than what I had actually become, and that it actually was about the music for me. Yes, drugs would still be a part of my life, but so would music. Now more than ever.

I would use that intoxication for my musical evolution. And, just maybe, I would fill the emptiness I felt inside while still keeping up to date with music—just in case I found myself in a band again one day. Needless to say, every dollar I started making went to growing my music collection. I started with everything I had missed over the past couple of years. I got caught up when I bought Rage Against the Machine's second album, *Evil Empire*. From that point on, I kept current. Know that!

The first thing I had to do when I got back was transfer my DUI shit from Oklahoma to Arkansas. Specifically, from Tulsa to Russellville. I did eighty hours of community service out at Lake Dardanelle, which consisted of helping the park ranger with his house the first week and then picking up trash around the lake the second week. I liked that better because I could smoke weed while I was out there. The state allowed me to drive to community service, but I wasn't getting my license back until August, which would end my six-month suspension.

It was about a week or so before I even looked for or talked to anyone. Eventually, I called Donovan and told him I was home. He told me to get my ass over there. We caught up. He also told me where Liam was. So, I surprised Liam at his job one afternoon. Liam had moved into an apartment with Theresa and her boyfriend, Pauly, in Russellville. Kelly was living with his brother, two apartments down from Theresa and Liam. Theresa and Kelly's became the new hangout area.

Christian wasn't in Russellville. He had moved to Louisiana with his parents after he left Tulsa. After that, he moved to Alabama with his parents. He didn't come back to Russellville until 1998. Robert was sent back to North Carolina to do some time. Ya see, he had come to Tulsa because he and his girlfriend had broken up. The problem was that during the breakup, Robert decided he was going to try and hit her with the car. Apparently, he succeeded a little bit because he had to do several months. He'll be back in 1997. And really quickly about

Pauly: he's a big guy. He stands well over six feet, and besides being tall, like I said, he's big. He's a pretty cool guy.

Jacob and Dane started showing back up again when they heard we were back. It was good to see both of them. We pretty much picked up where we left off. Except this time we were smoking crack. An old high school buddy started hanging out with us again. But now he dealt crack. Kelly would let our old high school friend come over to his place and cook it up. Needless to say, there was a little bit of crack around. Let me just start by asking: do you remember me smoking crack back in 1994? Well, I'll tell ya, that wasn't shit! I learned that it's all about the crumbs. Our old high school buddy taught us quickly. The rocks were good, too, don't get me wrong. But the small crumbs or pebbles left over from a fresh cook, that's the shit. I got my bell rung one day. I was over at Theresa's hanging out when my old high school buddy came over and said, "Try this." I took that first hit and holy shit! I literally heard bells ringing. I finished that pipe, and he loaded some more. I shit you not, the second time around I heard a goddamn freight train. "Whoo!" I shouted, smiling. He laughed. "Did ya like that?" he asked. "Damn, dude," I replied, "I ain't ever felt like that." He just started laughing. Then he rolled a joint and threw some crack crumbles on that. Need I say more?

Unfortunately, Jacob and Dane got strung the fuck out on crack for a short time. It was bad. During that month or so, they would make sure I would pick them up from work, or they would have someone drop them off over at Theresa and Liam's because that's where they knew Liam or I would be. Although, we didn't care. We were going to get fucked up, too. They would both spend their entire checks, an entire week's worth of wages. Can you imagine? They would each buy an 8-ball. I never would have thought it had I not seen it with my own eyes—several times. Then we would go park somewhere and sit for a couple of hours and get fucked up. It just goes to show how powerful a drug crack really is. I was sure glad that routine didn't last long.

Thankfully, one day Kelly came across some anhydrous. That brought us all out of our crack binge quite expeditiously. Just in case you don't know what I'm talking about, it's dope. Anhydrous dope. Dope made from anhydrous ammonia. Got it? Allow me to explain right quick.

The word *anhydrous* means: "free from water and especially water of crystallization," according to the Merriam-Webster Dictionary. Anhydrous ammonia can be used to make dope. Cooks can get these kinds of ingredients, specifically ammonia and anhydrous ammonia, from agricultural facilities and farmers. Like I said earlier, I'm no cook. I don't know the specific steps or process it takes to make dope. But I do know about some of the ingredients used to make dope. Dope made using anhydrous ammonia—extremely dangerous! Do you remember me mentioning it earlier? I was comparing the dope we were doing, which was made with pseudoephedrine or P2P, to the new way dope is being cooked, which is with anhydrous ammonia and lithium. Anhydrous ammonia is used to fertilize farms for fuck's sake. It's poison. Ammonia is used sometimes as a refrigerant and is also used to produce plastics. Poison! Don't get me wrong, I'm not saying pseudoephedrine or P2P is a fuckin' vitamin or anything, but it's not being used to fertilize farms or produce plastics. So there's that. But nonetheless, anhydrous-made dope will blow your fuckin' head off. I guarantee it.

We all went over to Kelly's to do it. All of us meaning Kelly, Liam, Jacob, and me. Kelly pulled a gram out of his pocket, and I swear it looked like salt. The rest of us were kind of looking at it like, "What the fuck is this shit?!" Kelly said that the guy he got it from was a junkie—I mean connoisseur—like we were and that it was good shit. "He said it's anhydrous," Kelly explained. At that time, I didn't know what the fuck that was. I don't think any of us did. I had heard of it once or twice before but didn't really understand anything about it. It sounded complicated. But it sounded good as well. Mmm, anhydrous! Yummy! Of course, I would do some. And ya know what? Just for clarification, even if I had known what anhydrous was back then, I still would have taken it. Because why not? I was a junkie. And that's what junkies do. Fuck it! Kelly poured the entire gram into one spoon.

Oh, and yes, unfortunately, Kelly had started slamming by the time I came back from Tulsa. On the bright side, I figured out how to hit myself. It's all about the keyring. Trust me!

He was just going to mix it all up, and then we'd split evenly among the four of us. Now, I understand that what I'm about to tell you won't make sense to the uninitiated. I will try to make things clear so you can understand the awesomeness—or maybe craziness—of what is about to happen. Even for the junkies out there, what I'm about to say is pretty fuckin' incredible. With the entire gram of dope in the spoon, Kelly put 50 units of water on it. Remember, we used 1cc insulin syringes. That means there are 100 units in a 1cc insulin syringe. Therefore, he filled half the rig with water, or 50 units, and then shot that water on the dope to break it down and start mixing it up. In contrast, and for additional clarification, we would usually put anywhere from 10 to 15 units of water on a quarter of dope, which is 0.25 grams. Four quarters makes one gram. With good dope, putting 10 to 15 units of water on a quarter would usually yield a shot of anywhere between 20 and 30 units. Make sense? So, like I said, Kelly put 50 units of water on the entire gram. By the time he was done mixing and drawing the dope back into two rigs to see what we had, well, we ended up with a total of 187 units of dope. That's almost 200 units. That's almost two full rigs of dope from putting 50 units of water on one gram of dope. Needless to say, we were all excited and giddy. We were like kids in a toy store. If there was someone other than the junkies in that room to share that moment with, we would have been jumping up and down with joy, pointing and screaming saying, "Look! Look! That's so awesome!" Ya see what I'm saying? Yeah, it's kind of funny. Yet, extremely sad at the same time. After that childish excitement swept through us, we decided on the best way to disperse it. Since it was already pulled back in two rigs, we decided it would get into our arms quicker if we just shot 40 units into two more syringes instead of putting it all back in the spoon and drawing it back again. So, that's what we did. Kelly and Jacob took the two rigs that already had the dope in them, and Liam and I grabbed two new rigs and had our 40 units put in those. Kelly took his extra 27 units and shot it back into the spoon, that way we were all doing 40 units a piece. And yes, that was my first time doing 40 units. All I can say is that I'm glad we didn't try to split that extra 27 units up. That would have been quite silly.

I say that because Jacob was the first one to do his—rather he was the first one to start doing his. It bears clarification because as Jacob was pushing the dope into his arm—by that time he had shot 20 units of that 40—he was warning us not to do all of it. When I say warning, it was more of a panicked yelling. "Don't do it all, y'all. It's too much! Put some back," he assertively warned. The problem with that warning from Jacob, though—as appreciative as I was for such warning—was that it was too late. We all had a needle in our arm already and were doing our thing. I already had blood pulled back in my rig. And now my buddy is over there with concern, telling me not to do what I was about to do. I looked over at Liam and he was in the same situation. He just sort of smirked and said, "Hmmph, well, too late." Keep in mind that we had never heard Jacob utter such a thing. And I'm telling you, we had already been doing the best-of-the-best dope over the past few years. So, needless to say, hearing Jacob express that as I was standing there with a rig in my arm full of dope and blood from my thirsty, swollen vein caused me some concern. Therefore, I did what any good junkie in that situation would do: I continued. Holy fuck! In a flash, I understood why Jacob was warning us off. I don't even think I made 20 units before I realized how fucked I was. It was amazing that I made all 40 units without missing. I remember going out the back door of the apartment at some point trying to get my shit together. I think we all did. We were either gagging, coughing, sweating, or all of the above. But it was quick. I coughed and then started sweating in the initial five to ten seconds. Within a couple of minutes, I was as high as I'd ever been—at least one of the highest. I don't think any of us formed a complete sentence within the first few minutes. At least not until Kelly's brother, Troy, walked in, which turned that situation from pure pleasure to a little chaotic and stressful. Kelly liked to keep his brother away from that kind of shit. And who wouldn't want to keep family away from that kind of shit? And keep in mind that Kelly's brother had just gotten off work. It's in the wee hours of the night, and this guy comes home to find a bunch of junkies in his place doing a bunch of junkie shit. That would irritate any rational person. With that said, Jacob and Liam proceeded quickly out the back door and walked over to Liam's apartment while Kelly kept me with him to get shit cleaned up before we bailed out. Oh, and to also do something with that extra 27 units that was sitting in a spoon on the living room table. Naturally, we went to the bathroom to take care of said issue. And on…and on.

It was about that time when Jacob and Dane started doing their own thing. We all kinda just started living different lives. There wasn't any friction or anything. We all hung out a few more times in 1997 and 1998, but not much. Jacob had met a girl and started focusing on that. Dane? Dane was doing Dane. And that's all that needs to be said. We'll come back to them later.

Enter my brother Roman. It was around that same time when he had gotten out of the Navy and moved back home. He had actually made it home before me, but only by a month or so. We were all over at Liam and Theresa's one night getting ready to do some dope. It was the anhydrous. Roman said he wanted to do some for the first time, and he wanted to shoot it. I immediately told him no. I told him that if he wanted to do some that he needed to snort it. He didn't like that. Kelly asked me if I wanted him to do it instead. I said no. Liam and I left for some reason to go do something, but we were going to be back. While we were gone, Roman decided he was going to shoot it anyway. Kelly hit him. When Liam and I got back, I walked in and saw Roman sitting on the couch engrossed in a drawing. He looked up at me, grinned, and said, "What's up!" All I saw was dilation. Blackness. "Well, what do ya think?" I asked. Roman smirked and replied, "What does it look like?" referring to his eyes and the drawing, which was a black, incoherent circle. It was a fuckin' absolute mess is what it was. I could only imagine by looking at that "drawing" that his brain and his thoughts were—at best—what he was illustrating on paper. I looked at Kelly. "Well, what ya want me to do?" he asked. "Let him hit himself and fuck up?" Kelly continued. "No," I said disappointingly. "I was just hoping he wouldn't go through with it," I said. "But I'm glad you hit him," I continued. "Because I sure as fuck wasn't going to do it," I said smirking. And that shit was true. Both statements. I wasn't going to hit that muthafucker for the first time and have that shit on me. But at the same time, Kelly was absolutely right to do what he did. We all had someone help us the first time, so it was only right that Roman had someone help him. I mean, he gonna do what the fuck he gonna do, regardless of what the fuck I think or say. Roman was a big boy. He just got out of the Navy. Who the fuck was I to tell him any different? Besides, I couldn't really say shit to the muthafucker. I'd had a needle in my arm for two and a half years at that point. Go on, homie. Do you.

Right after that, Roman and I actually got a job together at a furniture manufacturing place. But we both lost our jobs there pretty quick. I shot a nail through my finger after about a month working there and couldn't pass a drug test. I just left. Roman had already quit prior to that. By the fall of '96, things seemed to start getting darker. Both Theresa and Liam were moving out to a place called Gum Log. Gum Log was a little town about ten minutes outside of Russellville. It was actually pretty cool because Theresa and Liam were still living next door to one another. And it was out in the country, which meant we had a little more freedom to get fucked up and do fucked up shit. Ya know, kind of be able to stretch out and not worry about the things you have to worry about when you're in the city. Kelly moved in with Liam. We spent the rest of '96 doing dope. Gee, that's original. What other glorious news can you share with us, Shane? Oh, ok. Well, Tool's third album, *Aenima,* came out in late '96. So there's that. That was a long-awaited album, and it was good to hear from them again. Marilyn Manson released *Antichrist Superstar*. That album received critical acclaim despite the content, which was viewed by some political cocksuckers as graphic. The album was even put into the same "profanity-laced" category with greats such as Tupac and Snoop. And speaking of greats such as Tupac and Snoop, the end of '96 also brought us the end of one of the greats, Tupac Shakur. I'm sure by now you know the story. If not, go fuck yourself. *All Eyez on Me* had been released at the beginning of '96. I had just picked up the album when I moved back from Tulsa, so I had only been listening to him for a few months before his life was taken. To be honest, I've never been able to bring myself to buy his first three albums, nor *Makaveli - The Don Killuminati: The 7 Day Theory*. I guess I just felt like it was too late. I had only started listening to him on his fourth album. How could I go back and get all the previous shit when the legacy was over? I'd never be able to apply the music to anything tangible. Does that make sense? Maybe I'm just fucked in the head. Luckily, a couple of other great artists came out with new albums late in '96. Korn released their second album, *Life is Peachy,* and Snoop released *The Doggfather*. Ya know? Both albums kind of helped me move on from the whole Tulsa thing. It was the beginning of something new. A new era. I'm not sure if that makes any sense, but there ya go.

7 SAME AS IT EVER WAS

Did you think it was over? Bitch! I have only just begun. It was 1997, and I still wasn't playing music. Although, there were talks. Brian, Tyler, and I had patched things up, and the idea was to return to Tulsa in the spring. Therefore, I started saving money from the outage I was working at the nuclear plant. Although, it was a short outage. I bailed out within a month, so the only money I was saving was from unemployment. Meanwhile, in Gum Log, we had come across some morphine. It was liquid morphine. This girl we knew had a relative who had terminal cancer and had the morphine prescribed. But the relative received more than they ever needed, so there were baby jars of the shit stored. That is, it was stored until that girl we knew started bringing it over. It was gonna go bad if she just let it sit there, so fuck it. She didn't do any of it, but she knew our junkie asses would do it. And we did. We shot that shit for just over a week. I don't think we were supposed to be shooting it, but that's what we were doing. The initial feeling of the morphine kind of sucked. Every time I shot it, I would get a really warm sensation, followed by my body feeling like it wanted to lock up on me. That feeling would go away within a few seconds, and then the high was awesome. It was the first time that I could explain the feeling of being comfortably numb. It would only last about an hour or so. But that was alright. We would just stick our rigs into the baby jar filled with morphine and go back down that slide again. I'm glad we only had that shit for as long as we did. It started making us feel like shit.

Robert was out of jail and back home. It was good to have him back. He moved out to where Liam and Kelly were, except he moved next door with Theresa and Pauly. Kelly and I were looking for jobs with no luck. But we found plenty of dope. You know!

In March of '97, the music industry suffered another loss. The Notorious B.I.G. was murdered. The single "Hypnotize" had already been released, and people were getting pumped up for his new album to drop. Unfortunately, Biggie lost his life on March 9th. The album *Life After Death* was released on March 25 and hit number one on the charts.

In May, when I was supposed to move back to Tulsa, I wrecked my car the night before I was to leave. If that isn't a sign, I don't know what is. Needless to say, I didn't make it back to Tulsa. By the time I got my car fixed late that summer, life just kind of took over. Brian and Tyler were struggling to pay bills and weren't really focused on the band. And I had given up all hope of ever getting back with them or ever playing music again because I had been, and still was, a broke muthafucker. Not to mention, I hadn't even played my fuckin' drums in over a year. Shit was sucking. Things were just really dark. Besides all the dope I had been doing, I wasn't getting along with my folks and had been kicked out once again. Actually, both Roman and I had been kicked out. I was pretty depressed. I remember being over at Theresa's one day just sitting on her couch crying after having been up a couple of days. I was a mess. So, I decided to grab a big ass knife from the kitchen. Was I really thinking about that shit? Did I really want to go? No! I was just in pain. I didn't like who I was. As I was sitting there on the couch crying, contemplating what to do, Theresa came out of her bedroom. "What's up, man," she said as she was rubbing her eyes, having just woken up. "Holy shit!" I thought. I didn't even realize she was there. Or I had forgotten she was there. Regardless, it wasn't uncommon for any of us to be in that house, even if Theresa or Pauly wasn't there.

"Oh, nothin'," I replied. I had music playing, but it was turned down low. As she was walking over to the couch, I asked, "I didn't wake you up did I?" "No," she replied. When she got closer to me, she could see that I was upset. I hid the knife under my right leg as best I could. I was feeling very awkward and vulnerable at that moment. "Shane, are you ok?" she asked. Looking down in shame at the floor, I replied, "Not really. Sorry. I didn't mean for you to walk out on this."

How was I going to negotiate the fact that I was in my friend's house with one of her knives under my leg, deciding on my life? Oh, no worries. I didn't have to negotiate anything. "Is that a knife?" she asked. Wow! I really felt like a piece of shit then. I didn't think I could feel any worse until that moment. I was ashamed of myself. "Yep," I replied as I got up from the couch to put the knife back. She asked again, "Shane, what's wrong?"

We had a good talk. I told her the shit that was going on. She told me I needed to get off the shit so I could get my head straight. Of course, she was right. We sat and talked some more while we smoked a couple. I never told anyone about that day. Neither did she.

In the following years, I only saw Theresa a handful of times. She and Pauly split up not too long after the move. She made new friends and just kind of did her own thing. Kelly got back in touch with her at some point and even started taking care of her weed situation after a while. He told me he had been seeing her, and I mentioned that I would like to see her again. About a week or so before I was going to go down to Russellville with Kelly to see her, she was involved in a fatal accident. That was in 2019. Kelly and I were the only two from our crew who were able to make it to her funeral. Pauly was there as well. I'm mentioning this now because the previous situation I had with her in '97 was the last significant encounter with her. The other times I saw her, we were just coming and going. I love you, Theresa! Thanks for always being you. We're going to say goodbye to Kristie as well. The last time we hung out was also the summer of '97, and I'm keeping those times to myself and Robert. I don't mean that in a perverted way at all. It wasn't. It's just important to keep some things to yourself. After that summer, we just sort of lost touch. You know: life happened. She also died in a fatal car accident in 2013. We all made that funeral. I'm sorry that happened to you, Kristie. Thanks for the good times!

By the end of '97, Gum Log had run its course. Theresa, Pauly, and Robert moved, and so did Liam and Kelly. Theresa moved farther out in Gum Log with Pauly. They split up pretty quick. Kelly went back to his brother's. Liam bought his own property in Dover. Robert lived around the Russellville and Dover area for a while, but ultimately ends up in Dover on his own property.

Dover is about ten to fifteen minutes outside of Russellville. It was good that we were leaving the Gum Log area. Well, at least that area. We'll be back in Gum Log again later.

I decided to go back to Tulsa in October to visit everyone again. To make a long story short, I ended up getting pulled over on my way out of Tulsa for not wearing my seatbelt. Obviously, I had weed on me, just over a quarter, and I went to jail. Yep, I went to jail again. In Tulsa. Fuck! That was the third time. I went twice when I lived there and once when I was visiting. What the fuck! I was so done with going to jail. And I was so done with Tulsa. I couldn't escape the black cloud that hovered over me when it came to Tulsa. Colton and the girl I was dating at the time bailed me out. I'll close '97 out like this: Donovan got me a job working with him at a wood shop, so that was cool. And Deftones came out with their second album, *Around the Fur*. That was exciting because I had only just heard them for the first time—their album *Adrenaline*—earlier that summer. I love Deftones!

When 1998 rolled around, things had slowed down. Just kidding. Nothing slowed down. And now, besides Donovan's place, Liam had a place to hang out. No, but seriously, things were just as fast as they always were, at least the first part of '98. At the beginning of the year, Kelly and I took Anthony down to what was then Little Rock National Airport to catch a flight. I had talked to my cousin, Samantha, the night before, and she told me to drop by after we left the airport. And that's what we did.

It was a trip because she lived in a neighborhood right down the road from where I went to elementary school from third through sixth grade. I actually used to have friends back in elementary school who lived in that same neighborhood. And about a mile down the road from that neighborhood was the neighborhood I lived in from third grade through my first eighth grade year, until I moved to New Hampshire to live with my biological dad. I was already very familiar with the area.

When Kelly and I got to my cousin's, I wasn't expecting what we walked into. First, you need to know a little about my cousin Samantha. She's a sweet girl. We did a lot of growing up together. But over the years, she grew up hard and fast. Trust me. We were only there a few minutes, and she asked if we wanted to do some shit. I answered immediately, "Hell yeah, we'll do some shit." I looked over at Kelly, and he said, "Hell yeah!" Samantha said her ol' man would be back shortly with some. We were excited. But we had to come up with a story about Kelly to tell Samantha's ol' man, who we'll call The Cook from this point. Ya see, Samantha had just met Kelly that day, and if The Cook knew that it would be a no go. So, Samantha said she would tell him that she had known Kelly for close to seven years. When The Cook got back, he went to the bedroom in the back of the house. Samantha followed. A few minutes later Samantha came out and told me to go back. She left the bedroom and shut the door. The giant that stood in front of me was part of a white supremacy group. He was big in the sense that he was built. You could tell he had spent time behind bars. He had racist tattoos all over him. He had marks on his neck that indicated some form of ranking. I only say that because I was already familiar with affiliated folks from living in Tulsa. The guy I was getting dope from—through my weed connection—was Bandito. I didn't know who or what The Cook belonged to, and I didn't care. It was of no concern to me. Besides, my cousin just left me with the meanest and scariest looking muthafucker I'd ever seen in a room with the door shut and a shitload of dope on the bed and dresser. I wasn't about to start questioning and discussing affiliation. I already felt like I was in the depths of hell, about to be prison fucked by the devil himself. This fuckin' guy was standing there by the dresser mixing up some shots. He already had one rig ready and was in the middle of another. He asked me some basic questions about Samantha and then asked me how long I had known Kelly. I told him many years and that we had done a lot of dirt together over the years. He told me to go and get him. I walked out, got Kelly, and took him back to the bedroom. Handing him a rig full of dope, The Cook looked at Kelly and asked, "You ain't a cop, are ya?" Kelly replied with a little smirk, "Ha, fuck no."

I didn't understand the irrational question The Cook asked Kelly. We had just spoke of Kelly and my cousin. Obviously, if I'm not a cop, the person that I've known for years and that I brought up into my cousin's house isn't a cop either. Idiot! But whatever.

After The Cook handed Kelly the rig, Kelly started to put it in his arm, and The Cook actually walked out of the room. He wasn't even in there when we did our shots. It was a very confusing situation. The dope had broken down brownish black. We could tell it had been overcooked. Most of the shit we had been doing over the years broke down clear. The Cook must have had about forty units or more in each rig. I couldn't believe Kelly was doing all of it. I put some of the dope back into the spoon that was laying there on the dresser until my rig read thirty units. It took me a few minutes to get a vein. I couldn't tell when I had hit it. It was worse than that time in Tulsa with that dope that looked like blood. At least that dope was clear enough to see contrast between the dope and blood. This shit had no contrast. It looked like mud in a syringe. And for some fuckin' reason, I kept missing my vein. I would either go through it or not be in it good enough to pull back blood. I think I was just stressed out and felt rushed or something. Kelly, on the other hand, had no problem. However, as soon as he was done, he coughed. I stopped looking for a vein for a minute when I heard him cough. That threw me off. I had never heard Kelly cough before, and as far as I knew, that was the first time he had coughed off any dope. I got a little worried. There we were, two rigs full of dope, mixed up by someone else and given to us to prove ourselves, I can't find my vein, and Kelly is over there coughing. Holy shit! I knew I was about to be in for a ride.

A person will cough when the dope is really good because of the fumes or vapors of the dope going through the system and, apparently, back out through the lungs. I'm not a scientist or doctor or anything. I don't know if what I just said was true or bullshit. I'm just making an educated guess about what happens to cause someone to cough after shooting some strong dope. All I know from experience is that when people cough, or even when I've coughed, it feels like fumes of some sort leaving your body. And you can taste the dope when that happens as well.

"God damn!" Kelly said with surprise. As Kelly was standing there trying to get his shit together, and steadily getting higher by the second, I finally hit myself. Of course, by that point, Kelly was fucked up. We left the bedroom and went back out to the living room. Well, I did. Kelly could barely see and felt like he was going to throw up. He went outside to get his shit together. I stayed in the living room for as long as I could before I also joined him outside. I wasn't going to throw up, but I needed some cool, fresh air because I wanted to make sure I didn't throw up. That was some good shit! It may have been overcooked, but it was damn good dope. The Cook asked if we wanted to take some dope back home with us. We explained that we didn't have any money, but he said he would front us. Although, he had to go and cook some more, so it would be several hours before he got back. Kelly and I stayed a while because, well, yeah.

After about eight hours, The Cook returned. He gave us close to two 8-balls and told us to bring back $175. No problem! We went back home tore the fuck up with pockets full of dope. When we got home, Kelly and I split the dope up and went about our business. About a week later, we met back up, went back down there, and got some more. But this time we paid for what we left with, which was only an 8-ball. I knew we weren't going back after that second time. It took even longer for The Cook to get back the second time, and he came back with less. The dope was good, but not consistent enough for the unsafe trip back and forth to Little Rock. Besides, we could get all the dope we wanted in Pope County. The whole thing with Samantha was just an unexpected cherry on top anyway.

James and his brother, Mikey, came down to Dover from Tulsa in late February to early March. Obviously, we were up for a few days. It was good to see them again. Actually, I need to tell you about a situation when James had made another trip back about a month later. When he showed up that time, he was drunker than shit. He picked up Kelly and me, and we ended up going to Jacob's brother's place, Neil's, to take care of some business. I can't even remember where Jacob was that day, but he wasn't with his brother. By the time we left Neil's, we were pretty fucked up. James' driving was absolutely insane, which was nothing unusual. But the problem was that he was driving insane in an area he knew nothing about. Not to mention, we were on a mountain, which meant hills and curves. But that didn't matter to ol' James. As we left Neil's, James punched it. Mind you, again, that we were already on a hill leaving Neil's house. But like I said, that didn't matter to James. In less than a quarter-mile, there was a sharp turn to the left, which we didn't successfully navigate. Nope. Instead, with

James laughing the whole time, we ended up leaving the designated roadway and went flying into a front yard. Now, that wouldn't have been much to talk about had there only been a front yard. But our situation was much different because we were headed for about twenty fuckin' pine trees. And somehow, someway, through some divine intervention, we missed every fuckin' tree in that yard. However, we did manage to hit the front of the house that sat behind all those pine trees. After the chaotic and life flashing moment of dodging trees—as if we were on some type of speeder from the Star Wars classic *Return of the Jedi*—James miraculously managed to get the car turned just in time so that the entire passenger side of the vehicle slammed into the house. I was in the front seat. If I had wanted to get out of the car at that moment, I would have been trapped. I could have literally reached out the car window and touched the house. Amazingly, nothing happened when we hit that house. We didn't go through it. We just hit it. When we made impact, obviously, we came to a complete stop. I went ahead and calmly lit a cigarette as I figured we were all going to jail.

Why was I so calm in that moment? I'll tell you why. Because I had spent two and a half years riding with James in Tulsa. And in those days, riding with James, well, hell, you had about a fifty-fifty chance of coming back alive. Not so much because of the drugs or intoxication—but because of his car. When I first met James in '94, he needed new breaks for his car. After about a year of driving around and never replacing the brakes, I experienced that fifty-fifty chance I just mentioned. Not only did we experience it—we meaning Liam, Christian, Hawkin, and me—we experienced it in the middle of rush hour one evening. What did we experience? James' brakes finally failed. That's exactly what we experienced coming off the interstate exit. The brakes had finally gone completely out. Cars were lined up on the offramp. They were waiting on a green light. We couldn't stop. It was very sudden. I was in the front seat. James was pumping his brakes, but nothing was happening. As we approached two lines of cars—let me clarify: as we approached a shitload of cars that were stopped—everyone started yelling. But there was nothing for it. James quickly jumped the curb to avoid smashing into any vehicle. And there we were, in the grass, bypassing every car waiting at the offramp light, heading toward a very busy intersection at a fairly high rate of speed.

The curb did help slow us down, but we were still making our way toward the intersection. It was either that or smash into someone in order to bring us to a halt. And James wasn't trying to do that shit. He was actually doing pretty damn well considering the situation. As we were all yelling, screaming, cussing, and watching the last few moments of our lives play out, we entered the thriving intersection as if we owned that muthafucker. And I'll tell ya this, somehow, someway, not one mutha-fuckin' car was in the intersection as we plowed through. I couldn't fuckin' believe it. Either people saw what was going on and stopped all motion until we cleared the path, or the lights changed in our favor at the last second. I reckon it was the latter. Regardless, it was a relief. It was such a relief that, as we rolled through the intersection, it was pure calm and silence. We had either all accepted that death was knocking, or we had realized that we were going to actually survive that situation. Either way, it was a pleasant moment. When we finished through the intersection, there was a huge sigh of relief. Everyone started laughing and talkin' about how we just survived that shit. A block or so later, we arrived at our destination, which was dropping Christian off at work, at the same steakhouse where Liam and I worked. Why did so many of us have to go to drop one person off? Fuck, I don't know. We all just wanted to ride. Well, and yes, we were drinkin' and smokin'. Anyway, that was one of several instances with James at the helm.

But surprisingly, as James was devilishly laughing, he punched the gas and just drove the fuck off. I looked back at the house as we drove away. It was fine. There was a little impact mark. But that was it. But it wasn't the end of our little situation. You would have thought that would have been enough excitement for one day. Nope. Not for James' drunk ass. As we hauled ass away from the house we just hit, James, four-wheeling his vehicle out of the front yard and back on to the designated roadway, decided it would also be funny if we didn't stop for the road workers in orange and the heavy machinery that was blocking the roadway. Nope. Instead of stopping for said heavy equipment and the workers—who, by the way, were yelling at us to stop and who eventually had to run out of the way so they would not die from a car full of thugs doing thug shit—James went right through that shit like it didn't even exist. Meanwhile, James had us all yelling and screaming at him to slow down or stop—or something. Fuck! Let us out of the car. We'll walk. When we got to the bottom of Skyline, which was the neighborhood we just left, James had finally come back to his senses and started driving right. Well, better. I don't know about right, but he was driving better. Anyway, the rest of the day was quite intoxicating, to say the least.

Christian had also made his way back home from living in Alabama with his folks not long after that incident. It was good to see my brother again. He was back as if he was never gone. And we lived accordingly. Now, like Robert, Christian moved around Pope County for a few years, but ultimately ended up at Pauly's place in Gum Log.

Around that same time, I had my mom take me to my court appointment that had been scheduled as a result of the weed charge that I got back in October of '97. I wasn't sure if they were going to throw the book at me and open the master file that I had acquired a few years earlier in the stolen gun incident. I was told that if I had got into any more trouble within a certain timeframe, they could recharge me for that gun—on top of whatever I had just gotten in trouble for. For all I knew, I was going to do some time. Luckily, that didn't happen. All I did was pay a fine. The weed charge wouldn't even show up on my record. That was a good thing. Later that same week, I got the ball rolling to start college for the fall of '98. I was certain that I no longer wanted to live a life in and out of jail and that I was going to make something of myself. Keep in mind, that meant that I was no longer going to deal or do thug shit. I made it clear to myself that I wasn't going to play around any longer in the life of crime that had attracted me so much over the years. Fuck that shit! I didn't want to be a criminal. I didn't want to fuck with guns anymore or any of that shit. I just wanted to do drugs not sell them (except, of course, to close friends). This bit of information is important because the idea of continuing to do drugs at the level I was doing them—and the plan to re-introduce myself into society while doing said drugs—would be the beginning of learning how to be a socially functioning junkie. Interesting.

Liam and I went back to Tulsa in April to visit everyone. April of '98 was a badass month for music. We were in Tulsa the day that Clutch had come out with their third album, *The Elephant Riders*. I had heard

Clutch for the first time from Mikey when I was still living in Tulsa. The first time I heard them was on their first album, *Transnational Speedway League: Anthems, Anecdotes and Undeniable Truths*. When I had gotten back home, Clutch's first two albums were two of the first albums I had picked up. Hearing *Elephant Riders* for the first time in Tulsa sort of brought it back around. I picked up *Elephant Riders* as soon as I got back to Russellville. Oh, and I found out that Tyler was going into the Navy as well when we were in Tulsa visiting. That was a trip. Somehow, I also found a band called Soulfly in April of '98. Holy crap! Their first album was self-titled. I immediately turned Donovan on to the new Clutch and Soulfly. And yes, I was back at Donovan's again all the time. We spent the entire summer of '98 out by his pool, listening to music and drinking beer when we weren't doing dope. Donovan and I also heard of a new band from Jaxton, Donovan's brother. He told us to check out a band called Ultraspank. I added them to the collection. We also went to a badass concert in July of '98. Tool! It was Liam, Donovan, me, and our girlfriends. We went to Memphis to see the show. Melvins opened for them that night. That was my first Tool concert, and let me tell you: Magnificent! I had never seen or heard anything like that in my entire life. I was truly inspired. The rest of '98 was pretty kick ass. I started school like I had planned. However, I had to take preliminary classes before I could actually start taking classes that would count as credits towards a degree. In other words, I was stupid and had to catch up or learn the foundational shit that I never learned in order to start at a college level. Yep. Pretty embarrassing and sad. But what could I expect? Hell, I only took one class that first semester. Ya see what I'm saying? I was very intimidated and scared. In fact, the first year and a half I was in college consisted of those preliminary classes. I was going slow, put it that way.

In other news, Korn released *Follow the Leader* in August of that year, and Rob Zombie released his first solo album the same month, *Hellbilly Deluxe*. Oh, and I heard a band called Sevendust for the first time that same summer. I was talking to Mikey on the phone one day because he had left Tulsa for North Carolina and was giving an update on how things were. By the end of the conversation, we were talking music, and he asked me if I had ever heard of a band called Sevendust. I told him I had not. He told me to check them out. I did. Thanks,

Mikey! Holy Shit! That's all that needs to be said about the awesomeness of Sevendust. And then in September, Manson released *Mechanical Animals*. Actually, Anthony, Liam, and I went to Dallas in November to see him. We had, of course, been up. Wait, what am I saying? That's nothing new. Anyway, it was a little different than normal shows in the sense that while we were waiting to get in, we were talking with Christians who were protesting the show. Lol! Fuckin' hilarious! Although, I felt like the conversation went well. There was no anger or hate towards us. They were just asking us what we liked about Manson and why we were at the show. I thought that was special. Since both questions were one in the same, I summed it up like this to the protesters: "Basically, we really enjoy his music, regardless of his beliefs or our beliefs, which is why we're here at the show. There's a creativeness and artistic thing going on."

And that was that. They just nodded as if they understood and left us alone. There was no hostility or anything like that. As we were walking in, one of them even said, "I hope you enjoy the show." I just laughed and said, "Thank you. I will." Ya see what happened? What could they say to what I had just said? I broke them down, and I did it with style and grace—even to the point that we were being told to enjoy the show as we walked in. And indeed, I did enjoy myself. It was a great show. They opened with "The Reflecting God" from *Antichrist Superstar*. It was really badass. Liam even caught a pick that Twiggy, the bass player, threw out. It said "Coke Whore" on the pick. Classic! Oh, and I almost forgot: Godsmack released their self-titled album in August of '98. But they didn't show up on my radar until late fall of '98. Like I said, there was a lot of good music that came out in 1998. And we caught two badass shows.

For the new year, we all partied at Donovan's. Everyone was there except Christian. I'm only bringing this up because it's kinda important. Apparently, Christian and I had communicated poorly while making our new-year plans. Basically, it was a lack of clear, proper communication.

I say lack of clear, proper communication and poor communication because I'm not sure I believe in miscommunication or lack of communication. Change my mind. Communication means you have delivered a message or exchanged information interpersonally or to a group, either verbally, non-verbally, or written. Merriam Webster's definition of communication is "a process by which information is exchanged between individuals through a common system of symbols, signs, or behavior." A message or information was delivered. And a message or information was received. In other words, you have either communicated or you have not. Now, if you didn't mean to deliver the message or information you delivered for whatever reason—and there could be several reasons—then the communication that was delivered was done so incorrectly or poorly. But that doesn't make it a miscommunication. It just means that there was a lack of clear, proper communication. The message or information was just delivered poorly. Does that make sense? Merriam Webster Dictionary defines miscommunication as "a failure to communicate clearly." Therefore, there was a lack of clear, proper communication, or the communication was delivered poorly. (Oh, and a quick sidenote: the word communication, in and of itself, is plural. It takes two or more people to communicate. Otherwise, you are just talking to yourself. And that does not constitute communication. Also, one more quick sidenote if I may: I used the phrase "message and/or information" because a message doesn't necessarily constitute communication unless the receiving person or persons understand the message. For example, a code or sequence of special characters or emojis could be the message, or part of the message, right? It's the content within the message that conveys the information, which leads to communication. And information is what you obtain through communication. And, of course, there are different types of communication, whether they're print, broadcast, online, or in a multimedia format, which is the world we live in. The different types of communication allow us to—OH MY GOD! What has happened to my mind? Fuck off!)

Anyway, I was supposedly to go over to Christian's place to spend the new year. He was living with Pauly at that time. But the last conversation I remember was trying to figure out what we were doing and that Christian would call me at some point and we would decide. Then we said our goodbyes, and that was that. The problem was that Christian never called me, and I never called him. Look, I'm probably the worst communicator that ever lived. I take full responsibility for not calling and checking with him that night. Donovan said everyone was going to his place, so I just assumed that meant everyone. It wasn't unusual for Christian to just do his own thing. So, I really didn't think much of it when he didn't call. And for the record, I was the worst about doing shit like that. I would tell someone that I was on my way, and then two days later finally show up. Nevertheless, when Christian called me the next day, he was pissed. He felt like I had screwed him over. His feelings were hurt. And that is something I would never intentionally have done or tried to do. I was just an idiot, that's all. I tried explaining myself, but to no avail. I didn't like the situation I found myself in. It sucked! But trust me, that wasn't the first time Christian and I had bickered, argued, or disagreed with one another. Sometimes family members have disagreements, or they fight. Unfortunately, it would be April before Christian and I would see each other again.

It was 1999. The last year of the twentieth century. What to do? Oh, what to do? I've a great idea. We're gonna do a lot of dope. What do ya say? But we're also going to see a lot of unbelievable concerts and learn about a lot of new and incredible music along the way. It was a phenomenal year in music. Oh, and I might even pick up the sticks again. That'll be badass and is long overdue. Let's get started, shall we?

The year was off to a great start. Anthony had acquired a dope connection. His name was Gary, and he was connected to some pretty hardcore folks because of his family. Liam and Anthony had been telling me that I needed to come over, meaning come over to Liam's. But being that I was in school and all, I was trying my best to do as little as possible, and it was hard at first. Although, I was only taking one class. So, I thought, "fuck it." I went over one weekend in February, and it was on. It wasn't planned. I had just walked in on Liam waiting to get some. He said I was welcome to join him. Was there ever any doubt? Of course I would join him. When the dope arrived shortly after, that was the first time I met Gary. He didn't initially come in. Liam went outside, got the dope, and brought it in. Gary stayed outside. Oh, and in case you forgot, Liam is now living in Dover, in the country, on his own seven acres. Liam brought the dope inside and said Gary was going to wait outside. Gary was a little reserved at first.

Ya gotta understand, Anthony was the only person Gary had been fuckin' with until Anthony introduced him to Christian and Liam. It just so happened that it was Liam's first solo run with Gary—not the first time they had met, just the first time Gary dealt with Liam without Anthony around. And then, of course, my dumb ass showed up.

Liam started breaking down the dope. It stunk! And it was breaking down clear. Both were good signs. I must say, WOW! I know you may have heard me say that before, but that dope had just hit the top three. It was equal to the white rock we had been doing when we were young and the anhydrous we had done a few years back. That dope was that good. And yes, at that time, out of all the dope I'd done, that was how I was ranking things: 1-white rock, 2-anhydrous, 3-Gary dope. That is in no particular order. I'm just saying, those three I just mentioned were the crème de la crème of dope. As my arm was raised after I had slammed it, I tasted what appeared to be the smell of nail polish. It was crazy. I walked in the living room, and Gary was sitting there. Sitting on the couch, he looked at me and asked, "Well, what'd ya think?" I just smirked and replied, "That fuckin' shit is platinum, brother." Gary couldn't help himself. He had to come inside. He loved watching people get off. He didn't slam. He only snorted—at first. From that point on, Gary was fuckin' with all four of us.

In March, Liam and I went to Dallas to see Korn and Rob Zombie. Korn was touring off *Follow the Leader*, and Rob Zombie off his first album, *Hellbilly Deluxe*. It was a wonderful show! Rob Zombie had put on a show unlike anything I had seen. And Korn, well, that shit was just pure rawness. If you were looking at the stage in front of you, Liam and I were to the right, on the second level. Korn opened with a song called "Blind." The song starts with the famous and exciting ride bell from the drums and continues to slowly build with bass and guitars until, finally, the song launches into an explosive groove after Johnathan Davis yells, "Are you ready?!" Well, when that part hit, people who were in the back of the arena, in the stands, suddenly rushed the floor. Liam and I must have watched 500 people rush the floor all at once. There was nothing security or the police could do while it was happening. The only thing they could do was keep a second wave of people from doing that. It was pretty intense. Great fuckin' show! And wouldn't ya know it? A couple days later, Korn and Rob Zombie were announced for Little Rock. Damn right we were gonna go to that show too. Oh, we were gonna go alright.

Exactly one month after Liam and I went to the Korn and Rob Zombie show in Dallas, we were on our way to Little Rock to see the same show. But it wouldn't be the same show. That's because the entire crew did a bunch of dope before we left. Let me explain. It was going to be a hell of a night. We even had James and Bethany coming in from Tulsa. We started at Liam's. We meaning Liam, Anthony, Gary, and me. After blowing our fuckin' heads off, I told Liam and Anthony that I'd meet them at Pauly's. In the meantime, I went back to where I was staying, which was at the house of my girlfriend's parents. James and Bethany were staying with us there. I had brought back some dope so everyone else could get fucked up also. Although, by then, James was no longer slamming. So, I gave his the same way I gave it to Bethany and my girlfriend. In a capsule. You do that by literally filling up an empty pill capsule. Did I say filling up? Whoopsie-daisy! I probably shouldn't have filled those capsules up. I couldn't help myself, though. I liked watching people get off too. Evil, muthafucker! Not to mention, it was Bethany's first time ever doing dope. Although, I didn't fill hers completely up. It was only about halfway filled. It didn't matter. Those poor souls were about to get fucked up. Ha ha!

When we made it over to Pauly's, we were good and fucked up. Liam, Anthony, and Robert were already there; Kelly rode over with Donovan and his ol' lady, and they showed up shortly after I did. When I walked into Pauly's, everyone was in the living room except Anthony and Christian. That's because Anthony was making sure Christian got fucked up. We're all in the living room talkin' and hangin' out, happy and excited we're all about to go to Little Rock to watch a kick-ass show, when all of a sudden Christian came around the corner with a shotgun in his hand. He lifted the gun up, pointed it at me, and cocked it. Right before that moment, the living room sounded like a bar. Everyone was having a conversation. Then the sound of a pump-action shotgun silenced the entire room. Someone said, "What the fuck, Christian!?" As I was staring down the barrel of the shotgun, wondering why in the fuck my brother was tripping, Christian said, "If you ever ignore me again, I'll fuckin' kill you."

Then, before I even had a chance to react, he started smiling and laughing. He gave me a hug and said, "Man, I would never do that to you. I love you. You're my brother," he continued. Opening the chamber of the shotgun, he said, "Look, that shit ain't even loaded." Stress left the air. Everyone could breathe and laugh again. I was like, "Christian, bro, I didn't even know there was that much of an issue. Otherwise, I wouldn't even be here." "Well, you should have called or come over before now," he said in a hurt kind of way. He was right. I could have. I just didn't. "Sorry, bro," I replied, "I just didn't think you wanted to see me. I suck at communication, bro. Sorry." We hugged, and that was that. It was time to go to Little Rock.

We were rollin' three cars deep on the way to Little Rock. Either we were hauling ass, or we were that fucked up—I'll go with being that fucked up—but it seemed as if it only took a few minutes to get down there. When we walked into the coliseum, dope was in the air. I'm not even playin'. We were tore the fuck up. That was a fact. But there was a coliseum full of muthafuckers that were tore up. As we were headed down to the pit area, Pauly's big ass leading the way, we all noticed a rig on the floor. No shit! I'm tellin' you, muthafuckers were tore up and wired. A band named Videodrone opened the show. Videodrone was actually a band called Cradle of Thorns from Bakersfield, California, but they put one album out as Videodrone. Oh, and Korn is from Bakersfield. See the connection? Anyway, I thought Videodrone was pretty cool. Freaky from what I remember, yes. I think I was attracted to that as well. In between some of their songs, people were booing and heckling them. And wouldn't ya know it? Muthafuckers even started chanting for either Zombie or Korn. It was like a repeat of what happened during Alice in Chains' set years earlier in the same coliseum, no doubt. What the fuck?! But then the lead singer responded to the crowd that was booing and heckling with a classic response, saying, "How much did you pay to get in here?" Then there was lots of laughter. I didn't hear anymore booing and heckling after that comment. Just writing this made me giggle. That was a good response to shithead muthafuckers. Ya know? In between Videodrone and Zombie, we were huddled in a circle, smokin' a joint. We got on the subject about heroin for some reason. All of a sudden James looked at all of us and asked, "Did you guys give me heroin?" Everyone just looked at him and started laughing. "Man, we didn't give you no heroin," Liam said in an irritated voice. I followed up the same, "We didn't give you no fuckin' heroin, bro. We're just talkin' about heroin. That's all." James started smiling. "Oh, ok. Man, I'm fucked up," he said. Everyone just started laughing again. I responded, "No shit."

You have to understand, as the years progressed, James' rational comprehension of anything while he was fucked up went right out the fuckin' window. In a bad way. Eventually, James would no longer know how or be able to maintain in any environment, much less a public one.

We were on the floor, close to the front when Rob Zombie came on. It was rowdy! But it was fun and badass. We were having a great time. Being that we were so close to the stage, we found ourselves shuffled and moved around quite a lot. It also meant we found ourselves in one of the pits that had formed. Most of us quickly got the fuck out of that muthafucker. But not Christian. He stayed in. And I tell you what, I've never seen anything like it before. He must have bumped into everyone that was in that mosh pit. And he did it without his feet ever touching the floor. I shit you not! I couldn't believe what I was seeing. Christian was a short guy but muscular. Not fat. Muscular. And yet, there he was, literally moving in a circle while moshing, floating like a goddamn butterfly. I think that—between the mosh pit being so tight and packed, and Christian being one of the shortest people in the pit and moving as fast as he was—everyone he was coming into contact with was helping him stay elevated. But still moving, nonetheless. Does that make sense? It was fuckin' hilarious! When he was finally done moshing and came out of the pit, I asked him if he realized that his feet weren't touching the ground at times. He just smiled, all wide eyed and said laughing, "Shit, I was just tryin' to get every muthafucker that I could." I replied, "I think you succeeded."

We spent the rest of the night a little further back on the floor. Back far enough that we still had a good spot for the remainder of the show but didn't have to worry about mosh pits. Although, poor Robert had enough at one point. He made it about two songs into Korn and bailed the fuck out the rest of the show. When the concert was over, we finally found him sitting on some steps in front of the coliseum, by a group of cops. Kelly walked over and got him as I was standing there trying to figure out if he was okay and why the fuck he was sitting by the police. Kelly walked about halfway up to him and yelled, "Robert! Hey, it's time to go, bro." With nothing but dilatated pupils as he was walking up, I asked him, "Are you alright, bro? Why were you sitting by the cops?" I continued asking. "I felt safe," he said.

Let me tell ya something, that muthafucker was tore up. You gotta be TORE THE FUCK UP to feel safe around the cops while you're tore up. See what I'm sayin'? God damn! I just would have never thought to do that, especially as tore up as we were. The last muthafuckers I would have been hanging around would have been the cops. That's kind of like a dope dealer running up to some cops and asking for help after he just got jacked. Right? There ain't nuthin' for ya. The cops ain't gonna help you. And, in fact, you're probably gonna go to jail. You know what I'm sayin'? But then again, the cops that Robert was hangin' around didn't even look like they gave a fuck. Crazy shit.

When we got home that night, we went to bed, so to speak. That meant we turned the lights off. Like I said, I was living with my girlfriend's parents. It wouldn't have looked good to have the lights on all night. When we got up the next morning, James handed me a butter knife and said, "Here, dude. I kept it with me all night because I didn't know if you guys were gonna try to kill me or something." I was like, "What the fuck, Jim?! No one was gonna hurt you." "I know," he said with a little shame, "I was just fucked up." I just started laughing and put the knife in the sink. Good times!

By the way, we didn't see a lot of James after that. We saw him a few times, here and there over the years, but for the most part he just started doing his own thing. He'll be back later.

At some point in April, I lost my job working at the wood shop with Donovan. Apparently, I had gotten lazy in my work. That was bullshit, but whatever. I ended up collecting unemployment for a couple of months. Donovan left the wood shop himself, about two months after I did.
In the meantime, everyone was still pretty hard at it. I had taken a small break somewhere around the middle or end of April. But a week

before my finals, in May, I got caught up. I already knew where to go: Pauly's. Christian had been helping Gary get rid of some. So, I knew Christian would have some. Besides, we had been in touch, and he told me to come over. But I didn't know that we were gonna be on one for a few days. When I got to Pauly's, Anthony was there as well. I walked in and went back to Christian's room, and he was already making one up. He said, "Take those Xanax right there." He continued, "You'll get fucked up. It'll make ya see tracers," he said giggling. I asked no questions. I took two Xanax. I don't remember how many milligrams they were. Christian did the shot he was mixing up when I walked in. "You're next," he said, "I'm gonna mix you up a good one." After about fifteen minutes, he finished getting the shot ready. It actually only took him a few minutes. But he spent a good ten minutes getting his shit together after slamming one. Could I have mixed my own? No! That's because Christian said he was going to do it. That meant he wanted to blow my fuckin' head off. I hit myself. He just wanted to mix it up. Who was I to argue? After slamming it, everything was everything. Christian succeeded, once again, in mixing up a shot that blew my fuckin' head off. But I didn't experience any tracers or anything like that.

After what started on a Thursday afternoon, we finally finished up late Sunday night. We were back at Christian's after running around the past couple of days trying to help Gary get rid of some dope. Yeah, yeah. I know. I said I wasn't going to do anymore thug shit. Well, technically, I wasn't doing any thug shit. I was just along for the ride. Yeah, it was my car, but I wasn't driving most of the time. So, fuck it! Anyway, Christian, Anthony, and I were in Christian's bedroom figuring out how to get me home, which was back at my parent's house. Ya see, after doing all that dope and continuously popping Xanax the past couple days, well, I was having an episode. I wouldn't call it an overdose. More of a needing-to-go-to-sleep situation than anything else. Regardless, Christian and Anthony weren't going to let me drive. So, one of them called Gary. The plan was to have Gary come over and drive me home, and Anthony would follow in his car, and then Gary would take Anthony home. As we're sitting there waiting on Gary, Anthony's girlfriend showed up. Keep in mind that it's past two in the morning. She was out front making a bunch of ruckus because Anthony had been gone. Anthony tried to contain the situation, but the crazy bitch actually walked around to Christian's window, which we happened to have open, and just kept harassing Anthony. Being the situation that it was, there was really no need for her to be creating problems that late at night, especially after we had been up for a few days. After arguing for another good five minutes, Anthony's girlfriend threatened him with something. I don't even remember what she said. But I'll tell ya this, I remember Anthony's reaction. Whatever that girl said, the next thing I know, Anthony ducked down and jumped out the window like a fuckin' ninja. Now, that might not seem like much to the rest of you, but that shit was amazing. Anthony is tall and skinny, so to see him go out that window with such a quick and flawless action was pretty fuckin' cool. Not to mention, it took a lot to get Anthony mad. But to get him to jump out a window at you, well, you just succeeded in making him mad. We didn't see her anymore after that.

When Gary got there, the plan went accordingly. Except that Gary wasn't taking me home. He wanted to drop me off at a hotel. I told him I had finals the next day, but that didn't really matter to him. He didn't want me flopping at home, where he couldn't get to me. He wanted me at a hotel where, if something went wrong, he could at least take some kind of action—versus at my parent's house, where no one would know anything. At least that's what was going on in Gary's head. Or maybe he was just scared; if I did die, he didn't want it to be at my house where my parents would find me and possibly implicate him. I didn't give a fuck either way. I just needed some sleep. But I had to get my books and clean clothes and all that shit for school the next morning. So, he agreed to take me to my house so I could get all my shit together. Then he got me a hotel room, gave me some dope just in case I needed a "wake up" the next morning, and then he left. I got up the next morning after a great and much needed night of sleep, did the dope he left me, and went to school to take my finals. And yes, I passed my finals. Oh, and a guy I had been sitting next to all semester turned me on to two bands called Coal Chamber and Powerman 5000. I quickly became a fan of both. He also told me about a festival that was coming up. It was Woodstock '99, and it was taking place in July. Ya goddamn right I was going. But I sure didn't want to do something like that by myself. I went over to Liam's later that evening to tell him the good news. He told me to order him a ticket as well. I ordered them the next day. We were going to Woodstock '99, baby!

About a week or so later, after my parents had gone out of town, I thought it would be a great opportunity to get as fucked up as we wanted at the parent's house, to get out of the Gum Log area for a few days. There was plenty of room to spread out and relax. And we'd be closer to town so Christian and Gary could do their thing. So that's what we did. I knew when the parents were gonna be home, so I would have shit cleaned up and everyone out long before they got there. Well, there would be nothing to clean because everyone knew that my parents' house was to be left as it was when you started. That meant that things had to be spotless. So, I was never worried about that. My people knew the drill. All I had to do was make sure that I had all our junked-out asses the fuck out before they got home, which, of course, would be no problem, especially when I had the schedule. Because why would they come home early? Of all the years they had been going out of town, they adhered to the schedule. There was no deviation to the schedule. Two days before my parents were supposed to be home, Christian, Anthony, and I—several days in already—were starting to wrap things up at the house.

Gary and Anthony had been in and out over the past few days, and I was helping Christian on his end. Well, Christian and I were up at the house, tore up, kickin' it. It was daytime. Gary was sending a guy our way to pick up two 8-balls. Well, I put the two balls under a plastic or rubber Star Wars toy. The Phantom Menace was just about to come out, and I had gotten a toy out of a box of cereal. Why I still had it? I had no idea. But I did. And I hid the two 8-balls under it, in the back of the house—my side of the house—in my bathroom. Why did I put them back there and not just keep them on us? Christian suggested we do that because we didn't know the guy who was coming. Gary said we could trust him. But Gary was just as tore up as we were. He was always talkin' about how he thought people were following him and shit. Hell, just a couple days earlier he came haulin' ass up to the house and was on the phone with us tellin' us to open the garage door so he could park in there and hide. Apparently, he had slipped his tail and needed to quickly get off the road. Fuck, I don't know. He was slingin' a lot of dope. Maybe the police were watching him. All the more reason, Christian suggested, that we put the dope as far away from us as possible. That way, when the guy got to the house, all he would have to do was "go to the bathroom"—where he would get his dope and leave our money. I know. I know. Look, as tore up as we were, that made sense. No dope or money would have exchanged hands. Get it? Well, that was where our drug-induced heads were, and by god that was a good plan. Take that, coppers! You'll never catch us, see!

When the guy got to the house, Christian and I were in the den watching TV. I let him in, and there was some small talk, and I told him, "If you need to go to the bathroom, use the one in the back of the house." "Where is that at?" he asked. I took him through the kitchen, to the coffee room area, and then pointed to my side of the house, where he could see part of a bedroom and hallway. I said to him, "There's a pretty cool toy in there." He smiled and went to my bathroom. I went back in the den with Christian, sat down, and continued to watch TV. About 30 seconds later, he came back out to the den and tried handing me the money. "You were supposed to leave that in the bathroom, but ok," I said. Christian just started laughing at the guy like, "You fuckin' idiot." I told him to leave the money on the kitchen counter and go. Christian and I just looked at each other and shook our heads. We were both thinkin' the same thing: "So much for being discreet." A few hours later, Gary and Anthony came back over. Gary brought his sister and her friend. I had taken Christian back home earlier, and Gary was supposed to have gone and picked him up before coming to my house. Well, that didn't happen.

Christian called and asked if Gary was over there, and I told him that he was. Needless to say, that pissed Christian off. When Gary got off the phone with Christian, he was headed out to go pick him up. But before he left, he left some more dope for everyone. Anthony and I stayed with the girls while Gary picked up Christian. By the time Gary got back with Christian, it was about one o'clock in the morning. We spent the next few hours getting fucked up, hangin' out, and talkin'. About 4:00 a.m. rolled around, and we all decide it was time to do some more. So, Christian, Anthony, Gary, and I were all on my side of the house, utilizing both my bedroom and bathroom. Gary decided he wanted to slam one, which, by that point, wasn't gonna be his first time. Obviously, Christian was all over that for him. The four of us were in my bathroom getting shit mixed up. It was a pretty big bathroom. The two girls were in the kitchen hangin' out. I had bought some weed a couple days earlier and had about a quarter-pound left. I had it out all over the kitchen table where the girls were because I was going to bag the shit up. I just hadn't got to it yet.

Meanwhile, four junkies are huddled together in a bathroom. That's special. Just so you know. And what was it with the fuckin' bathroom? We had over 3,000 square feet to choose from. Yet, we congregated together in a ten-foot space. Interesting. Real bonding can take place in a bathroom. You'd be surprised. Or maybe ya wouldn't. At any rate, Anthony and I got our shots mixed and slammed first. I remember seeing that damn toy sitting on the bathroom counter. You know. The one I hid those two 8-balls in earlier? Anthony and I stepped out of the bathroom. He went to the other side of the house to enjoy his high. I stayed on my side of the house, and I just went up and down the hallway and in and out of my room until walking back into the bathroom where Christian was giving Gary what he asked for. As Gary started walking the same path that I did, Christian commenced to fixing his shot. For some reason, Christian, Gary, and I were all three in the bathroom with the door shut, watching Christian get his shit mixed up. There's that bathroom thing again. Why? Except for Christian, everyone had already done their shots. You'd think we would want to leave the bathroom. Nope. That's where we wanted to be. As Christian was just about to start drawing back from the spoon, Anthony walked in the bathroom and said, "Hey man, there's an old lady walkin' around in your house." He continued, "I think it's your mom." I frantically responded with both statements he made, as questions. "There's an old lady in my house and you think it's my mom?" I asked in horror. "What do you mean 'you think?'" I asked. Not letting him answer anything because of the panic I was experiencing—while trying to process the information he just gave me—I asked yet another question, "Do you not know what my mom looks like?" "Yeah," he calmly said. "And I'm pretty sure it's her," he continued. I asked where the girls were, and he said he told them to go wait out front. By that time, Christian had already evacuated to my bedroom and shut the door. Gary was obviously freakin' the fuck out. I told everyone to calm down, and I let Anthony and Gary out the front door of the house, which was on my side of the house and never used. That way, they could avoid any additional old people, specifically my parents. I let the two of them out, locked the door back, and quickly moved to the other side of the house where, when I got to the kitchen, I saw the tail end of my dad walking into his bedroom, and, of course, there's the old lady (aka my mom) walking through the den from the driveway with luggage in her hand. "Mom!" I said with a huge surprise, "What are y'all doing here? I thought y'all weren't supposed to be back until the next day?" "Well, we weren't, but your dad didn't feel good and was ready to come home," she said with disappointment. "Oh my god, mom," I said, "I'm so sorry. We were actually going to leave here in a little bit. I'm gettin' everybody out now. We'll be outta here in five minutes. Sorry about that, mom." I pleaded, and she replied with a disappointed, "Okay."

I cleaned the weed off the table and rushed back to my bedroom where I thought Christian would have already done his shot. No. He was waiting on me. He wasn't trippin'. He knew that if it was alright for anyone to be in that house at that hour, it would be him. "Wait on me, bro," he said whispering. I was like, "Dude, why haven't you already done that?"—referring to the shot sitting on my nightstand. "Because" he stated, "I was waiting on you to make sure it was cool." "Well, you need to do that shot, because we need to go," I said hastily. He looked at me grinning and asked, "Who's gonna do the rest of what's in that spoon? We can't just leave it there," he said. He was right. I couldn't hide the spoon properly with dope already broke down in it. What if it were to spill? So, I did what any responsible junkie would do. I did the rest of the dope. We had all used the same spoon. There had been a lot of dope in that spoon. And I wasn't about to go throw it in the sink. We had been using the same spoon for several days. I was all for each of us having our own spoon. But Christian said that might look suspicious if my parents got home and saw a bunch of spoons in their dishwasher. That was a good call. Because any time my parents went out of town, they never left any dirty dishes. Everything was clean and picked up. And that was how they expected it when they returned. And except for that night and the night that Walter poured whiskey on that bitch's head, they always came back to the same house they left.

Gary told us to meet him at a hotel and that he was getting us rooms. Christian and I met up with the four of them and got the rooms. Christian and Gary ended up leaving. Anthony and I stayed in one of the rooms until they got back. By eight or nine o'clock that morning, Anthony and I were still at the hotel room waiting on Gary and Christian. All of a sudden, my phone rings. It was my mom. I answered the phone and heard, "Shane, I think you left something behind." I immediately asked, "What are you talking about?" She said, "In your bathroom…under that toy." I was still trying to figure out what the fuck she was talking about. Did I accidently leave a rig out? Was there a spoon that I had forgotten about? And why the fuck was she back there digging around? So, I asked, very hatefully, "Mom, what the fuck are you talking about, and why are you in my bathroom digging around?" "There's a baggie full of stuff underneath this toy on the bathroom counter. And I was making sure everything was cleaned up so your dad wouldn't come across anything," she continued. Ignoring the part about her covering for my ass with dad, I instantly asked, "Are you telling me that you found dope underneath that toy?" "Well, I don't know what it is," she said irritably, "But there's something there, yes." Again, throwing my poor mom to the side, I looked at Anthony and said, "That muthafucker didn't take both those 8-balls. He only took one of 'em."

All I could do at that point was kind of stutter in a shameful and confused response to my mom, saying how sorry I was and that I was fucked up. I did manage to acknowledge the fact that she was trying to protect me and that I appreciated what she had done. I'm most certain that came out in a shameful and incoherent acknowledgement, though. My sweet, precious mom: bless her. Oh, and no, I didn't deserve her graciousness.

Obviously, that guy who had come over to take both 8-balls only took one. Yet he gave us the money for two. That whole time we were at my house, in and out of the bathroom all night, one of those fuckin' 8-balls was still sitting there. And the person to find it, of all people, was my mom. We called Gary to tell him the situation. At some point, many hours later, we all hooked up again, but I ended up going with Gary to drop off the dope that dude didn't take. Anthony and Christian went back out to Christian's place. Meanwhile, I'm rollin' down the interstate with Gary. It took about thirty minutes to get where we needed to go. I waited out in the car while Gary went in to drop the dope off. The whole situation seemed kind of weird to me. Yeah, I had been up for a few days. But fuck that! I didn't like that muthafucker, and when Gary came back out to the car, I told him as much. Who the fuck leaves an entire 8-ball behind yet gives the money for two? A moron? A cop or narc of some sort? That guy was acting too much like he didn't know what the fuck was going on. Gary agreed that he wasn't gonna fuck with him anymore. But as far as the guy being an idiot, Gary said that's just how he was. I told him that was all the more reason to drop that fool. I told him that even though he had known the guy for a while, he just couldn't take those kinds of chances in that kind of game. But it's not like it would have mattered at that point, anyway. That guy had already been in my house and picked up an 8-ball, and now Gary was directly handing one off. And the shit that happened next was sure to create even more paranoia for my white ass. Was it just a coincidence that—as we were travelling down the interstate at dusk after having just dropped off some dope—we passed a state trooper who immediately got on our ass? I mean, it's not like we were speeding. That muthafucker came up on us with a mission. It was like he was sitting there specifically waiting on us. Thankfully, we had already dropped off the dope, so, besides the strangeness of the cop getting on our ass, I was okay for the moment. I was maintaining. I didn't feel that I had to worry about jail if the trooper ended up pulling us over. But then, of course, as the trooper was following us—and when I say following us, he was less than a car length behind us—Gary handed me a rolled-up ball of electrical tape and said, "Get ready to throw this." I asked, "What's this?" He said, "Dope!" "Well, how much is in there?" I asked in a panic. "I don't know," Gary said. "Close to two grams," he stated.

"Well, god damn!" I thought to myself. You remember that feeling about worrying about going to jail that I was talkin' about? Yeah. There's that feeling. Adrenaline pumping. Your heart racing. Every thought goes through your mind: How much time am I gonna get? Maybe I should run. I've ruined my life. How can I get out of this? Your legs might even have a small tremble to them. Enough of a tremble that if you tried to stand up, you feel like you would fall. And then, maybe from shock or because of defeat, you start to accept what is about to happen. Because it's the only thing you can do.

The trooper was on our ass for a good two minutes of pure hell before he eventually hung back a little further, about two car lengths at that point. I kept thinking about how Gary was always saying that he was being followed or watched. Is that why this fuckin' cop was fuckin' with us? Was Gary really being watched? Those questions kept bouncing back and forth in my head.

Gary kept saying, "Get ready to throw the dope out." About a minute later the trooper looked like he was about to make his move on us. He came rushing up on us again, and as he did, Gary yelled, "Throw it!" I threw that muthafucker out as inconspicuously as I could. Literally, as I threw it out, the trooper pulled around us and hauled ass past us. I couldn't fuckin' believe it. That cop was fuckin' with us. Bad! "Holy shit, dude!" I yelled. "I told you!" Gary shouted. "I fuckin' told ya'll they were watching me." I was like, "Dude! I'm just glad he didn't pull us over." "Did you happen to see where you threw that?" Gary asked.

As a matter of fact, I did know, which was pretty fuckin' awesome. "Actually, yeah" I responded. He looked at me with shock. I continued, "You actually told me to throw it out at the same time we passed the sign that said Russellville was a mile away." He started laughing. Look, that shit was pure luck! I couldn't believe where I had thrown it. I couldn't believe I actually had a good idea of the vicinity. Yeah, it skipped and rolled and all that, but it was a rolled-up ball of electrical tape about the size of a ping pong ball. How hard could it be to find? We went back later that night, dressed all in black. We pulled over on the side of the interstate, around the spot that I had thrown it, and we looked for about fifteen minutes with flashlights. I know. I know. But what do you expect? We're junkies. If a cop would have rolled up on us, we were gonna say that Gary and his fiancé got in a fight, and she threw the ring out the window. It sounded good. But how would we have explained being dressed up like ninjas? Can you say *junkie*? After our unsuccessful attempt at locating the dope, we spent the rest of the evening at Gary's, unscrewing all the vent covers in the ceiling, looking for cameras. Good god! It was time to go to bed.

Gary pretty much stopped coming around. I'm not sure why. Maybe he decided to go a different route. I saw him one or two more times, and that was it. He left as quick as he entered our lives.

A couple days later, after some much-needed sleep, Christian and I hooked up, got some food, went up to my house, smoked out, and got ready to go watch the new Star Wars. Kelly unexpectedly showed up before we left. He could tell we had been up. He asked if we had any, and I said no. But I did have a spoon from which he could probably get a good rinse. He saw the spoon and liked that idea. You remember that spoon from earlier? Well, that's the spoon he was about to get a rinse out of. A rinse is basically putting a little water in a spoon that has had massive amounts of dope in it to get the residue. The spoon we had been using was a good rinse. Kelly got the fuck off. Right after he did the shot, we left to go to the store for a couple things. As we were headed back to the house to drop off Kelly so we could go to the movie, there was an asshole stopped in the road on the right side. You know, the side ya drive on. He had no blinker on or anything. So, being the asshole driver I was, I didn't miss a beat. I just proceeded to go around him. Well, at the last second, that muthafucker decided to start moving and put his left blinker on as if he was about to turn. Because I had ninja reflexes, I was able to brake quickly and get back behind him so I wouldn't T-bone the muthafucker. But then he decided to stop again and not make the turn. By then it was too late. I rear-ended him. It was just a fender bender. That's it. The problem was the guy I hit, quickly got out of the car and opened the back car door. Christian already knew what I had just done and said, "Oh shit! He's got a kid." At first we were all like, "What the fuck is this guy's problem?" But then he pulled a baby out of the back seat. Christian got out and immediately asked if they were both ok. The guy said yes. I went up to him and apologized. As he was holding his kid, I told the guy that we'd call the police. After an hour, the sheriff's deputies finally showed up. They explained that they had been eating dinner. They thought that shit was funny. One of them asked Kelly something. But Kelly could barely talk he was so high. He said something about being in the backseat and that his name was Kelly. The cop left him alone after that incoherent conversation. I got the ticket, and everyone moved on their way. We dropped off Kelly, and Christian and I went to a later viewing of the movie.

A week and a half later, we were out of dope. We had been out of dope for a few days. Gary was out and was taking a break. I was over at Christian's. We were kind of jonesin' to get high. We were both talkin' about how it would be awesome if we could find a little bit. But wait! "There's two grams laying on the side of the interstate right now," I said to Christian. "I know we can find that shit." He grinned, and as he was smoking a cigarette, he looked at me like only Christian could and said, "Let's go!" We went in the middle of the day. I shit you not, after it had been sitting out on the side of the interstate for a week and a half, we found that shit. It took about five minutes, and I located it. I yelled to Christian, "Let's go!" He just looked at me and smiled. He could tell by the smile on my face that I had found it. We got in the car, and Christian asked, "Did you find it?" "Sure fuckin' did!" I responded excitedly. I gave him the ball of tape. We didn't open it until we got back to his place. We never told Gary we found it. Like I said earlier, he started doing his own thing and pretty much got out of the game. We told Anthony, though. He came over. It turned out that we had a gram and three quarters. Need I say more? Good times!

June was pretty uneventful as far as dope. And that was a good thing. June presented lots of good music, though! Liam and I went to Tulsa that month to see Soulfly perform, which was badass. I spent the rest of June and July up at Donovan's, until it was time to leave for Woodstock. We spent that time hangin' out by the pool, drinking, smoking, and listening to good new music. The music that was coming out in '99 was awesome, and I found a treasure trove of wonderful music. For example, I heard a band called Static X for the first time. They had come out with the album *Wisconsin Death Trip* back in March of '99. Then I heard Staind for the first time. Their album *Dysfunction* had come out in April. Snoop put out *Topp Dogg* in May. It was nice to hear from him again. Plus, a band called Limp Bizket, who I had heard for the first time back in 1998—on their album *3 Dollar Bill Y'all*—came out with their second album, *Significant Other*. Oh, a band by the name of Slipknot had also come out with their debut album, self-titled, in June of '99. I didn't pay a lot of attention to Slipknot at first. We'll get back to them shortly. And an artist who was creating a big buzz was introduced to us in 1999. Eminem (aka Slim Shady) released his first album, *The Slim Shady*

LP, in February of '99. I really didn't catch on to him until that summer. I heard he had been produced by Dr. Dre, so I had to check it out. Holy shit! Enough said. As you can see, 1999 was literally rockin'!

Liam and I left around three o'clock in the afternoon on July 20, 1999. We were on our way to Rome, New York to attend Woodstock '99. We were so excited! I couldn't believe we were actually going. We may have had about seven or eight hundred dollars between us. Yeah, I know. Of course, you couldn't do that today. Hell, you'd spend that much on gas just getting there these days. But it was a different time. We had a tent, two coolers, a couple pairs of clothes, and some weed. We had a good twenty-hour drive ahead of us, if not more. God, it was really exciting! Just the journey there was an adventure. We were both crossing new territory, driving through states we had never seen. Crossing countryside we had never seen. We took I-40 East to Nashville, where Liam started driving. We continued on I-40 East through Knoxville until it eventually turned to I-81 North. We finally stopped to rest when we hit Virginia. That was about a fourteen-hour drive. Liam parked in a hotel parking lot where we slept for the next four hours. We woke up and continued on I-81, which took us through a small part of West Virginia as well as Maryland, then on through Pennsylvania and into New York, where we finally reached I-90 East. From there we hit 365 East into Rome. It was about seven o'clock in the evening on Wednesday, July 21, when we hit town. The gates to the festival would open the next day. In the meantime, we had to find a place to crash. There were instructions that came with our festival packets on how and where to find a place to lay our heads. We called one of the numbers, told them where we were, and they instructed us right to an area that was letting early arrivers crash for the night. I think it cost us five dollars for the night. There were several hundred people in that area already. We found a spot to set up the tent. Afterward, we started drinking. It was just a big party. We were havin' a great time. Later that evening, we even found some acid. We decided we were gonna take it first thing in the morning. That way, we'd be trippin' as we walked into Woodstock '99. Epic! That didn't turn out exactly as we planned. The next morning, right at sunrise, Liam didn't even let us finish waking up before he pulled that acid out of his pocket, took it out of the cellophane, and said, "Here." Well, that was all fine and dandy except for the fact that Liam accidently gave me both hits. I guess he thought he had only given me one, but then he couldn't find the other one. "Oh shit, man," he exclaimed. "What?" I asked. Liam continued, "I just accidentally gave you both hits." "Really, dude?" I asked. "Yeah, I'm pretty sure," he said. "Well, that fuckin' sucks," I said. "Not for you," he said laughing. I responded kind of frantically, "Yeah, because now I'm gonna be trippin' by myself."

And so it was. I had to take that ride solo. That was alright. I mean, we were only 1,000 miles from anyone we knew, in a place we were completely unfamiliar with, and I had a head full of acid. Actually, looking back on it, I'm glad only one of us was trippin'. It was already chaotic as hell when we got into the main part of town, waiting on the gates to open to let us park. I couldn't have imagined both of us trippin' because Liam held me down while we were waiting to get in. He was my safe sense of reality that everything was going to be ok. We were waiting in a McDonald's parking lot for about an hour before Liam went in and grabbed some grub. I went to the bathroom. When I came out, I was frying my balls off. I'm glad Liam got us food when he did and that I went to the bathroom when I did because it was like the whole world just descended on this one little town, specifically McDonald's. I sure was glad Liam was sober. After another three or four hours, the gates opened and started letting people in to park. We were in a really good spot for parking. The closer our parking spot was, the closer we were to the main gates that actually got you into the festival grounds. I'll tell ya this, as close as we were, it still was a good 200-yard hike to the main gates. And once we got to the main gates, we were at a standstill—not because we were waiting in a long line, but because they weren't letting us in yet. As far as placement in line, we spent about an hour waiting to get inside.

While we were waiting, festival officials said that the coolers we were told we could bring were not going to be allowed. That was the first thing that made people unhappy. What the fuck was everyone who brought coolers of food and drinks supposed to do? Some people drove 1,000 miles to get there. And we were told that basic things—like coolers, water, and other non-perishables—would be allowed. Now they were tellin' us those things wouldn't be allowed. That was bullshit! What did they want us to do, spend money on their shit all weekend? Well, yes. That's exactly what they wanted everyone to do. And that was the beginning of the end, right there. Ya see what I'm sayin'? Liam and I hadn't brought our coolers yet. We were gonna go back and get them once we got a camping spot. I guess we wouldn't need them. When the gates opened, it was a race. It was a race to get a decent camping spot. There were hundreds, probably thousands, of people at that point, moving as fast as they could with their tents, sleeping bags, and coolers. I think we hauled ass for about a quarter-mile until we saw a nice little spot that was taped off with caution tape. We saw someone rip that muthafucker down and start setting up. We followed. It was the first shaded area that we saw.

Turned out that there were very few shaded areas for campers. That was another situation that pissed off people. After all, it was only late July in New York. And if you think for a second just because you're in New York that it's not hot, you would be dangerously miscalculating the level of heat. Especially when you're surrounded by concrete and asphalt. I'll tell you why in a few.

It had been taped off because there was a tree there with a metal rod to absorb any possible lightning strike. Then, separated from that one fuckin' tree, there was a nice little cluster of about seven other trees. Look, they had no business taping off that nice area. It was perfect for camping. And they were going to ruin it because of one tree. And like I said earlier, there weren't very many shaded spots. So, fuck it. Besides, it was fine. We weren't right by that one tree anyway. There was plenty of space between us and the tree with the metal rod in it. The festival officials had tried taping too much off. That's my story, and I'm stickin' to it. No, but really, it was a nice spot. So, we set up camp. There were probably twenty of us in our area. But just a few feet from us were about 1,000 other muthafuckers. It was alright. The people we were camping with wanted as much distance and privacy as they could get, too. We almost had ourselves behind a circled wall of tents. You could only get into our little circle one way, and if you weren't in our initial camp area, you weren't in our camp area. I liked that. It helped keep things a little less chaotic. We soon learned, after being out watching shows all day in the heat, that it was nice to have a little safe haven in which to go and relax. Everyone in our camp area quickly became neighborly. We had folks from Virginia with us, North Carolina, West Virginia, and Georgia. We even had two Georgia cops with us. Can you believe it? We drive a thousand miles to go to the one place where a muthafucker shouldn't have to worry about a cop, and we got stuck camping with two of them. It was all good. They were actually cool. They didn't give a fuck about the drugs. They were there to listen to music. In fact, over the weekend, they smuggled several cases of beer for us to our campsite. Once we got settled in, we took off back for the car to grab anything else in order to make our stay a little more pleasant. On the way back to the car, there was a couple of guys standing a few feet apart from one another. One was selling t-shirts, and the other guy was selling "massive doses." "Massive doses," the guy kept repeating. I finally realized what he was saying. I immediately stopped and asked, "How much?" "Five dollars a hit," he responded. We bought seven hits. As we got back to our campsite area, we noticed a guy standing and selling weed in the middle of one of the main walkways, announcing loudly that he had weed. The amazing part about that was that he was doing it right in front of cops. I couldn't fuckin' believe it. It was as if they didn't care. Maybe the cops were told not to fuck with people. I mean, after all, it was Woodstock. Whatever the case was, I knew I was at the right location. We brought him into our campsite, and he smoked one with us. Let me tell ya, that guy had good weed! It was the kind of weed that is common today. But back in those days, remember, the dominant product was called Mexican brick or schwag weed. Well, that muthafucker had what we referred to back then as "the chronic." We started with an eighth. The guy actually became our official drug dealer the rest of the festival. He would make frequent stops at the campsite throughout the time we were there to either smoke with us or hook us up.

Believe it or not, it was damn near three in the afternoon before we finally got settled in. Then, we took a bunch of acid and went walking around to start checking everything out and get familiar with the area. It was Thursday, July 22. The actual main shows didn't start until Friday morning. That gave us plenty of time to get acquainted with our home for the next three days.

Remember me talking about being surrounded by concrete and asphalt? Well, the festival was taking place at an old air force base. Ya see what I'm sayin'? Planes and jets tend to roll better on hard surfaces, right? So, yeah. It was a huge area. Both main stages, the east stage and the west stage, were at least two miles apart. Between all three stages—there was a third stage in a hanger—you were looking at well over two miles of walking just to get to stages. Make no mistake, you had to pick and choose the shows you attended based off the schedule because you weren't making every single one. Period.

By dusk we found ourselves outside a hanger where a live band was playing. As we were walking in the hanger, people were having a great time throwing frisbees. There were so many people throwing frisbees up in the air that it looked like a continuous swarm of alien beings, dancing a dance of visual splendors. When we entered the hanger, weed smoke hit us in the face with a welcoming breath of fresh air. As the chaos in my head cleared, I noticed the badass music playing. And no shit, I looked up at the stage and George Clinton was playing. He was walking back and forth smoking a bong. Holy crap! We were watching George Clinton & the P-Funk All Stars. Not only did we start Woodstock '99 with a christening of excellent acid, but we finished our first night with one of the best artists in the industry. We were both all smiles as we were watching the show. We fired up a fatty because that's what the fuck you do when you are in the presence of the Godfather of Funk. Wow! We just couldn't believe what we were witnessing. After George Clinton was done, we spent a couple of hours going to both the east and west stages. We knew that would be the only time that we would be able to walk all the way up to the front of either stage to just look. The acid flowing through us made the artwork on the walls of both stages seem as though it was breathing. Both were inviting. No one was out there yet. In those moments, things were still nice. Seeing both the stages the way we saw them that night was peaceful.

We woke up early the next morning. James Brown was opening the east stage, and we wanted to catch it. But after James Brown we bailed to find some food. We hadn't really eaten anything since McDonald's on Thursday morning. We had some snacks in the car from the trip, but other than that we hadn't had anything else. As we were looking around for some grub, we noticed that the prices for everything were outrageous. For example, a hot dog would cost you seven dollars. And a burrito? That would be ten dollars. Burgers? Anywhere between seven and ten dollars. Cheeseburgers? Ten dollars and up. A slice a pizza? Ten dollars. Oh, and a bottle of fuckin' water? Between seven or eight dollars, depending on which vendor you visited. We knew we wouldn't be able to afford those kinds of prices the whole time we were there. We were gonna have to figure something out. We both got burgers and some water. We wouldn't eat again until Saturday—that short of crackers and pop-tarts from the car. Yet, more reasons why people were pissed off: no one could afford to eat. What the fuck?!

A little later we caught some of Sheryl Crow's show. But I wanted to also get to the west stage to see The Roots. Both shows were really good. After that, we went back to camp for a while to rest before the Korn show, which would finish our day as far as shows. They were playing later in the evening, and we already knew that after seeing Korn previously we would have no energy left when they were done. And we were right. Of course, Korn put on a wonderful performance. We were a little to the left of the stage and pretty close as far as having that many people in one spot. We were well past the soundboard and mixing area. There was no fuckin' way we were getting close to any kind of mosh pit. Fuck that! After Korn, we went back to camp, and we smoked some weed for a while and then crashed.

Saturday morning we woke up to raging hunger. There was a deep-dark cloud that had developed over the entire festival. By Saturday people were pretty fed the fuck up. The cops I told you about? They had already started smuggling in the beer by Friday. Getting a beer at Woodstock '99 would cost anywhere between seven and ten dollars. Needless to say, the beer gardens they had at the festival pretty much stayed empty, short of the rich folks. And there weren't very many of them around. People had started bringing in grills regardless of the rules, and they were cooking their own food. Everyone started bringing in coolers of food from their cars. The vandalism had also started. Little spots all across the festival grounds were getting fucked up. Whether it was part of the fencing that surrounded the festival grounds or trash cans and porta-potties, it was apparent that people were tired and angry due to the lack of proper and affordable amenities. Liam and I heard about shuttles that were taking people into town where there was a grocery store. We went right away. The plan was to get water, bread, peanut butter, and whatever else we could find and afford. While we were waiting on one of the shuttles to arrive, Kid Rock started playing. A few minutes later a shuttle arrived, and we were off. When we got to the grocery store and walked in, the goddamn place looked like the end result of a zombie apocalypse. I've never seen a grocery store that empty. We did, however, find a twelve-pack of water, some bread, and peanut butter. We were rich!

We got back to the campsite as quick as we could. But this time our coolers had some water and food in them. And no one said a fuckin' thing to us as we were bringin' them in. At some point early during the day, we found a band called Full Devil Jacket playing in the hanger. They were really good. But we were waiting on three artists that day: Ice Cube, Limp Bizkit, and Rage Against the Machine. In the meantime, we drank beer and smoked weed. According to the schedule we had, Ice Cube ended up starting early. From our campsite, I faintly heard him performing. We hauled ass to the stage he was playing, and it was so awesome! I finally got to see one of the artists who had inspired me early in life. As of this writing, it is the only time I have seen Ice Cube perform live. Between that show and the next two shows we wanted to see, we relaxed back at the campsite. After a while, I had decided that I wanted to take a shower. Or at least rinse off. The last two-and-a-half days had been pretty intense. I thought it would be nice to get wet from something other than sweat and rain. Holy crap! That was a mistake. I should have known by the fact that there was no line to get in. That's because it had already turned co-ed, and the water in the shower area wasn't draining. It was up to my shins. And it was not clean water. It was brown, dirty, soapy, muddy water. There were quite a few people in there. Most of them, like me, had swimsuits on. But some of them didn't. And I would say they just didn't give a fuck: fully naked and showering as if they were at home with soap, shampoo, and all. There was even a couple making out in there—for some god-awful reason. That was nasty! But at that point, I didn't give a fuck. I took my shirt off and let the water from the shower head run. I didn't even bring any soap with me. I'm glad, too. That shit wouldn't have done any good up in that muthafucker anyway. I rolled my swimsuit up to my thighs and then pulled my trunks down enough to get some water down in that area as well. And then I got the fuck out of there. I was smart and didn't bring a towel. I didn't need to dry off. I would be dry by the time I got back to camp.

Limp Bizkit, Rage Against the Machine, and Metallica were scheduled to play back-to-back. Shit went nuts during the Limp Bizkit show. Liam and I were on the right side of the stage, closer than we had been at any show during the festival thus far. It was a great show! There was a little technical difficulty at one point, but it was cleared up pretty quickly. Unfortunately, it turned out that during that show, there were sexual assaults taking place along with vandalism to the stage. That was the only time I ever saw Limp Bizkit. Rage Against the Machine was next. Absolutely incredible! I wish I could say that I saw Rage again after that night, but I never did. After Rage was over, we went back to the campsite. We were tired. Luckily, when we got back to camp, no one was there. Everyone was watching the Metallica show. We listened to it from our campsite. They sounded really good!

By Sunday, shit was really fucked up out there. When we woke up Sunday morning to go to Willie Nelson's show, we saw quite a lot more vandalism on the way. Lots of vendors were already shut down and had left. Other vendors had been vandalized and looted. When Willie Nelson was done, we stuck around that area so we could catch Everlast. From there, we went to the west stage to watch Sevendust and Godsmack. Except this time, we were in the fuckin' back, sitting down on the grass. We were both fuckin' exhausted. We smoked a couple of joints while we were listening to the show. I made the mistake of lying down on the grass. I don't remember anything after the song "Crumbled." Liam woke me up and asked if I was ready to go. We never made Godsmack. As we made our way back to the campsite, little fires were being set in random spots. Once we got back to camp, it took us about thirty minutes to get our shit packed up and bail. As we made the final tiring trek to the car, most of the fencing that was standing when we arrived on Thursday had been destroyed. Fencing, gates, barriers, and walls were tore the fuck down. I was glad we were getting the fuck out of there. We had close to a quarter of weed left and about ten hits of acid that we were bringin' back home with us. Liam drove us out. About an hour later, Liam stopped at a rest stop that had a restaurant. Hell yeah, we got some food! A few hours later into our trip back home, we heard on the radio how shit was going down back at Woodstock. Fires! Looting! Rapes! Fighting! Pillaging! Vandalizing! Complete chaos and disorder. We were glad as fuck that we got out of there when we did. I'll tell ya this about Woodstock '99. It was fun. But it was miserable. According to *The Washington Post*, somewhere between 225,000 and 250,000 people attended the festival. I also heard reports saying closer to 300,000 as well. Either way, that's a lot of muthafuckers in one area. Would I do it again? Probably.

It felt good to get back home. A couple of days after we got back, I hooked up with Anthony and we went up to Donovan's. I took some acid because Anthony, Liam, and I were gonna trip, and I knew Donovan and his ol' lady would want some as well. I had the acid in cellophane. I sat down at the kitchen table to cut up and divide everything. Anthony and I each took two, and Donovan and his ol' lady each ate one. As I was getting ready to put the other four hits back in the cellophane, I looked to grab it, and it wasn't there. Where did the cellophane go, Shane? Well, Donovan's son was walking around the kitchen with it in his mouth. As soon as I noticed, I immediately grabbed it out of the child's hands and informed Donovan that I had been carrying the acid in it. Needless to say, that freaked everyone the fuck out. Anthony expressed his need to get the fuck out of there immediately, and I agreed. I told Donovan we were leaving and to keep me updated on the kid and that I was really sorry about what just happened. I also apologized for the fact that we were bailing. But besides the situation that had just transpired, we had to get to Dover to get Liam his two hits so that he wouldn't be too far behind Anthony and me. A couple hours later, I called Donovan to make sure everything was alright. The kid was fine and already in bed watching movies. And he and his ol' lady were fryin' their balls off. That was a relief. I could continue with my trip without the thought of Donovan's four-year-old son trippin' his little peanuts off. I mean, shit, can you imagine? Fuck that shit! Liam, Anthony, and I continued our frying out at Liam's. There was no reason to go anywhere else. Although later that night—after the hardcore tripping was over and I had left Liam's—I stopped off at Donovan's. I didn't want him to feel completely abandoned. He was cool. He understood what happened and why we left and didn't come back. He did say that the first hour and a half were kind of stressful, though. I mean, shit. He had to wait a good hour just to see if his kid was gonna start freakin' out and shit. But he knew that when he started feeling the acid really good within the first hour or so, and his kid was eating dinner and still acting normal, that he was in the clear. Still, though! I imagine that first hour or so was kinda shitty. Over the next two months, there wasn't a lot that happened with us. That's alright. We had been pretty busy. Don't ya think? Oh, I had found a job at a distribution center right before I left for Woodstock. That was good because I needed the money.

As far as music goes, Sevendust released their second album, *Home*, in August. And in September, Nine Inch Nails released *The Fragile*. Both albums were fantastic. When I listened to *Home* for the first time, I realized that I had seen the band perform some of those songs at Woodstock, which I thought was really cool. And *The Fragile*? That was and still is a fuckin' masterpiece. When October rolled around, Kelly and I went down to Tulsa on Halloween and saw a show at a place called Brady Theater. Bethany even came to the show with us. It was a badass show! It had an incredible lineup. We saw Machine Head, Orange 9mm, Dope, Slipknot, Sevendust, and Coal Chamber. I walked away that night with two bands on my mind: Dope and Slipknot. Don't get me wrong, all the bands were kickass, but Dope and Slipknot acquired a new fan that night. Oh, and one other artist I need to mention who put his long-awaited second album out in November of that year: Dr. Dre released *Chronic 2001*. I had that shit turned up! That year—the last year of the 20th century—was absolutely fantastic as far as new music coming out. It is important that I mention that shit. And as far as the end of a century, what was next? Where would it go from there?

8 THE BEGINNING OF THE END

In January, Anthony and Liam went to truck driving school. I know, right? Not only were they going to learn how to drive big-ass trucks, but they were going to do it as a team. They were both going to have their CDL, driving down America's interstate and highway systems. Yes, sir! The start of a new beginning. I was really excited for both of them. I would definitely miss them. We'll get back to them directly.

Meanwhile, I had been talking with Donovan about playing music again. It was time. Actually, it was way overdue. Donovan said he was down to play, so that was a start. I was so excited to have my drums set up again. I cleaned everything up and also purchased some new drumheads. Man, I was so excited! I even dreaded my hair around that same time. It was a new beginning!

[BREAKING NEWS UPDATE:
LIAM AND ANTHONY WERE INVOLVED IN AN ACCIDENT AND LOST THEIR CDLs BY APRIL OF 2000—JUST FOUR MONTHS AFTER RECEIVING THEM. THE POLICE REPORT INDICATED THAT BOTH LIAM AND ANTHONY WERE STILL INTOXICATED AFTER A NIGHT OF HEAVY DRINKING. THIS, JUST A FEW HOURS BEFORE HAVING TO GET BACK BEHIND THE WHEEL AND HIT THE FUCKIN' ROAD. POLICE SAID THAT IT WAS A MINOR FENDER BENDER, AND THERE WERE NO CASUALTIES.]

By April of 2000, Donovan had met a guy named Ian at school in one of his classes. He said that the guy was a musician. So, Donovan brought him to his house one night to do some drinkin', smokin', and introductions. I was unsure about Ian at first. And I told Donovan. To me, Ian seemed to act a little snobby and full of himself. At first, there wasn't a lot of conversation between either one of us because he and Donovan did nothing but talk science, chemistry, and other scholarly topics that were way over my head. Although, to be fair to Ian, I wasn't trying to talk to him, and I'm sure he was looking at me and wondering, "Who the fuck is this guy, and why does he look like he wants to kill everyone?" After Ian left that night, Donovan told me that Ian was just one of those guys that ya gotta get to know—that he was actually really cool and that he was a lot more like us than I thought. Donovan was right. After hangin' out a second time together, we clicked. The three of us started playing music at Donovan's. Ian was playing bass. At first, we just played some covers from bands like Coal Chamber, Manson, and Korn. Eventually we came up with a couple originals. They sucked. A couple of weeks later I met a guy named John. I had John in a sociology class. After a test one day, he came by my desk on the way out and dropped a note off with his name and phone number. So, I called him that day as soon as I was done with my test. Apparently, he heard I played drums. I can't remember how he found that out. Maybe it was from Ian. Anyway, he said he was wanting to form a band. I told him that I thought that was awesome and that I knew a guitarist and a bass player.

Real quick about John. John was into music as much as any of us. Probably more. He was part of some kind of street team group. Street teams introduce new music to people at clubs and concerts by handing out demos and other promotional merchandise. He didn't get paid, but he got the latest demos of music coming out along with concert tickets and other merchandise. It was a pretty cool gig. He turned me on to a band called Disturbed. Good shit!

Well, after that, John introduced me to a guy named Addison. We went over to Addison's apartment one day, and Addison started playing the acoustic guitar. While we were smoking one, I asked Addison if he wanted to play in a band. He nodded his head no, which made me wonder why in the fuck I was brought over there in the first place. But then, another week later, when we finally had plans to meet up and start playing, Addison showed up. Except that he showed up with a bass. And Ian? He showed up ready to play guitar with Donovan. Apparently, I missed all the communication that was going on behind the scenes with John, Addison, and Ian. Oh, and our first practice took place at what we used to call headshops. John was friends with the owners and had agreed to let us set up in the back of their business, which was a huge club-like room with a stage. It was pretty nice. The first jam session was pretty horrible. By the second and third jam sessions, we had definitely started making improvements. However, Donovan just couldn't keep up. He wasn't used to playing the style of music we were playing, which was shit like Deftones and Sevendust. The originals started coming out quickly, and everyone was tuned to drop D, a different tuning style with a lower pitch. Plus, Donovan had two kids and a wife that didn't want his ass back in that kind of life. So, Donovan had to leave. No worries. Addison knew a guy named Matty. So, Matty took Donovan's place. That was a good thing. Nothing against Donovan. But Donovan was behind in the game and couldn't produce at the level needed. Soon after that, we left the headshop and set up at Addison's dad's place for a short while. But that only lasted a couple of months before we needed a new place to practice. So, Liam said we could practice at his place. I love that man! It was very kind of him to have let us be there for as long as we were. We would end up being at Liam's until the beginning of 2001. I knew after a while that he was regretting it. I didn't blame him. But he had brother's love. So, that's where we started practicing.

Now, let's talk band members. First of all, Ian was a wonderful guitarist. He was better on guitar than bass. And he was a good bass player as well. Speaking of bass, Addison was the best bass player I had ever seen or played music with. Matty was just as badass at guitar as Ian. Matty just had a more jazzy and classical sound. And then John. Let me tell ya something about John. He was a cool muthafucker. Nice guy! But he couldn't sing a note to save his life. He could scream great. But he just couldn't hold a note. And his timing was just as bad. He would constantly be singing off key and off rhythm as well. We worked with him often. He would never get it.

By the summer of 2000, we played our first show. Besides John's singing, the music was great. Oh, and speaking of great music: I had gone to Dallas in May to watch Nine Inch Nails perform. And the opening act was A Perfect Circle. APC was a new band that the singer of Tool, Maynard, helped put together with his friend Billy Howerdel. Oh goodness! That was and still is one of my favorite shows of all time. As soon as APC's album came out, which was around the same time I saw the show, they were added to my collection. And continuing with great music in the summer of 2000, Liam and I went down to Little Rock to watch Soulfly and a band called Shuvel. That same night, after we got back home, Liam and I drove down to Dallas to go to Ozzfest 2000. That was a great time and a great show. We all met up down there: Liam, Anthony, Kelly, Robert, Donovan, and me. We saw Pantera, Static-X, Incubus, Godsmack, Methods of Mayhem, Disturbed, Kittie, Soulfly, and Taproot. It was so fuckin' bad ass! Later that summer or early fall, Matty, Ian, and John went to Memphis to see Ultraspank for their second album, *Progress*, and a band called Mudvayne for their debut album, *L.D. 50*. I was definitely jealous that I didn't get to go to that show. But anyway, about Mudvayne—holy Shit! When I got that album and listened to the whole thing, that was the best shit I had heard since Slipknot. I had become really inspired by all the new music that was entering my life. Not to mention, the guys I was playing music with loved the same shit and wanted the same thing, to create great music like the bands that I've been talking about. And speaking of, I'm not recapping bands' albums and the music that was dominant during that time for my health; I mean, if you wanna know about the bands I'm talking about, then Google them. You can get all the info you want. Rather, I'm talking about that shit because the bands I'm mentioning not only helped to revolutionize the music industry, but they helped shape who I was becoming, both as a musician and a person. But I wasn't the only one inspired. All of us were. And when I say all of us, I mean Addison, Ian, Matty, and me. Although, it'll mainly affect Addison, Ian, and me. All the music I've been talking about was important on so many levels. It's so important to talk about because it helps to illustrate the commonality in music and creativity that I found with these new guys. Unlike with Brian and Tyler in Frustrated Cruelty, every single one of us liked and listened to the same music. Another reason I'm talking about all this music is that it was the only thing that kept me going. I would say it was the only thing keeping me alive. And finally, like I said earlier, never again would I be ignorant to new music and the culture with it. Now, besides our similarities in music, the thought process and the communication amongst ourselves—and even the engagement we had with the outside—was damn near mirror like. We thought very much alike. We had developed such a cohesiveness in such a short amount of time that it almost seemed as if the four of us—especially me, Ian, and Addison—had literally been created to find one another and play music together. I had found my new Frustrated Cruelty. And that was something that I never thought I would see again. We were creating a bond together as a band like I had never felt with Tyler and Brian. In fact, the only other people I felt remotely close to in the same way were my brothers. Music quickly absorbed and consumed every part of me. I approached music as if it were the last time that I would ever hear or play it. Besides school and drugs, music was the only other thing I gave a fuck about outside of my people.

The mood and vibe of all four of us was very dirty and evil, what we would refer to as "devil." For example, we named our band Sin 7, not because we wanted to make people aware of sin or because we even believed in Christianity's thought process of the seven deadly sins. No. We named ourselves that because we thought we *were* sin. And we allowed ourselves to be covered in it, from our behavior and attitudes to our thought processes and actions. And trust me, it would live and breathe in our music. If a group of people could have been more "anti-Father" than we were, I would like to have seen it. Hate and anger flowed through my thoughts as if I were raised in such a way. And that's not the case at all. But, for some reason, hate and anger consumed me. I hated myself, The Father, Satan, life, and whatever else I could come up with to hate. But I was a pretty nice guy, all things considered. I would do anything for the people I cared for and loved. With that being said, if a group of people could have been more ignorant and ate up than we were, well, knowing what I know now, I would have really felt sorry for those people.

We eventually went into a studio not far from Donovan's house and recorded an EP. It was done in a few hours. Unfortunately, we had to use an effect called auto tune on John's voice to put it remotely in tune. Nevertheless, we produced as many copies as we could and handed them out. Donovan even helped us produce copies on the new computer he had bought for school. But behind the scenes, we knew what we had to do. It was just a matter of doing it, which sucked because it had to be done to one of the nicest guys we knew.

On the job front, well, things had been going well. I was at that distribution center I told you about. I was over six months in, and I changed jobs from filling orders to loading trucks.

Now, there are many kinds of distribution centers and warehouses. And when we talk distribution centers and warehouses, it could mean any kind of distribution center or warehouse, from food to electronics and everything in between. I was working at a food distribution center. Real quick, let me tell ya just a little bit about some of the fine folks who work at distribution centers and warehouses. Ya see, those are the folks who take products off trucks to store until it is time to ship. Or they're the folks who put the products on the trucks when it is time to ship. And I'm being very generic in my description. There are many different jobs and levels within a distribution center and warehouse that bring everything together to ultimately get the products on the trucks and to the customers and consumers. Either way, we have products on the shelves when we go shopping due to those fine folks at warehouses and distribution centers all across our nation. The other part of that fine logistical piece, of course, are the wonderful truckers who travel this nation to drop off those products at the stores for your shopping convenience. Well, those folks at the distribution centers and warehouses? Don't fuckin' worry about it! You got your food, yes? You got your bath soap? Did you get that new set of wireless headphones you ordered online? You goddamn right you did. So don't fuckin' worry about how ya got it. Anyway, I digress.

It was a good night right up until I had to get a couple pallets of bananas to put on the truck I was loading. I thought using a forklift would have been the quickest way to get them. And I was right. Except that on my way to get those bananas, as I turned the corner to go down the aisle to get them, a smart ass backed up out of a slot on another forklift to fuck with me, as if he was going to back into me. Well, when I reacted to prevent a collision, I over corrected. When I looked behind me to make sure I was clearing him, I ran right into one of the rails of the pallet racks. Imagine aisles of pallet racks, each slot in each rack going up three to four pallets tall, and each pallet with product on it could weigh as much as 1,000 pounds or more. And aisles of pallet racks with product on both sides could be as long as seventy-five feet or more, I'd guess. Now imagine hitting one of the foundational beams that help hold those muthafuckers up. No, imagine hitting one of those beams holding thousands of pounds of freight, hitting it so hard with your forklift that you total the forklift. That's what I did. I fucked up that forklift! I didn't know a person could fuck up a forklift like that. I'm not sure anyone else did either. I hit that fuckin' beam so hard that I came to a complete stop. Only the forklift came to a complete stop. I, on the other hand, flew out that muthafucker about five to ten feet. I kept my balance the whole time and never hit the ground. Those are ninja-like skills right there. Luckily, the beam I hit was one of several beams holding that rack, and I only dented it. Don't get me wrong, they would have to fix it. And they did. But that forklift? Nope! And that meant I had to take a drug test. I won't lie. I was sweating the whole situation.

I knew I hadn't done any dope in about a week. So, I was good there. But it was the weed I was immediately worried about. What the fuck was I gonna do? I guess I was gonna lose my job. But wait! Not so fast there, skippy. The folks at the DC were a pretty tight-knit group. I went to my locker to put my gear up. Then I went to the bathroom to take a piss. When I came out of the bathroom to wait in the hallway for the operations manager to drive me to the clinic to take a piss test, one of my buddies came walking out of the break room, gave me a hug, and said he'd see me when I got back. Now, that was no ordinary hug. That was a we-got-your-back hug, fresh with a sealed, brand-new bottle of clean pee. Some kept containers of clean pee on them, or we knew guys who didn't participate in extracurricular activities and were clean who didn't mind peeing for us, which is what happened in my situation. When I finally got to the clinic, about 11:30 at night, I was still nervous. What if the pee I had was losing too much temperature? Oh well! It was gonna be what it was gonna be. And it turned out in my favor. When I handed the nurse the pee and my ops manager and I started to walk out, the nurse said, "Wait a minute. It's not reaching temperature yet." The ops manager got mad and was like, "Oh c'mon! Just take the piss." Then the nurse replied, "Oh there it is. It just took a second."

Man! That last part about got me. I thought the scam was up and I was caught. But it worked out the only way it was supposed to work out. When I got back to the DC, the guy who gave me the clean pee had been interrogated while I was gone. He said our manager kept asking him, "What did you give him?" and saying shit like, "We got you on video giving something to Shane." He never broke. He knew the manager didn't have shit. Even if he did have him on video giving me a hug, our manager couldn't prove that he gave me anything because he couldn't see anything. Fuck that manager! The operations manager was cool, but our regular manager was a dick. Needless to say, until my piss test came back, I couldn't operate any equipment other than the wrapping machine. It took about a week for it to come back. Of course, I was good.

And speaking of being good, that reminds me: the *Up in Smoke* tour that Liam and I went to in Dallas, in early August of 2000—that was a great show. You Know! Holy shit! Dr Dre, Snoop, Eminem, Nate Dogg, Kurupt, Warren G, Xzibit, and the list goes on. You get the picture. It was nothing less than one of the most bad-ass shows I've ever seen in my fuckin' life. I wish I could say that I've seen any of those artists more than that one time, but I haven't. Oh, well. I'll always have that night in Dallas. Of course, Liam's ol' lady remembers that night differently than the rest of us. I managed to get us pulled over on the way back to my brother's house from the show. They pulled all of us out of the car. They could smell that we had been to the *Up in Smoke* show. I know that because the officer asked, "You guys just come from the *Up in Smoke* show?" I responded, "Yeah." He replied with a grin, "I can smell." Everything was fine until some weed fell out of Liam's ol' lady's pants. Yep, the whole bag fell right out the bottom of her jeans. I'm not quite sure why she put it where she put it. But, nonetheless, that's where she put it, and it came falling out onto the ground. I was just going to get a warning, which I still got. But Liam's ol' lady walked away with a ticket, which meant a fine. Oh well. At least they didn't find the rest of the weed that we had on us. The drive back to Arkansas the next day would have sucked without it. I'll tell ya this, too: I was gonna have to try to be much more careful from now on. There was no reason I should have gotten us pulled over. Must be more careful.

Speaking of being careful. Have you ever seen a demon before? I have. Not a demon in the sense of something from the movies, but rather a demon in real life—a demon in human form. Have you ever talked to a demon before? I have. Well, that or I was just sooo fucked up that I couldn't for the first time truly see the difference between reality and fantasy. Or maybe I couldn't tell the difference between reality and intoxication. Or maybe I was sooo fucked up that what I thought was me meeting a demon was, in all reality, misinformation based off poor communication due to intense intoxication. Maybe I blacked out of the original conversation and come back in on the "Hey, Shane! It's good to meet ya." Please, allow me to explain. It was a Sunday evening on New Year's Eve, and I was in Austin. I was visiting a girl. Actually, it was me, one of her friends, and a buddy of mine from work. We had gone down a day or two earlier and were heading back to Arkansas on the 1st. The girl I was visiting had hooked up some good coke and some good X (ecstasy). Oh, and I don't know if I've said this before, but, besides Pine Bluff, Dallas and Austin have the best coke. Period. Anyway, she had gotten us an 8-ball of some excellent coke with some tasty X for our New Year's outing. So, needless to say, by the time we had all shown up to a club downtown called The Ritz, I had already done massive amounts of coke and had popped some X. Now, what I'm about to explain next is really simple. There's not a lot to it. No one else that I kept company with that night saw or heard what I'm about to tell you. And that, too, will make a muthafucker think: Did any of this just happen? Am I being fucked with?

Hanging out at The Ritz was to be our last club for the night before a short stint at a house party that no one but our host attended. We had waited in the car. As we walked into the club single file, I remember hearing Tool on the club system. The song "Third Eye." Only in a bad-ass club in Texas would you be hearing that song in rotation on New Year's Eve. We were walking towards the back of the club where there was another bar and a couple of pool tables. Our host had some friends that got us seats ahead of time. When we got to our destination, everyone veered left towards the booth-like table where we were going to be sitting. Except that I was stopped by a man before I was able to get to the table. He was literally tall, dark, and handsome. He was wearing jeans with boots and a black t-shirt. He had a shaved, bald head. And with his simple demeanor he displayed confidence and a welcoming smile. And with his hand extended, he said, "Nice to meet you, Shane. I'm…." I have no recollection of what he said his name was. It evaporated from my thoughts as quickly as he said it. I responded to him, "Hey, bro! Nice to meet you." Then he pointed to his wife who was over at the bar and said, "That's my wife at the bar." I just responded, smiling as I was trying to get to my company, and I said, "Awesome!" There was no hostility from that man. He was as friendly as the morning sun in Arkansas on an early Autumn morning. When I finally made it to my table, I said my hellos to those I was meeting for the first time, and then I quickly turned to my host, leaning over in secrecy and asked, "Hey, you see that guy over there playing pool?" She looked, then responded, "Yeah." "Do you know him?" I asked. She looked over at him again and said, "No. Why?" I responded, "Well, because he knew me. Even introduced himself to me using my name." She kind of dismissed what I had just told her by smirking, and then she turned around to continue her conversation with those we had just met. Me? I asked if anyone needed anything from the bar and made my way in that direction.

When I got to the bar, there were just a few people up there. But one of the beautiful people at that bar was the woman that the terribly handsome man had pointed out just minutes earlier, claiming to be his wife. She was blonde and not as attractive as her counterpart. You would have thought that maybe he had settled but that she had definitely married up. Know what I'm sayin'? But that didn't matter. She quickly came over to me after noticing that I couldn't seem to get the bartender's attention. She stood next to me and screamed, "Hey!" The bartender turned around and looked at her. She turned to me and asked, "What do ya want?" I told her three beers. She turned to the bartender and ordered them. They were Miller Lights. "Thank you," I said nervously. "Ya gotta' yell at muthafuckers around here," she explained. We introduced ourselves, made small talk, and she said something about her handsome husband, and that was it. She walked back over to her handsome husband. I walked back over to my table with three beers. I was very confused. When I got settled in and made my rounds of small talk with the rest of the fucks that were at that table, I turned to my host and asked again in as low a voice as I could in that loud, chaotic environment, "You sure you don't know that muthafucker over there playing pool?" She looked again, turned back around, and said, kind of irritably, "No." Then, our kind host turned to everyone at the table and asked, "Do any of y'all know that guy over there playing pool?" My cold host explained to whom she was referring. Everyone said they didn't know who that guy was. With my head down and my hand covering the bottom part of my mouth, my host turned to me. "See? No one knows that guy. Are you sure you're alright?" she asked. Luckily, by that time, everyone else at the table had gone on about whatever the fuck they were going on about—except for the four of us: me, my buddy, our host's buddy, and our host. "Oh, I'm good," I responded angrily. "That guy knew my name. That's all. I mean, for fuck sake, his wife even ordered my beer, and no one here knows who the fuck that guy is," I said in a mocking way. They were just looking at me like, "What the fuck, Shane? What do you want us to do?" I told them it was all good, and we went about our night. I even played pool at the same table as the demon and his wife after they had left the club or the state or the earth or the dimension or wherever. The point is, well…I don't know what the point is. Have you ever met a demon?

We let John go in early 2001. Matty broke the news to him. We would go a while without a singer after that. In the meantime, we moved out of Liam's and into our own studio. Matty had a pretty good job back then, and he could afford the rent. He even invested in recording equipment. We changed our name to Studio 202. That was going to be a hell of a ride. But we'll circle back to that in a minute. Oh, and by spring of '01, I had left the distribution center and transferred to one of the company's local stores. I started taking on more classes at school, and I needed a more liberal schedule to accommodate my education.

Meanwhile, we weren't long at the studio before a couple of guys from Houston showed up. They were friends of Addison's originally. They heard what we had going and wanted to get in on it. They found out the suite next to us was also for lease. They were checking things out. They decided to get the place next to us. We had the rock and metal covered. They had the techno and dance covered. Ok. Alright. Sounds fine. Oh, no, no, no. Things quickly became not fine. We'll start referring to the Houston guys as "the neighbors." Within about a month, Addison was selling ecstasy for the neighbors. You know: XTC, E, rolls, X. But they soon realized that I had access to the good shit. Addison approached me one day to ask what I could do. Of course, I could hook them up. What kind of question was that? So, that's what I did. I started hooking up Addison, and he would hook up the neighbors. Other than that, the rest of us didn't have any dealings with the neighbors. Well, not long after the neighbors moved in next door, not even a month after, something happened.

Now, I'm still not sure exactly what happened because we only had Addison's story. But, according to what Addison told us, this is what went down: We were at the studio. We being Matty, Ian, and me. Addison arrived shortly after. When he got there, he went next door to the neighbors' studio to drop some money off that he owed for some X. A short while later, Addison came through the door extremely upset. He wasted no time explaining what had just happened. Apparently, when Addison walked into the neighbors' place, they threw him up against the wall, asking about money he still owed. Addison said he insisted that he was all paid up, that he didn't owe them anything. He said they kept saying he was lying and threatening him. Eventually, he said they let him go, which was when he came back over to the studio. Of course we believed Addison. Plus, I had gotten them a lot of dope that Addison sold to them. I figured they were tweakin' or trippin'. There was no more relationship between us and the neighbors. Although, we would have another encounter with them on Halloween. We'll get to that shortly.

In the meantime, at Studio 202, we wasted no time. We started playing and recording constantly. The only time we weren't at that studio was when we were at school or at home sleeping. Other than that, we were there. Matty even got a business permit so he could start recording other local bands to make some money. But we really never made any money off that. We did make money off throwing parties and having shows, though. But it was mainly for us to have a practice space free from interference. After we got the place, people showed up there daily—mainly just hanging out, smoking, drinking, and listening to us play. It was only people we knew, of course. Except for my crew, who would make an appearance from time to time, it was mainly folks we had classes with or people that Addison, Ian, and Matty already knew. And during shows and parties, the inside part of the studio was only open to a select few. Besides the artistic creativity that was being produced (unlike I had ever experienced up to that point), the studio was a place of debauchery. We got fucked up and did some fucked up shit in that muthafucker. Hell, within the first two months we were there, I found myself in a situation where I thought I was gonna die.

Let me explain. You ever heard of ketamine or ketaset? Fuck that shit! The first time I ever saw it, it was in a rig. Actually, it was in a fuckin' syringe that looked like something you would put in a large animal. You couldn't really consider it a rig because that's exactly what that shit was used for: animals. And it came straight from a vet clinic. That's because the guy who brought it over worked at a local clinic and would steal the shit. His name was Dominik. I can't remember who knew Dominik. I know that Donovan worked with him at the same clinic, but that was about it. Dominik came over to the studio one day with three syringes of the shit. I can't remember if it was ketaset or ketamine. It really doesn't matter. They're pretty much the same from what I've been told. Anyway, Ian, Dominik, and I were the specimens that evening. Really, it was just Ian and me. Dominik had already done it several times, but it was my and Ian's first time. Dominik hit us both and then hit himself. This wasn't the kind of drug you put in your vein. You just put it right into your muscle. Not that it mattered. Within two minutes I was fucked up. Within five minutes I was really fucked up. Within seven minutes I was in trouble. I was in big trouble. Ian and Dominik were fine. Ian said he was nice and high. Shiiiit! I was beyond high. I couldn't believe Ian was maintaining like he was. He and Dominik were fine. Not me. I was so high that I thought I was going to die. I had literally accepted the fact that I had finally overdone it and was on my way out. There was peace about the whole situation, though. Not at first, mind you. I was scared at first. Then I was mad at myself for what I had done. Then I was sad because of what I was going to do to the people who loved me. After all that, I just accepted what was going to happen. It sucked. I was perfectly rational with the thought process in my head. I was talking to myself clearly. And I could hear everyone around me. But I couldn't see a fuckin' thing. Nothing. But still, I had made peace with the fact that I was going to die. I remember Ian kept checking on me. I would lift my hand to signal that I was still alive, but eventually I couldn't even do that. Ian said he had turned me over and opened my eyes at one point, and he said that he saw nothing but grayed-out eyes. He said there was no pupil or color. Eventually, Ian found me out in the garage throwing up. He made sure I stayed on my side. I don't remember how I got out there. I guess I had come back to life enough to crawl out the door. Throwing up was the best thing that could've happened. It sobered me right up. The entire episode took all of two hours. I was jamming later that evening.

And speaking of jamming: we were writing a bunch of shit. Tool had come out with their album *Lateralus* in May, and we were listening to a lot of it. We were very inspired and creatively influenced by that album; that or it was all the acid we were doing. I'd say it was both. And, of course, the guy hookin' us up with all the acid was Dominik. This guy was hooked the fuck up. He was getting eye-drop containers full of liquid LSD. And because he liked us so much and was always hangin' out at the studio, he sold it to us cheap. He'd sell us eye-drop vials with 100 hits for $300. It was awesome! We'd put a drop on a piece of candy and sell that shit for seven and ten dollars a hit. We did that shit all summer. Oh, and speaking of summer 2001: we all went to Ozzfest again. Except this time, Ian, Addison, and Matty were there as well. We were at the July show in Dallas. Ian and I went up the night before, stayed with my brother, and went downtown fryin' our balls off. That Ozzfest was a damn good show, my friends. Black Sabbath, y'all! The original lineup. Plus, Marilyn Manson, Slipknot, Disturbed, Linkin Park, Papa Roach, and Black Label Society. And that was just the main stage. At the second stage we were caressed by the sweet sounds of Mudvayne, Taproot, Nonpoint, American Head Charge, and several others. Oh, and we were introduced to a band called Otep on the third stage. Hell, Ian damn near started a riot during Slipknot. Crazy muthafucker. I couldn't believe it. He must have had about a hundred people in one area ready to storm the pit. He was tellin' everybody how we needed to just rush the pit and fuck the police and the security and all that shit. Screamin' that shit! Putting his fist up and all that shit. I mean, he had these concert goers ready to take it to the next level. In fact, we were about to rush that fuckin' pit. And at the last moment, a hoard of police and security came running over to block our path, and they forced everyone to either sit down, go to the lawn, or go to jail. That was enough for me. I went and sat my ass down. So did Ian. It was for the best. That was a great day, y'all!

A couple of days later, I ran into someone I hadn't seen in over a year. Dane! It was good to see him. He asked if I knew where to get a bump. And for the first time I was able to help him out. I couldn't believe it. It just so happened that I had access to some pretty good dope. Dane said all he wanted was a bump, so he gave me twenty dollars. I asked where he wanted to meet back up, and he said he wasn't sure when he was gonna be back in town from running errands and to just leave it with Robert. Ya see, Dane just wanted something until his normal things came back into play. And I was happy to help him out. All those years hookin' us up, it felt good to actually return the favor in some very small way. So, I went and got the quarter and immediately brought it to Robert's. I stayed for a little bit, hoping I would catch Dane again, but I left after about forty-five minutes. Apparently, he didn't show back up for quite a while, according to Robert. A couple of weeks later I ran into Jacob. He told me that Dane was hurt by the dope I had gotten him, that it was not enough dope for what he paid. I couldn't believe what I was hearing. It didn't make sense. I would never short Dane. In fact, I added to his quarter from my stash before I had dropped it off, just to make sure he had a nice bump. I'm not saying the quarter I got him was short to begin with because it wasn't. But it was Dane. I knew he would do that quarter with no issues, which was why I wanted to make sure he had a little extra for his evening. I told Jacob as much. I argued my case. I stated that I couldn't believe Dane was mad at me. Jacob corrected me and said, "He's not mad at ya. His feelings were hurt." Well, that made me feel like the biggest piece of shit on the planet. After telling Jacob exactly what I did, he told me he believed me and that he would let Dane know the next time he saw him. And then Jacob said, "To be honest with ya, I think Robert dipped into it." Now, that had never even occurred to me until that very moment. When Jacob said that, he saw the light bulb go off in my head and kind of smirked. That had to have been the situation. I told Jacob that I thought he was spot on. What the fuck!? Why would Robert put me in a situation like that? Oh, I know. Because he was a fuckin' junkie! We all were! I couldn't blame the muthafucker. But at the same time, I was gonna bring the shit up the next time I saw Robert. We needed to make that shit right.

Another great day arrived a couple of months later. We left for Chicago to see Tool perform. We all left from my parent's house in two vehicles. Matty, a buddy of ours named Jeremiah, and I went in Matty's truck. And Ian, Addison, a guy named Jay, and a girl named Chainey took Chainey's grandmother's minivan. Real quick about Jay: Jay would soon become our vocalist. He was, well, Jay. I didn't understand him, nor did I respect him. Although, he was creative. That's about all I'm going to say about it. Regarding Chainey: if you haven't been able to tell by now, I've only talked about a handful of women in this story. Chainey is one of the last women I will talk about. I met her through Addison. She's one of the sweetest and most loving people I've known. I'm honored she considers me a friend. And that's that.

We left on September 8, at about seven o'clock in the morning. Tool was to perform the next day. It was rare to find a crew like us up that early and ready to hit the road without having had some major help. But we were already wired. Tool was our drug. We were so pumped. It would take us twelve hours to get to Chicago from Russellville. I had booked rooms via my parent's credit card, and I gave them the cash for the tickets and rooms. We pulled into Chicago, actually Rosemont, at about 7:30 that evening. Rosemont is about twenty miles outside of Chicago. The next morning, Matty and I went down to the lobby, ate breakfast, and then we immediately started drinking. The rest of the gang followed closely behind our early-morning start. Later that afternoon, we decided to try and find an authentic Italian restaurant to do a late lunch/early dinner sort of thing. I'm not sure we found the best Italian restaurant, but after asking several people from the hotel, they all seemed to agree on the same place, so that's where we went. Although I can't remember the name of the place, I do remember that it was really good. And I fancy myself an Italian connoisseur, for my part as a southerner anyway. I had no doubt they could tell that we weren't from around those parts. Especially because when Jay ordered his meal, he actually ordered "a side of fries to weight that down with." What the fuck did this muthafucker just say? Had I actually heard him, in all his southern glory, in Chicago, at an Italian restaurant, order a lasagna, and then ask for an order of fries to "weight that down with?" Yes. Yes, I did just hear him request that. I don't even think that fries were actually offered as a choice except from the kids' menu.

Meshuggah opened the show that evening. They were good. That was the first time I had seen them. When Tool hit the stage, they opened with "The Grudge." Holy crap! I couldn't believe my ears or my eyes. Look, I've seen Tool many times since then, but I must say: that show in Rosemont is still one of my favorites. All I saw was the look of happiness and satisfaction on everyone's faces that had just witnessed that show. I slept well that night. We took our time going home the next day. It was a beautiful morning that September day. We went and grabbed some doughnuts and then did a little sight-seeing. Ian and everyone with Chainey went to the Sears Tower and did that whole thing. Oh, and speaking of Ian and Chainey: they became a couple during that trip. Beautiful! Matty, Jeremiah, and I thought driving around the downtown area was enough after a while, and we started on our way back home before the other crew. It was around midnight when we made it back to Russellville. I had class the next morning. Although, it turned out that I didn't have class the next morning. Why? Well, September 11, 2001, was not a good day. It seemed that, once again, our country suffered at the hands of terrorism. Except this time it wasn't domestic; it was foreign. When I woke up that morning, the first tower had already been hit. I walked out to the living room and my grandmother was watching the news. I asked what was going on because watching the news wasn't routine for her. She said that a plane had accidently hit a building in New York. She didn't know what was going on. Hell, I don't know if very many people at that point knew what was going on. But then, all of a sudden—and, no shit, on live television—we watched the second plane hit. It was at that moment that I and the rest of the country knew that it was not an accident. Then, of course, a third plane hit the Pentagon, and a fourth crashed in a field in Pennsylvania. We were under attack. The country was under attack. And since that time, this country has...well, I'll let you decide.

A couple of weeks later, we threw a party at the studio. Hell, my mom and grandma unexpectedly showed up to that one! Not that it was a big deal or anything. We were only in our element, getting fucked up and doing fucked up shit. There were probably fifty or sixty people at the studio partying it up. Several of us, myself included, were in the back of the studio getting fucked up; meaning we were smoking weed. No biggie—until, of course, the guy you're paying to watch the front door for any unwelcome visitors comes walking to the back of the studio and says, "Hey, man. There's a woman out there who says she's your mom and that she's with your grandma. You want me to let them in?" Everyone just started laughing. I hauled ass past the few people who were allowed in the studio and got to the front door as soon as I could. And there they were, two little cuties surrounded by a host of debauchery. My mom had a cup of wine in her hand, and my grandma had a cup of whiskey in her hand. We all just hung out for a while and partied. Everyone had a great time talking with my mom and grandma. I didn't really have to keep them entertained. Everyone was entertained by them. Good times!

Come October, though, things changed…again. In fact, the rest of the year pretty much sucked. I remember the day Kelly came rushing into the studio, crying. I was in the lounge part of the studio, so I was right there when he swung the door open. "Dane's dead, bro," Kelly said as tears ran down his face. "Whoa, whoa!" I responded hastily. "What the fuck?! What?" I was very confused and startled. "Dane's dead, bro," Kelly repeated in a little calmer tone. "How? What the fuck happened?" I asked. Kelly explained everything. I was supposed to go to work that night. I didn't. Instead, Kelly and I made our rounds, letting everyone know and just trying to make sense of what happened. Well, turned out, the lab exploded. Besides the burns one suffers, the oxygen is also sucked out of the room during this process. The person he was in the room with delayed getting him to the hospital because she decided it was best to put him in the bath to rinse him off, hoping no one would suspect a lab had just exploded. Of course, by then, it was too late. Dane never woke up from the explosion, and he was declared brain dead due to the amount of time he had gone without oxygen. I'm so sorry that shit happened, Dane. Thanks for all the good times. I'll never forget them.

On Halloween, we were gearing up for a huge party. A Halloween party at the studio. Live music and alcohol! And, of course, weed. Duh! Well, our neighbors decided they were going to throw a Halloween party as well. Yep! You are correct. It turned out exactly how you would expect: with the cops showing up. But this time they actually weren't fuckin' with us. They were fuckin' with the neighbors. I don't remember exactly how it happened. All I know is that one minute, between both parties, I'm surrounded by about 200 people having a good time, and the next minute I'm being asked to come talk to the police. When I walked up, Ian, Matty, and Addison were talking to the police, and one of the neighbors said something, and I shit you not, right there in front of the police, with a large-ass knife attached to his belt, Ian looked at that neighbor and said, "I'll fuckin' gut you, muthafucker." I couldn't fuckin' believe it. One of the cops just said, "Now hold on, wait a minute. Let's just calm down here." At that point, for some reason, I knew we weren't going to jail. I know. You would think the opposite. But for some reason, the statement Ian made seemed to calm everything down. Hell, I walked off dying laughing. Addison followed right behind me, laughing his ass off as well. Ian and Matty stuck around a few more minutes to clean things up, and that was that.

If November of 2001 wouldn't have come around, things would have been better. Much better. But that wasn't the case. Because there is no avoiding time. And eventually, that time comes to an end. I had been working that night. My phone was off. Donovan had left a message on my phone telling me I needed to go to his house as soon as I got off work. So, obviously, I went to Donovan's when I got off work. Somehow, Bethany from Tulsa had tracked me down through Donovan. Apparently, she didn't have my number yet. Anyway, she had told Donovan to deliver a message and to call her as soon as I could. The message? Tyler had died. I could see that Donovan didn't like delivering that message as much as I didn't like receiving it. He already had a couple rolled. Tyler died while in service to his country. Apparently, he had been given prescription meds that he shouldn't have been given. We don't know the full details. He died in his sleep. We had a memorial service for him in December, in Tulsa at a veteran's memorial park. Liam, Anthony, Bethany, Brian, James, Mikey, Colton, and I attended—along with Tyler's mom and dad. I miss you, Tyler. Thank you for everything you taught me musically and for all the good times.

It seemed that 2001 had started out well. And then it suddenly went to shit. 2002? Let's start slow. It was March or early April of 2002. We were having a little get together at the studio. When, all of a sudden, who drops by? Anthony, Christian, and Jamie. Real quick about Jamie. I met Jamie back in '97 or '98. Jamie, Donovan, and I worked together at that woodshop. Jamie was a crazy muthafucker. But he was a cool muthafucker. Anyway, the three of them dropped by. That was unusual. Not the Christian part but the Jamie and Anthony part. That was the first time Jamie or Anthony had come to the studio. And actually, I would never have expected Jamie to come by. He just showed up out of nowhere. It had been a while since anyone had seen Jamie. And I don't remember how Christian and Anthony had hooked up with him. But they did. And I'll tell ya this, when they showed up, I could immediately tell they were tore up. In fact, they were on their way to the studio to get me. However, before they got to the studio, they got pulled over. And since they were specifically targeted for what they were carrying, Christian, of course, did what Christian would do. He swallowed that 8-ball before the pig made it to the driver's window. Actually, Anthony said he was gagging on it as the cop walked up. After being interrogated and even asked if that's what Christian was choking on when the officer walked up, they were released. Needless to say, they then had to make an extra stop before coming to the studio. That stop would be the grocery store to get some laxatives. And thus, there we were, at the studio hoping that Christian would shit out that 8-ball. Not only would Christian not overdose, but the mission would continue. I would get high, and then the four of us would run away into the night to continue said behavior. You see, the plan was to stop off at the studio, let me do a bump, then all four of us would go out to Dover and finish cooking. But alas, that did not happen. That did not happen because Christian never shat out that dope. Nope. Instead, he took the ride. He had no choice. His body was not going to release that dope except on its own time schedule. And that's what happened. I checked on him the next day in between classes. He just went to his bedroom window; he gave a whammy followed by a thumbs up and a small peak out the window—just enough to let me know that he was okay but tore up. Luckily, for whatever reason, when I finally talked to him a couple of days later, he said the dope only came at him one time with a rush. The rest of the time Christian said that it was a rollercoaster, small rushes with intense wiring. That was a good thing because that was the issue we were worried about. The main concern was this: was he going to be able to survive eating an entire 8-ball of Jamie-cooked dope once the baggie dissolved in his system? Did ya see what I did there? This was no ordinary 8-ball. That 8-ball was like the old school days. Ya see what I'm sayin'? This batch of dope, my friends, was a Jamie batch. And if you knew Jamie (and the elite junkie would), then you also knew that when he cooked a batch, it should be handled with care. Everyone in

Johnson and Pope County knew that. Even the cop who pulled them over that night knew that. Of course, that cop knew everyone in that vehicle, which is why he made the stop. Ya see what I'm sayin'? Anyway, Christian was fine, and no one went to jail. (To be continued.)

Around that same time, I met another guy named Matty. We'll call him Elliot. He was a manager at the place I worked. He sang and played guitar. He had heard of Studio 202 and came by to check things out one night. I was excited because I had heard a demo of this guy. He would be the perfect singer for us. And he could actually sing. I think we scared him that first night. We didn't see his ass for a year after that night. He even quit his damn job. We'll get back to Elliot a little later. Little Bitch! LOL!

Right before the spring semester ended, MTV came to the college I was attending as part of their *Campus Invasion Tour*. The fact that a big media group such as MTV would show up to a small college in Russellville—and bring with them national acts such as Default and Nickelback—was pretty cool. It was healthy for Russellville on so many levels. Because, trust me, ten years earlier that would have never happened. It was definitely a step forward. By that time, I had finally declared a major: journalism with an emphasis in broadcast. It was fortunate for me to be majoring in journalism when MTV came through because I got to help produce and direct segments for the college TV station that ran throughout the day. Plus, the journalism students got to interview the bands and be backstage. It was a great experience. It was my first live-broadcast experience as far as an event goes.

By the end of April, we were out of the studio and in a different location. The studio had run its course. It was loads of fun, but Matty could no longer afford the bills because he lost his job. That was alright because I had hooked us up a new spot. I did an interview for the college newspaper about a new facility that had opened and was free to the public. It provided arcade games, basketball, shows, and all kinds of shit for the youth. During the interview, the guy asked if I could help him get the word out about his facility. He said that if I could, he would let us set up our studio in his place to jam and record.

Help get the word out? What? Of course I could help. And so, we did. After I got the word out, things started moving right along. We took control of two rooms in the facility. One was the actual sound booth, and the other was the jam room. We cut a hole in the wall between both rooms and put a soundproof window in so we could see from one room to the other. Then we sound-proofed both rooms so that we and the owner wouldn't disturb each other. Then we were recording and jamming. Remember Jay? He started singing for us. After a while, we started throwing parties. But there was only so much we could do. We weren't making the owner any money, and he wasn't making himself money. The whole place shut down less than three months later. We moved over to Jay's parent's house and continued to write and jam.

Anthony and I had decided that we needed a vacation. So come July, we went on vacation. We left Russellville and went to Six Flags Over Dallas. Then we moved on to Austin later that day and stayed the night. From there we made our way to New Orleans. New Orleans—put it this way, we ended our night at a strip club. Enough said. The next day we went to Florida. When we arrived in Pensacola, it was packed. There were people everywhere. And actually, we stumbled upon an air show. The Blue Angels were performing. It was badass! Afterwards, we found a room at a hotel. And then it was jet ski time. We were having a great time. But then my dumbass got pulled over. Have you ever been pulled over in the water? Specifically, have you ever been pulled over by the police on a jet ski in the ocean? I have. Can you believe that shit? They said I was making waves or some shit. I wasn't even near the shore. I could understand that charge if I was near the shore. Whatever. They didn't give me a ticket or anything. They just told me to stop doing whatever I was doing. Anthony was over there laughing. I had to have Anthony explain to me what the hell I was doing wrong. Apparently, I couldn't make waves and then jump those waves. Fine. Whatever. We continued our fun for the rest of the hour that we had left. Then we went and ate seafood at a restaurant on the beach. We stayed a couple of days and then bailed out back home to Russellville. A couple of weeks later, though, we went to Atlanta for Ozzfest 2002. That was a great show! We saw Down, Hatebreed, Flaw, Otep, and several others on the second stage. And then, on the main stage, we watched Drowning Pool, Rob Zombie, System of a Down, and, of course, Ozzy. That was a great show! Unfortunately, not long after that show, the lead singer of Drowning Pool, Dave Williams, was found dead. Reports indicated that he died from heart disease. He was thirty.

As school started back up for the fall semester, so did the dope. By that point, I was a socially-functioning addict. I had learned to do school and dope, and, as Ian used to say, to "still be able to maintain." Maintaining was important, and it still is when one remains intoxicated for longer periods of time. Look, all I knew was this: I wasn't going to fuck up my entire college career by doing dope. But I wasn't gonna stop doing dope, either. So, yeah. Anyway, Christian had told me to go out to Liam's dad's place when I got out of class one day. He and Jamie were up there cooking. Yep! They were at it again. That was fine with me. Although, I did feel sorry for Liam. He didn't want those muthafuckers out there doing that shit at his dad's place. But that's what brothers do for other brothers. Liam's dad was out of town at that time working a cattle ranch, so the place was free range. And it was out in Dover on plenty of property, so no one was gonna be fuckin' with anyone. And make no mistake about it: Liam would get his for even allowing the situation to exist. But when I got out there that day, it was just Christian and Jamie. I could tell that they had been up all night. I saw the labor of their work on a plate. It was a pretty big pile. It was damn sure over two 8-balls. And they were in the middle of another batch. Christian set me up while Jamie continued his duties. And then I tasted the labor of their work. Good god, man! Remember me telling you about Jamie's dope? It was everything previously reported—and then some. That was some good shit, my friends. After having my head blown off, I went back to school. And that was how it was going to be until I graduated. I wasn't planning such things, but…well, fuck!

A few weeks later, Christian and Jamie ended up at my place. I don't know why the fuck we chose my place, but we did. Because, keep in mind, I didn't live in Dover. I lived in the middle of Russellville, in a tri-plex. I know, right? Anyway, there we were, at my place, cooking. Luckily, at the time, I didn't have any neighbors. Well, I was on an end, and there was no one living in the middle part of the tri-plex, and the guy who rented the other end was literally never fuckin' home. And when he was home, it was for no more than three days at a time, and then he would be gone again. So, needless to say, we weren't keeping anyone up. Well—you know what I mean. It actually only took Jamie about three hours to finish the batch. Although, I remember him saying that he was doing a "stripped down" version of what he had previously done. He yielded close to an 8-ball. He wasn't happy about the yield. I could tell he was ready to go somewhere else and get better results. But fuck. What are ya gonna do? We were in the middle of Russellville in a fuckin' tri-plex. We were already paranoid, which brings me back to what I had originally mentioned. I have no idea why the fuck we were at my place. I guess to get fucked up. We did our shots; Jamie left me some dope, and he and Christian bailed out. It wasn't until the following evening—just over 24 hours, mind you—that I had a visit from the monster. Remember me telling y'all about the monster? Well, it had probably been since the Gary dope that I had any encounter with those little tweaksters. Alas, there I was, watching those little shadow monsters. Damn that dope was good. Too good. I had every light in my place turned off, and for some reason my attention was drawn to the front yard, across the street, in a huge drainage ditch. Yep, I was tweaking my ass off. So much so that I got to the point of paranoia. But why was I so fuckin' paranoid? It's not like I had been up for days. Oh, but wait. I know why I was so fuckin' paranoid. It was that can of whatever chemical left behind that Jamie had used when he was cooking. I really don't remember what it was. It may have been acetone. But I remember what the fuck I did with it. Now, keep in mind that I was tore the fuck up and half naked with only boxers and a pair of slides on. I ran across the street with that can of whatever, and I poured that muthafucker out where the shadow monsters resided. The main problem with that situation—besides everything I just told you—was that it burned the area where I poured it out. It didn't set fire to it. It just burned it. It burned it so bad that smoke filled the air for a good fifteen or twenty minutes after I poured it out. It looked like there was a fire, but there was no fire. There was a huge fuckin' chemical burn, though. Holy shit! I thought I was paranoid before. Thankfully, no cops or firetrucks showed up. It was about three in the morning, so I think that helped the situation. You know, everyone being asleep and all. Shit, that was fucked up.

The next morning I looked out of my front blinds. Yeah, there was a bigass burn mark where there had not been one before. Damn!

Whoopsie-daisy! All I can say is: damn that dope was good. A couple of months later I met someone I wasn't expecting to meet, and she was damn near my counterpart. Her name was Alexis. I had met her once before, and the next time I had any dealing with her was for some weed: a quarter-pound. It was quite a silly situation. I had acquired what was supposed to have been a quarter-pound from her. I was doing it through the person who had initially introduced me to Alexis. Well, when the weed was brought back to me, it was an ounce short. I was furious! I demanded that I be taken to her place to confront the situation. So, I was taken. When I told Alexis what was up—in a pretty hostile way—she just smiled, told me not to worry, and that she would make it right. She just needed a ride. As we got in the car, I had forgotten in my rage that I had actually brought a huge kitchen knife with me. It was sitting on the middle console. When Alexis got in the car, she giggled and asked, "Was that for me?" Embarrassed, I tried explaining myself in a way that she could understand my frustration. She just smiled and said to the person that had brought me there, "I like him already." From that point on, Alexis and I were cool. We were down. I feel I need to bring this up, and even though you pretty much won't hear about her again except for one other time, she was significant in my life for a while. We did a lot together. I won't talk about it because it doesn't necessarily have much to do with the remainder of this story. Oh, and there was never anything sexual between us. We just enjoyed each other's company. We knew where the other was coming from. We would get fucked up and just hang out and talk.

By the end of 2002, we had left Jay's house and moved everything to my place. Because why the fuck not? We had to get rid of Matty as well. Or maybe he just quit. Either way, he was no longer with us. He stopped showing up to practices. I think he was just burned out. Shit, I don't blame him. Let's see…what else? Oh, Ian and Chainey got married as well. That was awesome!

I'm pretty sure that when 2003 hit, the band was in full devil mode by that point. We had changed our name from Studio 202 to A Unit. We were all fucked up.

I don't remember exactly how it happened or if I was even the person to have given Ian his first shot. But, unfortunately, and maybe because of influence, Ian asked for a bump one day. Now keep in mind that when I say influence, I don't mean I asked him, "Hey man, ya wanna shoot up?" I never, ever did that to anyone unless, of course, it was someone directly from my crew. In which case I would never have to ask anyway. Rather, he just came up to me one day at practice and said to give him a good one. I thought he told me he had done it a couple of times before, but I can't take an oath to that. But I'm pretty damn sure it wasn't his first time. What I can tell you is that I gave him a bump. And yes, I hit him. And yes, it was a thick thirty. After that, Ian would have me mix him one up from time to time. So, I would always ask, "You want a thick thirty or a thin ten?" And that's how that came about.

We were writing songs like "Thick 30" and "Thin 10". We even had a song called "PTFF". I can't bring myself to explain that one. "Thick 30" and "Thin 10" are no problem. (Just a reminder: the 30 and the 10 referred to how many units we wanted to inject.) Did you want a thick 30 units? Because, as you know, from previous situations, when someone in my crew mixed up 30 units, it was most likely always thick. Or did you want a thin 10 units? Which was the opposite of a thick 30—because why the fuck would you even wanna do 10 units? Well, it actually started with 15 units. But after a while, our standard of at least 15 units went out the window. Because when you're a junkie, even 10 units of dope can make a difference, especially with the kind of dope we were always doing. Plus, we knew how to mix that shit. We could make 10 units feel like 30 units to an amateur. But besides all that, "thin 10" just rolls off the tongue a little better than "thin 15." What do you expect? We were artists, god damn it. We may have been junkies, but we were artists, nonetheless. Anyway, I would always joke around with Ian when he saw me shooting up. He would ask, "How much ya doin', Shane?" "Well, I ain't doin' no thick 30," I'd respond. It was something between Ian and I, a kind of comedy mixed with tragedy, if you will. Ya see, it got to the point where we were able to do a shot, eat, and then go to bed. Wait a minute, that sounds familiar. Where have I heard that before? I think I see a pattern here, folks. Anyway, mixing up a thick 30 for us would get us off and keep us up better. Obviously. And mixing up a thin 10 would give us just enough to get through a practice session, or maybe through a few hours of class. Ya know what I'm sayin'? Anyway, the point is: besides getting fucked up, we were writing some pretty badass shit. And I will admit that Jay was writing some creative lyrics. It was what it was. It was working…for now.

A couple of months into 2003, we went to Tulsa and played a show. It was a small bar with a small stage. We could barely fit on it. It was one of those bars that had regulars. And we weren't any of them. We had no business being there. Not to mention that we were the only band playing, and we had only seven songs. On top of all that, I had already been up a few days. But, to my surprise, after we got through the first song, the ten people who were there went pretty nuts for us. I couldn't believe it. It was like they hadn't heard that kind of music in their area. And having played progressive music for a couple of years in Tulsa, I was surprised at the reaction we got. They made us feel right at home. And Jay, during some incoherent speech, confided in the crowd that I had been up for a few days and that we were all fucked up. Of course, our set was over thirty minutes later, and the crowd was like, "What the fuck? That's it?" When we told them that was all we had, someone screamed, "Play it again!" To be honest, I can't remember if we did or not. I hope we didn't. Knowing me, especially after three days, I was ready to go. Just guessing. And that's pretty much how it went. Playing music and getting fucked up. Although, Addison did have a beautiful baby girl. And Ian and Chainey had a beautiful baby boy. That was pretty cool. Oh, and in December of 2003, we saw Sevendust in Little Rock.

They actually dedicated one of their songs, "Angel's Son," to John. If you remember, John was our first singer. Unfortunately, John had committed suicide earlier in the year. It was horrible. None of us had really talked with John since the day we let him go. I saw him in passing a couple of times; we talked, but that was about it. He was a really nice guy. It was sad to find out that he was in so much turmoil.

In fact, we—Me, Addison, and the women we were dating—even got VIP afterparty passes. I will admit, the only reason we got those afterparty passes was because the girl that Addison was dating had shown her tits to some radio guys. So, she won four VIP passes. Gotta love it! Shit, I know I did. It was awesome to hang out with the guys from Sevendust. They're good folk. We even got to smoke out with the singer. It was kick ass! This guy called Ice Smiles was there. He seemed to know the band. He was also a musician, and he and three other guys had just come out with an album. They were called Official. The album was *Welcome to Little Rock*. He was a nice guy. He had a huge mason jar of weed. I'm talkin' bout a big-ass jar, filled with luscious, green bud. He rolled a fatty, and we all smoked out. At some point we went outside from the back of the club to where the tour bus was parked. Ice Smiles had a razorback-red car that was sittin' on huge spinner rims. I don't remember what kind of car it was, but that muthafucker was nice. We spent the rest of the night drinkin', smokin', and hangin' out. At the end of the night—about three or four o'clock in the morning—Ice Smiles walked us to the front door of the club, gave us a copy of his album, and told us to have a good night. We left with smiles on our faces. It was a great time. Like I said, the guys from Sevendust were awesome, just as humble and friendly as could be. And Ice Smiles was as well. Good times!

9   THE END

Around the same time of that Sevendust show, A Unit had separated. I'm not sure what happened. Everyone just said, "Fuck it!" However, do you remember the guy I was telling you about earlier, Elliot—the guy who could sing? Well, in the beginning of 2004, Addison and I hooked up with him. It was about a month after that A Unit split up. For some reason, at first, Ian wasn't a part of it. There had been some friction going on. And why not? For fuck's sake, if we weren't playing music together, we were getting fucked up together. Hell, we didn't even see each other in school. All we did was play music and do drugs. I reckon that we had worn ourselves out on each other. Shit, I don't know. The point is, there was life, again. Addison and I had found the person we had all been musically looking for all those years. And his name was Elliot

Look, finding a singer, apparently, was just as hard as finding a drummer. I'm not sayin' that because I'm a drummer but because of what I know from personal experience as well as listening to other musicians. And finally, we had found our singer. Not only could he sing, but he could play guitar. And he could write. That was important. You really don't have a band until you have a vocalist who can define the sounds that are being projected. I'm not saying a band can't have instrumentals. Of course, they can. I'm just saying: when you've been an instrumental band for the majority of your existence, it's nice to have a muthafucker that can bring further definition. So, Addison, Elliot, and I started playing together. We were playing out at Elliot's house. He had an okay drum set. It was good enough to practice on. That way I didn't have to bring my shit out. All I brought out were my cymbals, hi-hats, pedals, snare, and drum throne. And let me tell ya, that may seem like a lot, but it's not—comparatively speaking. And there we were, the three of us playing music. It was wonderful! Finally, musically, after all the music I had played over the years, I had a vocalist, a musician that I would take the Pepsi Challenge with. You know what I'm sayin'? I knew that Addison and I had finally absorbed what we needed to complete our expression. For me (as the drummer)—and even for everyone else—the vocalist was the key to the riddle. Right?! I mean, we had spent our entire musical careers expressing in the music what we were trying to say verbally. And to finally have a person who could express what I and the rest of us were saying musically, well, that was pretty fuckin' cool. Ya see what I'm sayin'? After a couple of months, Ian joined us. We named ourselves Paperface.

Creatively, the music was immature. The four of us were still finding our way with one another. Not so much with Addison, Ian, and me as with the three of us with Elliot. We were so used to playing hardcore, technical music that we had to almost relearn our instruments in a more straightforward and standard way. And there was nothing wrong with that. A lot of great music has more of a standard and basic rhythm and beat to it. Again, absolutely nothing wrong with that. I'm just sayin' that the three of us had to get used to Elliot; we had to play a more basic format versus the hardcore riffs and crazy time signatures we were so used to playing before. Eventually, we went into a studio in downtown Russellville and recorded a demo. The sound quality was definitely better than what we had been recording ourselves. But it was still a pretty bad recording. To be honest, we really had no business recording yet. But we did. And actually, we got a surprisingly good response from folks. And so it was.

By the summer of 2004, Paperface was coming along well. We entered some kind of bullshit contest to perform in front of record executives at a club in Dallas. Although we had a good time, we had no business being there. We were absolutely not ready for any type of record deal. But it was an experience. My mom, dad, and grandma traveled to Dallas just to support me. My brother Thomas even showed up. Of course, he lived in the Dallas area, so it was easy for him to attend. It was great to have family there. I love them so much. They've always been so supportive in my music. And to go all the way to Dallas to support that moment—a moment where we were allowed three songs—showed an incredible amount of love. But alas, I said it was a bullshit contest because no one that day walked away with a record deal, and there were a couple of bands that damn sure should have. After getting drunk at the club where we performed, we all finished our evening at my cousin's house. It was a good time! A couple of months later, we played the Pope County Fair in Russellville. To our surprise, there were at least 50 people there, if not more. We couldn't believe it. So, what did we decide to go and do after that successful turn out? We decided to play another Halloween party. Except this time it was my fraternity and one other that got together to throw it. Yes, I was in a fraternity for a short time. I was part of the alpha chapter of a fraternity. There's no need to mention the name. The point is, my fraternity and another one with close ties threw the Halloween party. We rented out a local armory in Russellville. I should have seen it comin', but I was too fucked up and consumed. Fucked up and consumed. It was a funky party. We had music, booze, drugs, and people. The perfect combination for any disaster. But nothing fucked up happened. I mean, we got fucked up and did some fucked up shit, but it was a successful party…except for what happened afterward. I was kind of responsible for making sure that the fraternities made their money back. And that happened. My fraternity and the other fraternity broke even. Paperface made about $150. But I told everyone, when they put money in for supplies, that we probably wouldn't make the money back. Everyone had chipped in as far as decorations and shit. We all wanted it to be properly decorated. The fraternities put the money together to rent the armory. So, everyone had money in on this thing. Addison even had one of his buddies make us a badass stage to play on. So, like I said, we were all in. Everyone.

At the end of the night, Addison and I were in the bathroom dividing the money. I'm not sure what went wrong after that, but about a week later Addison texted me sayin' that he thought I took some money—or some shit. I couldn't believe it. I couldn't believe that muthafucker would think that. Especially since we were both in the bathroom counting the fuckin' money we had brought in. Well, apparently that shit didn't matter. Anyway, I was so upset by the accusation that I left right in the middle of class. I called Ian's house, but there was no answer. So, I left a message on his answering machine. Obviously, I was horribly upset and very emotional as I was explaining what had just happened. And yes, I was cussing while I was talking. Well, that didn't help my situation. Not one damn bit. Ya see, I had left a message once before on Ian's answering machine, and it was much like the one I had left when I was bitching about being accused of stealing money. Well, Ian had told me to never do that again because he didn't want his kid hearing that shit. Now, this was comin' from a guy who would leave his kid in my bedroom while we played heavy-ass music in the other bedroom not ten feet away. This, comin' from a guy who would do dope in my kitchen with his kid not ten feet away. And cussing? Was he insane? We cussed around that kid constantly. But for some reason it was different on the answering machine. Look, I think it came down to this: some muthafucker was calling (that muthafucker being me) and ranting and raving on a machine about whatever the fuck he was upset about. And ya know what? I don't blame him a bit. Who wants to come home to some bullshit like that? I wouldn't. I'd be a pissed muthafucker, too, if I walked into my house after being in school or work all day and then hearing a message on my answering machine from a piece-of-shit muthafucker who was cussing and being belligerent. Fuck that shit! All I'm sayin' is that it would have been better if Ian would've at least framed it that way instead of talkin' like it was all about the kid and shit. I even said all that to him, but it didn't matter at that point. He had already scolded me about doing it again. So, apparently, it didn't really matter what the fuck I said or was being accused of. It was over. Apparently, I had run my course. I had wronged those guys in some way over the years and didn't know it, I guess. Or maybe it was the fact that I was so selfish. Or maybe it was all the drugs that had everyone all fucked up. Like I said, at that point it didn't matter. I even pleaded my case to Elliot. He said he believed that I didn't take any money. I even offered him the money that I had in my pocket, like forty dollars or something, which Addison and I had divided up from the leftover cash that we paid the frats and the band. But that shit didn't matter. He didn't want the money. He said he was going to "stay where the creativity was." And according to him, Addison was the creativity.

He and Addison were doing most of the writing at that time. So, I understood why he said what he said. But it didn't make it any less hurtful. Not only was I being accused of shit I didn't do, but now I wasn't creative enough. Great! Addison and I were on the outs. As far as I was concerned, fuck 'em all! Within twenty-four hours, we were through. I called Ian the next day and left yet another message on his answering machine. But this time it was to reassure him that everyone's equipment would be safe until they decided to pick their shit up. He and Addison came over later that same day to get everything. There was great hostility between Addison and me, but not between me and Ian. Ian was calm and peaceful. He responded to the message I had left earlier that day saying, "I wasn't worried about our equipment, Shane. And I don't think you took any money." I appreciated him saying that. And that was that. We parted ways. I'll tell ya this, though: never again would someone tell me I wasn't creative enough. Whether it was my drumming or anything else, I wasn't gonna hear that shit again. But that meant going beyond just playing drums. That meant getting back into playing guitar. It meant writing. Writing! It meant producing. Producing! And that's what I was gonna start doing. And I was going to do it on all levels—from composing to writing, playing, and producing. Bet that!

I graduated college the following month. Can you believe it? I had a fuckin' bachelor of arts in journalism with an emphasis in broadcast. Can you believe that shit? So, what does a junkie do after getting a degree? What the fuck do you think he does? Yeah, I did the typical partying, drinking, smoking, eating, and all that. But later I did the other kind of partying. The kind of partying that involved intravenous drug use. Besides, I was off until January, out of school I mean. But I was still working. In fact, I was working retail, radio, and at an advertising agency. I was keeping busy. I mean, I had no band. I, once again, wasn't playing music. And, apparently, it was my own doing. So, fuck it! Like I said, I didn't have anything to do until January. But come January I was enrolling back in school. That's right! I was going for my master's degree. It would be a Master of Arts in multimedia journalism. And yes, I was doing it at the same school. When you're a non-traditional student, there's no time to waste on the college experience. That shit was long gone. As a non-traditional student, one usually already has bills to pay and jobs to work and all that shit. Hell, in Donovan's case, he had all that and kids to feed. Besides, I wasn't interested in going anywhere else. School wasn't fun for me. I mean, don't get me wrong, I had fun experiences and all that in college, but it was a means to an end. I was already behind the 8-ball. No pun intended. But I was thirty years old with nothing to show but tracks on my arms. I was going to blaze through the master's program as fast as

I could. Oh, and really quick, an important situation to note: Darrell Lance Abbott, better known as Dimebag Darrell, one of the best guitarists in the world, was murdered in early December. Dimebag was from the mighty, mighty band, Pantera. Nothing else need be said. But it is important to note.

In January of 2005, before school had started, I went with Anthony and Liam to the cattle ranch that Liam's dad was runnin'. I had already been down there once, but it was just to hang out and ride four-wheelers. This time, we were doing more than just riding four-wheelers. This time we were helping with the cattle. And by that I mean we were corralling, separating, loading into trailers, and castrating. And this was no small farm. There were at least 100 head of cattle out there. This was a big ass farm. Have you ever worked a cattle ranch? Well, neither have I really. I can't say that one day amounts to having worked a cattle ranch, but I got a little taste of it. I used to picture muthafuckers working a cattle ranch with horses. And I'm sure there are many cattle ranches that do use horses. But not this one. We were using four-wheelers to corral the cattle. It was an interesting day. I never knew that cattle could jump the way they do. I'm talkin' over the corral gates and all that shit. These muthafuckers were like olympic livestock and shit. And I'll tell ya what, I never knew that cattle had the feelings they have. You separate a momma from her baby and see what happens. You separate friends, mates, or cattle that have kicked it together for a long time—see what happens. Hey, man, that shit was rough on all levels. Whether it was corralling or separating, that shit was tough and rough. I reckoned I didn't wanna do it again unless I had to. But it was an experience I would never trade.

Later that month, I started my path on the road to getting my masters. Let me tell ya something, getting a bachelor's degree is one thing, but going on to graduate school is something else entirely. Going on to a higher academic level is pretty awesome. All that shit you learned while getting your bachelors ain't shit. When you're getting a masters or doctorate, you will experience an academic pinnacle that you never thought possible. For instance, you learn different levels of communication theory, laws of communication, speech patterns, theory, etc. And, of course, on the creative side of a multimedia degree, it's all about website and content creation as well as creating documentaries, music videos, etc. Then you have the professional project. And you better give yourself a good year on that. Your professional project is when you come up with a scholarly topic to research and address, maybe even make some kind of unprecedented breakthrough at the end. The point is to continue to grow, to figure out what those before you have not done, to dig deeper, to question and answer, and to hypothesize. Ya see what I'm sayin'? And your professional project is something your advisor will tell you to get going on the first day you meet. Trust me, it takes time. My professional project was going to address the topic of the media. A topic that is a button pusher these days. Specifically, I was going to address: What do the news stations in a local market consider newsworthy, and who or what factors play a role in the decision-making process? To help answer those questions, I used a scholarly research theory on media called *Agenda Building*. So, yeah. Grad school.

By February or March, I had hooked up a new gig. I was playing drums for a band called First Place. I had to readjust my playing style again. But that was no problem. Besides, it's important to be versatile in your music on as many levels as possible. I caught them in the middle of some pretty good shit. They were ready to record a demo, make a music video, and play shows. Perfect! As soon as I learned everything, it was on. We were playing shows. In fact, Ian, Addison, Elliot, and Matty opened for us one night in Little Rock. They had a new drummer, and they had changed their name to Wasting Days. I noticed the music they were playing. I had composed the drum parts already on a few of those songs when we were Paperface. There were some new songs, but some of the music had been written and recorded by me on the drums before I had left—I mean—got kicked out. But that new drummer wasn't playin' the shit I wrote. They knew it. And I knew it. I ain't tryin' to suck my own dick. I'm just stating facts. But none of that mattered at the time. And that was cool. Actually, Ian, Matty, and I talked. I didn't say much to Addison and Elliot, but I really didn't have any beef at that point. Yeah, I had been hurt. And maybe I was still hurt a little. But I was no longer angry. And that was important. Life was changing for me. I was feeling different about things. My outlook was changing. Or at least I was thinking a little more about things—beyond what was right in front of me. Anyway, playing a show with my old bandmates was no big deal. It was a good show. After that show, Ian and I started talking more and hanging out more. I even hooked back up with Matty. We weren't playing music or anything, just hangin' out. And I would go to Ian's here and there to smoke out. It was good to hang out with either of them from time to time. By late 2005, Addison and I had hooked up again. When I got his text, I will admit that I was kind of shocked. I really wasn't expecting it. Although, Ian had told me that Addison had been wanting to hook up. I, of course, being the master communicator that I am, never reached out. But he did. When I read the text, it was classic Addison. "Wanna smoke a blunt?" he asked in a fashionably late kind of way. My response, "Does Howdy Doody have wooden balls?" So, we hooked up later that day and smoked out.

In 2006, things were going to change again. My life was going to change. Again. Apparently, that's just the way it goes. Right? Here's a little somethin', somethin' for ya. I had a little girl in May. Can you believe that shit? Things definitely started lookin' different. I had a baby girl. My princess. It was the most wonderful day! And what did I go and do a couple weeks after she was born? Well, what the fuck do you think I did? Once again, I found myself in the fuckin' bathroom with a fuckin' needle in my goddamn arm. My daughter was two rooms down the hall. Was I insane? My precious princess deserved more from her dad. Blah, blah, blah! What the fuck did you think was going on by that point. JUNKIE! Alice in Chains said it best at the beginning of the song "Junkhead." The first word you hear in that song is *Junkfuck*. And that's what I was: a junkfuck. I didn't give a fuck about nuuuuuthiiiiiing. Apparently, not even my baby girl. Of course, I thought about that shit as I was doing it. What the fuck you think I'm talkin' 'bout it for? I was devastated. I thought shootin' up was a low point in my life. That was nothing compared to what I just described to you. For once, I was in tears as I was shooting up. But not for me. My tears were much deeper than that. Keep in mind, I was a master at maintaining, as Ian would always say. I was a successful, socially-functioning junkie. I could work, do school, take care of a kid, and remain a junkie all at the same time. Congratulations, Shane. I mean, ya know—yay for me! But what kind of father was I going to be? And did I even give a fuck? Shit, by that time I was runnin' around more with Alexis than I was at home where I was supposed to be. Typical, right? I mean, the girl I was with had stopped partying. So, what the fuck? I wasn't ready to call it quits. I still had to feed the monster. But besides being a junkie and possibly ruining my child's life, things seemed to be going in the right direction. I was working at an advertising agency out of Dover. Yeah, that's right. Who would've thought? But it's true. In fact, I was working at a national advertising agency. That means I was producing and directing commercials on a national level. This agency had clients everywhere, from Russellville to the west coast, the east coast, and everything in between. So, it was no surprise that I was directing a shoot locally one night. Locally meaning in Russellville, at an old furniture store that had been around for many years. It was actually a national campaign I was working on, but I was shooting it locally.

As the evening came to an end, the blackness crept in. It was dark as fuck outside, not because it was night, but because there was a storm brewing. It was to be quite the storm that night. Lightning, high winds, rumbling thunder—a scary-ass Arkansas storm. When the storm had started, we were in the middle of putting some of our equipment and props back in the storage area at the furniture store, which happened to be on the second floor and was where the furniture store kept additional product. The only way to get the additional furniture and our stuff to the second level was by using a service elevator. Now, this service elevator was not like a service elevator you would imagine: you know, modern. No. This service elevator was like one of the first service elevators ever made or some shit. It was just a big, open-like cage. And to operate it, you had to manually switch up or down and then push a button. Or something like that. It was an old fuckin' service elevator. Anyway, we were in the middle of our final load when, all of a sudden, the fuckin' elevator stopped. Not only did it stop, but whatever dim lighting we had also went out. Now, keep in mind, the first floor to the second floor was not a long distance. We could see the next level when we were in the elevator. So, it wasn't like the three of us were scared that we were in danger or anything. We were all just like, "What the fuck?!" It was pitch black, and we were in a fuckin' elevator at night. Luckily, within about twenty seconds, the lights came back on, and we were able to finish our night.

I mention this story because at the same time that all of that was happening, Ian had been performing magick.

I say magick with a 'k' because Ian had first mentioned it to me a couple of years earlier. He corrected me when I looked at him and asked, "Magic? Like m-a-g-i-c, magic?" He said, "No. Magick with a k." And then he explained a little. Not much. Just a little. And yes, he mentioned Aleister Crowley, but he also mentioned wicca. But some would argue that there is really no difference between magick and magic. An article by Catherine Beyer on learnreligions.com titled "The Difference Between Magic and Magick" says that scholars think such word usage, with the k, "is unnecessary" and that "academics discuss magic in ancient cultures all the time, and no one thinks they are talking about the Celts pulling rabbits out of hats." That could very well be the case. I don't know. The article goes on to discuss the other reasons Aleister Crowley and others may have used the word with a k. On the other hand, dictionary.com defines magic as 1) the art of producing illusions as entertainment by the use of sleight of hand, deceptive devices, etc.; legerdemain; conjuring: to pull a rabbit out of a hat by magic; 2) the art of producing a desired effect or result through the use of incantation or various other techniques that presumably assure human control of supernatural agencies or the forces of nature. Compare contagious magic, imitative magic, sympathetic magic; 3) the use of this art. However, they define magick as 1) Archaic, magic; 2) a power of effort associated with wicca.

Now, let's go scholarly. I'm trying to cover the basics. I found a 2008 thesis paper by John Payne that covers some of what I'm talking about. It's called "True Will vs. Conscious Will: An Exploration of Aleister Crowley's concepts of True Will and Conscious Will and its Possible Applications to a Midsummer Night's Dream, Marison, and Wicked." Obviously, for this story, we're going to be focusing on what the student's findings were as far as the terms magick and magic. And by the way: true will is ultimately the basis around magick, or Thelema. Anyway, Payne found that Crowley defined the term magick in his writings as "the Science and Art of causing Change to occur in conformity with Will." Crowley explains this in what Payne describes as "somewhat general"; because Crowley goes on to write that "[i]t is my Will to inform the World of certain facts within my knowledge. I therefore take 'magical weapons,' pen, ink, and paper; I write 'incantations'—these sentences—in the 'magical language,' i.e., that which is understood by the people I wish to instruct; I call forth 'spirits,' such as printers, publishers, booksellers, and so forth, and constrain them to convey my message to those people. The composition and distribution of this book is thus an act of MAGICK by which I cause Changes to take place in conformity with my Will" (Crowley xii-xii).

So, I just want to illustrate things here. In conclusion, I don't know what the fuck Ian was talkin' about, or what he was doing when he was practicing magick. But I can tell you that he thought he was doing some shit outside the common reality of a human.

And, apparently, during his "causing change to occur," he had taken down a huge tree branch, or piece of a tree, or something like that. I know because I had talked to him after my little ordeal. Magick, as it pertains to—I have no idea. Look, I had only dabbled in that sort of thing in my time. And it was only with Ian and a friend of his. So, I can really tell you nothing about it other than what I just wrote. The next day, a Saturday morning in July, I got a knock on my door. It was Matty and he was in tears. I had heard that song before. I just wasn't sure what the name of it was. "Shane!" Matty said, "Ian is dead." I was immediately in confusion and disbelief. What did that man just say to me? Ian was dead? I talked to the man less than twenty-four hours ago. What the fuck!? I asked all the frantic questions one would ask when they're in shock from hearing about the death of a loved one. Apparently, Ian had od'd. He went to sleep and never woke up. Yep. A fuckin' overdose. I couldn't believe it. Ian had taken a fatal combination of Methadone, Xanax and Seroquel. He was twenty-five, married to a beautiful woman with a handsome little boy, and he had just graduated about a year earlier with his bachelor's degree. What the fuck?! Addison, Matty, Elliot, and I—along with Chainey and Ian's family—all convened at Chainey's house to comfort her. Well, at least to try and provide comfort. At the tribute (Chainey had him cremated), Elliot and Addison played some music. Then we listened to "10,000 Days (Wings, Part 2)" from Tool's album *10,000 Days*. The church was full. And it was a big church. I don't think there was a dry eye in the house. Afterward, those close to Ian had a gathering where we did exactly what Ian would want us to do: we drank and smoked for hours. Eventually, we all moved Chainey out of her place just outside Conway to Northwest Arkansas. And there she stayed until her job moved her to Houston three or four years later. I love Chainey. I loved Ian. He was a good friend, musician, and bandmate. I have missed talking with him over the years. I can only imagine the kind of music we would have created. Not too long after all of that, Chainey took us out to Richland Creek, a beautiful area outside of Dover where people would camp and just hang out. And that was where we scattered Ian's ashes.

By the fall of 2006, the band First Place had dissolved. It was alright. I needed to focus on graduation. By the end of 2006, I was back with Addison and Elliot. Apparently, their drummer just wasn't cutting it, and Wasting Days was about to record a new album, a tribute album to Ian. So, they had to call in the pimp: ME, muthafuckers! Look, after I put the first track down, they all looked at each other smiling, and one of them said, "Yep, we just needed a Shane beat." And everyone shook their head in agreement. I'm just sayin'. I didn't say that shit. They did. And I was very appreciative of that comment and the gestures and smiles and all that. But most of all, it was clarification for me, reinforcement that I was actually valued as a musician, that I had something to bring to the table. Right? I finished recording all my parts for the album by March of 2007. Addison had already moved to Northwest Arkansas and was going to lay most of his tracks from there and work digitally with Elliot. In May of 2007, I graduated with a master's degree. It was a master's in multimedia journalism. Yep. Can you believe it? I can't. All I knew was that I needed to put Russellville in the rearview mirror. I loved my people, but I wanted my daughter to have opportunity. Hell, I wanted opportunity.

So, I eventually settled on Northwest Arkansas. My parents had moved there a couple years earlier when they retired. And Addison had just moved there a couple months earlier as well. Northwest Arkansas is like a mini corporate America: Walmart, Tyson Foods, J.B. Hunt, and Arvest Bank just to name a few are headquartered there, plus there's all the vendors and other companies that have offices located in Northwest Arkansas because of the major companies. Northwest Arkansas is absolutely beautiful. It's perfect for outdoor activities, food, music, and there's tons of culture. It was the place I knew I needed to be. A few weeks before I left for NWA, I saw Christian. I hadn't seen him in about a month, maybe a little longer. And when I say I saw him, it was in passing while driving. I saw that he was two or three vehicles behind me. We were stopped at a redlight, so I thought I would jump out of the car and say hi. So, I jumped out right quick and with my arms up I said, "What's up, bro?!" He kind of grinned and waved. I jumped back in my car, and that was it. We went about our way. A few days later, Anthony and I were hangin' out. I rode with him to drop off some weed. Christian needed some, so he asked Anthony to get it. When we got to where Christian worked, we parked and waited for him to come outside. When he did, we all said our hellos, and then he started bitchin' at me about yellin' hi to him that other day. I was like, "What the fuck?" I asked him if he was serious, and he said yes, that it was embarrassing. I tried explaining to him that all I was trying to do was say hi. I explained that I was excited to see him because it had been a minute. It didn't matter. He wasn't havin' it. And he told me to never do that again, like what I said didn't matter, or like I didn't just say somethin'. So, I just smirked and told him what the fuck ever. Even Anthony was lookin' at him like he was a little overboard on how he was actin'. We could tell Christian was tore the fuck up. I even asked him, but he didn't say nothin'. He just smirked. After that, we bailed out. I was like, "fuck it." It was just Christian.

I moved to NWA a few weeks later. The first year was rough. I had graduated in the middle of the Great Recession. It was hard to find a job. I was getting work here and there. Eventually, Addison and I got a place together, a place where we could practice what we had finally finished recording. Elliot had been laying all his tracks—guitar and vocals—as Addison was getting his shit done. As he would get shit mixed, he would send it to Addison and me, and we would tell him things like add more bass drum, more toms, less bass, more guitar, etc. We would do that until we thought we had a good mix. After a while, we had an amazing album recorded, most of it from Elliot's bedroom in fuckin' Gum Log. The rest was recorded from Addison's bedroom in Northwest Arkansas. Incredible! This album was unlike anything we had ever produced. It may have all been done from Elliot's bedroom, but it was all done using Pro Tools. Elliot had done a fantastic job. Impressive! We tried getting it mastered, but we couldn't find anyone who didn't want to change too much about the creativity of the album. Everyone wanted to put their dick on the table because they apparently knew better than we did. Fuck that! So, it never got mastered. We called the album *Beautiful Shame*. The title was based off a poem that Ian had written for his son before he died. Eventually Elliot would make trips up to NWA to practice. By the middle of 2008, I had finally found a job. But that shit really didn't matter because I got a phone call from a person who surely didn't want to make it. Christian had been in a horrible accident, and it didn't look good. He had been taken to a Fort Smith hospital because everyone knows that you don't wanna end up in the Russellville hospital. Needless to say, we all gathered in Fort Smith. I felt so horrible for Christian. I felt so horrible for Cheryl and Miller. Obviously, everyone was an emotional wreck. I don't remember another time that we ate that much Xanax. We were eating handfuls. All of us took turns being at his bedside. We did that for about a week until his mom transferred him to Tulsa for one last attempt to save his life. He died a day later. About a week later, we buried our brother. There was a tractor there to fill the hole after the funeral. That tractor wasn't needed. We had about seven shovels. And with them we all took turns filling up the hole. This team of brothers consisted of Liam, Anthony, Kelly, Robert, Donovan, Connor, Jacob, Pauly, and me—along with a few other folks who became close with Christian over the years. Respect! Love!

By 2009 I had found a different job, which was short lived because the place got shut down. It was one of those payday loans places. Arkansas shut those muthafuckers down. But none of that shit mattered to me. I didn't give a fuck at that point because Wasting Days had just won a statewide battle of the bands contest. That's right! Out of all the bands in Arkansas, the people voted for us. Can you believe that shit? I couldn't! We had won a statewide contest. And it meant that we would open the Edgefest concert in Little Rock. Staind, Slipknot, Chevelle, Drowning Pool, and a few others were going to be playing that show. I couldn't fuckin' believe it. The day of the show, we were rollin' deep. Shit, we brought everyone. But then some bullshit happened while the stage was being set up with all the bands' gear. A drenching, unforgiving storm came through. People's shit started getting rained on. My gear might as well have been thrown in a fuckin' swimming pool by the time they got it covered up. Don't get me wrong, everything was immediately being covered up, but the rain came in so fast and so hard that response times didn't much matter at that point. There we were, the first musical break in our careers, and it was fuckin' storming. Hard! The show was delayed to the point that we were told we weren't going to get to play due to time issues. My stomach sunk when I heard that. I couldn't fuckin' believe what I was hearing at that moment. None of us could believe what we were hearing. Basically, too much time had passed due to the rain, and play time was getting shortened. So, if they bumped us, the other bands would have more time on stage and the schedule for the two big acts wouldn't be fucked with. Okay. Look, I understood what was happening. I got it. We had won a battle of the bands. That was it. We weren't a signed band. Everyone else who was playing the show was signed. Well, according to what we were told, word of us getting bumped had luckily reached one of the big acts, and they apparently refused to play if we got bumped. Can you believe it? We got to play! Although, when we started playing, the gates to the concert hadn't even been opened yet because of all the chaos that had happened. We were behind our instruments looking at an empty, wet, muddy field. But as soon as I hit that first drum fill at the beginning of the title track song "Beautiful Shame," we heard everyone who was waiting to get into the show start screaming, clapping, and yelling in excitement. And at that moment, the gates were finally opened, and hundreds of people started running towards the stage. It was intense. I think we were allowed to play four songs. I must say, we had a good show. Things had been chaotic and iffy for a while. But there we were, jammin' our shit and doing it professionally. I was told we sounded good. By the time we were done playing, there were a lot of people in front of us. We had been heard!

Later that day we were hangin' out backstage with a vocalist from one of the big bands, and he confirmed that had we got bumped, they wouldn't have played. He also said that there would be consequences for how the show was turning out. And he was right. Hell, even a couple of the signed bands only got to play a few songs due to all the time constraints from the chaos that had taken place. The fans had kinda been fucked from seeing more of the bands they came to see because of the storms. But bad planning was also to blame. Apparently, it's not a good idea to schedule a show of that size to take place in the middle of an open field where all the bands are playing from one stage and to not take into consideration possible weather issues that might create problems. I guess it would have been a little different if it had taken place in a more controlled environment rather than farmer Fred's pasture. Look, it got so bad that by the end of the concert Edgefest was changed to Mudfest. The field was completely fucked up. Muddy as fuck! I mean, should it have been in any other condition? For fuck's sake, you had thousands of muthafuckers listening to music in an open field with random storms all day. What the fuck?! And because of that, people, of course, had stopped giving a fuck. Everyone was throwing mud, moshin' in the mud—all kinds of shit. Hell, mud was even being thrown on stage during Slipknot. Of course, the guys of Slipknot didn't care. They were in tune with the crowd. They knew what the muthafuckers had been through all day. Like I said earlier, it was an intense day. But ya know what? We got to open a major concert. It was a badass, great time! I'll never forget it.

And not only will I never forget that show, but I'll never forget the Edgefest we played a few months later as a "redemption" show because of what had happened at the previous Edgefest. By the second show, though, we were a signed band. Now, when I say signed, I don't mean big-time signed. I mean signed as in signed to a little piece of shit, corrupt, so-called record label out of St. Louis. And that's all I'll say about those fucks. The point is that we were opening another Edgefest. And this time there were two stages, and the festival was held in the parking lot of Barton Coliseum in Little Rock. We, along with several other bands throughout the day, were on the second stage. The main stage? Mudvayne, Korn, Static-X, Black Label Society, and several others performed there. Our show on the second stage was right before Mudvayne played on the main stage. We played a good show. And we were heard by more people that time. It was another exciting day in my musical career—more progress as a musician. And that's exactly why I was so ashamed of myself that day. It had been weighing on my mind since that morning when I rolled out of bed. There I was, playing another once-in-a-lifetime show, and I had yet again put a needle in my arm. And for what? It was hotter than shit that day, and I felt like shit. Heat and dope don't mix. But nonetheless, I had gotten up early that mornin' and done one. Not a thin ten or a thick thirty, but a thick fifteen. That was me trying to take it easy before a big moment in my life. Fuck that! I was done. That was it for me. I was so ashamed of myself. I had justified it because I hadn't done any dope since I had moved to Northwest Arkansas. I had done some coke here and there, but I wasn't doing any dope. So, I thought I'd do a little one. But I hated it. Yeah, I got off. And, like I said, I felt like shit the rest of the day, mentally and physically. On my way down to the show that morning, I made a promise that I would never shoot up again. That was the last time I stuck a needle in my arm. You noticed I said that was the last time I stuck a needle in my arm. And that's all it meant. That's all it meant.

A little over a month later, I met the woman I would spend the rest of my life with. I had found a new job as a call center representative, and this woman was one of the trainers for new hires in the facility. I remember the first thing she ever said to me. I was still training at the time. They had us on the call center floor taking calls with experienced reps sitting next to us. The trainer was making her rounds up and down the aisles. As she got to me, I just happened to have done something wrong. I don't even remember what it was. I said something or did something during the call that was against customer service policy. But I remember that the agent I was with was laughing at whatever had just happened, and she was explaining what I had done wrong and why I couldn't do it. I guess the agent's laughter got the trainer's attention, and she asked what was up. When the agent explained what it was that I had done, the trainer started laughing. And then she looked at me while she was still giggling and smiling, and she said, "You ever do it again, I'll bust ya kneecaps." Then she walked off. I immediately fell in love. About two months later, we were planning our wedding. That's right. Wedding. We both just fell madly in love with one another. Snoop was right. It was "the good, good." I really didn't even care about having a wedding. However, being as thoughtful as she is, she knew that it would break my mom's heart if she didn't get to help plan something that, honestly, no one—not even myself—thought would ever happen. But like I told my mom the night we told her we were going to get married: "I'll marry her right now and never look back." And I meant it. I actually had found the woman I wanted to spend the rest of my life with.

The new year couldn't come quick enough. We were hoping as a band that 2010 would be the year that we would take off. But that shit never happened. In less than a year of signing that so-called record deal, we had fired those fucks; that was sometime around March or April. Stupid-ass, lying, corrupt, tryin'-to-steal-a-muthafuckers-art, piece-of-shit muthafuckers! And I'll leave it at that. After that shit fell apart, Wasting Days fell apart. There was nothin' for it. Elliot was still livin' back home and tryin' to raise a family. Shit just didn't work out. And that was that. I haven't played music with Elliot since. That was alright. I mean, it was alright that Wasting Days didn't work out. We were behind our time anyway. We had missed that train. It was time to move on. And that's what I was doing. Addison and I took a short break to try and figure out what the next move was. Plus, I had started a new job. I was finally back in media.

In the meantime, my fiancé and I were making trips every now and then to Dover. One: I wanted everyone to meet her. Two: Kelly was up to some "good, good" as well. And I mean good. Yeah, I know what you're thinkin': this fuckin' guy got this poor girl strung out. Well, no. Not really. In fact, we were just comin' back from an Edgefest show when we decided to stop off at Kelly's place. Well, it just so happened that Kelly had just cooked up a batch. My fiancé was interested, so I thought, "Fuck it!" And we did some dope. And it was really fuckin' good. Kelly asked if I wanted him to mix me one up. I told him no, that I would snort it. And that was that. I started going down there a little more. Besides, it was good to be with everyone again, with Liam, Anthony, Kelly, and Robert. Yep! I hadn't seen Robert in about a year, and it was good to see him. I had made plans with him to come down the following weekend to hang out. At the time I saw him, I was only down for the day. It was a weekday. I was there long enough to get some shit cooked up. We may have all been up to no good, but we were together—at least for a short time. The week after I talked to Robert—two days before I was supposed to go back down—I got yet another familiar phone call. Apparently, Robert had a heat stroke. And that's all I can say about it. What else can I possibly say? What feeling or emotion can I express that I haven't already expressed since I started this writing? There is no more describing the pain, heartache, and sadness. But I can tell you this: we buried our brother about a week later. And that day, I could finally understand, just a little, what it meant to face your demons.

Afterward: The New Beginning

Well, that's it. This is the end. The fuckin' book is done. Yes, it is the new beginning. And that's why it's the end. I bet you're wishing for some grand finale. Sorry. The ending is short because it is sweet. And that's because the new beginning was quick. It was quick for all of us. Let's wrap this shit up. Drum roll please............. I married the greatest woman of my life in the fall of 2010. It was a small wedding at my parent's house in Northwest Arkansas. Some of my family, her family, and most of my people were there. My daughter, sweet princess, was the flower girl. It was a wonderful day. And guess what? I've never looked back.

As far as looking back—the Tulsa crew? Well, Colton ended up moving to Arkansas in the early 2000s. He lives closer to Little Rock. I haven't seen him in years. James and Mikey? Mikey ended up moving to North Carolina. I haven't talked to him in years. And James actually moved to Northwest Arkansas for a while. But then he got all fucked up and bailed out. He left a note on my door one day saying he was moving to Arizona or Nevada or something like that. I haven't heard from him since. I think about them often, hoping things are good for them. And as far as looking back the other way? Well, my attention did turn to dope again. But it was short lived. I had decided that I just wasn't ready to stop doing dope and that I was going to continue my junkie career until I saw fit to stop. So, I started making lots of trips to Dover. All I had to do was bring Kelly the supplies, and he'd cook the shit up. For instance, I would bring the pseudoephedrine pills and batteries, and he would have the other stuff. Again, I'm no cook. Then we'd have a shake-n-bake party. I shit you not. It would be Kelly, Anthony, Liam, and me swapping bottles to shake. Ya gotta keep that shit shaking for thirty to forty-five minutes. We would have four or five bottles going at a time. Oh, but let me tell ya, Kelly knew how to cook some good shit. We'd get fuuuucked up! We probably did that for a year before shit started going the wrong way. Really, I think we were all just tired of being tore up all the time. Hell, I ended up overdosing again—or crashing, really. Lack of food and fluids is what it was. But I got fucked up. That scared my wife, so she swore it off. And that basically meant that I swore it off. Although, I would never actually set myself up for failure like that. Because as soon as I would say it was the last time, it wouldn't be the last time. Ya know? Anyway, I was done—for the moment anyway. It felt good.

Things were happening with Anthony and Liam as well. They were sick of doing dope all the time, too. We all were. It wasn't fun for us anymore. Besides, it was time. It was time. Shit, it was *way* past time. It was time to live. All of us but Kelly cleaned up about the same time. Kelly would stay on it for a while, but he cleaned up eventually. Oh, and don't think I forgot about Brian and Bethany. Yep! That's right! They ended up together. They had a beautiful baby girl in early 2011. And later that same year they tied the knot. They live outside of Oklahoma City. We visit as often as possible. Around that same time in 2011, Addison and I started a new band. We did a bunch of good shit with that band. We were called Eye for a Lie. We played a lot of shows. We played a lot of big shows. And really quick about one of those shows, we were at a local, well-known club in Fayetteville playing a show one night. And wouldn't ya know it? My mom and grandma showed up. They came walking towards the stage before the show started. Now keep in mind, the place was already packed with people ready for a rock show. The floor was pretty full. That shit didn't matter. Have you ever seen a floor of people in a packed club separate on both sides to leave the middle open for two little ol' ladies to walk through? I have. And that was a sight to see. My grandma and mom walked right up to the front of the stage and stayed there for at least two or three songs. Wow! That was a great time. Eye For a Lie was a great time. But in 2015, it was time for me to go. I was burnt out. It wasn't fun for me anymore. And that was alright. I needed to focus on my wife, my daughter, and me. So, that's what I did. I donated all my shit to a local music academy in Fayetteville. Well, I did keep my snare and my throne. Since then, I've just been working. As of this writing, I'm in media. News. Yes, I'm a producer. Go fuck yourself! I like delivering information to people. And because of where I live, I'm able to do that for my community without misinformation and false narratives. I understand such things takes place and that the media can be a poison, but local news isn't the same as national news. We actually do care about our community and deliver accurate information. The local markets, the local news stations, papers, magazines, and so on—they are the only true forms of journalism left. Anyway, here we are. Not what you expected, I know. Me neither. I must admit, I have fallen off the wagon a few times. Kelly and me. The only promise I've been able to keep to myself was not shooting up again. That day in 2009 really was the last time. The few times that I have done dope since 2011, I snorted it. I'm not sayin' that's any better. I'm just illustrating the promise. That's all. It's all the same. Doing dope is doing dope.

As of this writing, in 2021, things are calm. Well, calm for me. I am at peace. Writing this has helped. I'm happy. I've started writing music again. Addison and I are back at it. I'm alive! Although, I'm damaged. Ohhhh the irony. How many years did I spend with a needle in my arm? About 16 years? And then a straw in my nose the rest of the time? Well, I was diagnosed with multiple sclerosis back in 2019. Now I take three shots a week so I can keep my MS tamed down. Ohhhh the irony. Today, Liam, Anthony, and Kelly are doing well. Like me, they're family people. Donovan? Donovan moved to Oklahoma. He became a veterinarian. Jacob? Don't ask. Phillip? In Texas. A family man. Connor? Back in Texas as well—a family man livin' life. You already know about Betty, Dane, Tyler, Heath, Ian, Christian, Robert, Kristie, and Theresa.

So, what was it all about? What was the point? I wish I could tell you. My conclusion? I'm lucky I'm sitting here writing this. I'm lucky I have a beautiful wife and daughter along with two stepsons. I'm lucky to have the wonderful and loving family I have. Could my parents love me anymore than they do? I don't think so. I'm lucky I still have Anthony, Liam, and Kelly in my life. Oh, and speaking of life, Alexis lost hers during this writing, in 2021. I'll just tell you: she wasn't doing well. Miller, Pappa Miller (Christian's dad), was taken by COVID this year. Both a fuckin' tragedy! And bless Momma Cheryl. I hope The Father will bless her and keep her.

The past couple of years have been insane. Along with COVID, hate has ravaged our country. We are a divided people—politically, racially, lawfully, spiritually, culturally, and in every other way you can imagine. It shouldn't be that way. But it is. Today we have social media. And, apparently, we have social media influencers. What the fuck does that mean? Influencers? FEED THE CATTLE! FEED THE CATTLE! MOO ALONG. THERE'S NOTHING TO SEE HERE. Whatever it is they're influencing, I'm sure it's fuckin' retarded. That's right! I said it again. Retarded! Today, when you don't agree with someone, it becomes war. Today, you have to be careful what you say and how you say it. At some point, you're inevitably going to insult someone or something, even the day itself. Today, because you're offended, all of a sudden there's no longer freedom of speech. Today, we are spoon fed to the point that we are gagging. The cattle keep feeding and feeding. The rest of us are sick with disgust. We're fuckin' fed up! We? The ones not sleeping. Today, it's black, white, brown, red, blue, green, pink, yellow, bisexual, gay, lesbian, transexual, transgender, queer, he, she, we, it, they, non-binary, hate, racism, reverse racism, cancel culture, sex trafficking, child exploitation, abortion, no abortion, global warming, guns, no guns, equality, no equality, vaccine, no vaccine—hold on, I'll be right back. I need to go throw up—

Okay, I'm back. I needed to smoke a bowl after that one. By the way, go fuck yourself! Today, we're monsters. But then again, we have always been monsters. Today, we get to see ourselves in action being monsters because we're all being digitally fed a bunch of streamlined trash, directly to our brain and senses. Everything is interactive. Everything. Today, if I don't jump on the bandwagon with everyone else by catering to your incoherent bullshit about your gender or lack thereof, then I'm the piece of shit. Why? Because you wanna make up some stupid-ass shit, I'm supposed to play along in your fantasy? I'm supposed to play your games? Fuck that! Get fucked! I don't need your acceptance. You surely don't need mine. Own your shit, muthafuckers. Stop harassing us. I mean, c'mon. My wife has to specifically put down that she is a woman when she goes to the gynecologist. What the fuck! Stop harassing us. Today, apparently, because I'm white, I'm genetically prone to being racist. And to think that all this time, I thought I didn't give a fuck about skin color, or what school ya went to, or where ya grew up, or what ya do for a living. But it turns out: I guess I suck. Of course, I had a professor once who said, "Well, in order for you to suck, someone else has to be involved." Yeah, I like that. Today, well, you tell me, muthafucker, which way to go. Today, law enforcement is out of control. They tell us to trust them. Trust? How the fuck am I supposed to trust people who lie and murder? How the fuck am I supposed to trust people who hide around corners waiting to generate revenue and then trample on your rights in the process? I was always taught not to trust a sneaky muthafucker. I think I'll stick to that motto.

Today, religion is money and politics. Religion has nothing to do with The Father. Religion is manmade. If you believe in The Father, then it's just you, The Father, and HIS people. Also, church and state are no longer separate. And I really don't know if it has ever been. Why can't I buy beer on Sunday? Because some asshole, many years ago, decided that Sunday is the so-called sabbath and that it should be a day on which I can't drink. Liquor stores are closed, but everything else is open. Last time I checked, that's not separating church and state. In fact, that would be the opposite of separation. I don't believe in your bullshit. Stop trying to make me play along in your games. I don't need your fuckin' permission for when to drink and when not to drink. Religion only exists to control, manipulate, and brew fear. It's very similar to government. Today, your government is not for you. They do not give a fuck about you. You have been lied to and abandoned. Money, big corporation, and the religious institutions control government. It is no longer We the People. Republicans and Democrats are no longer working for the people. They work for their own party. Government is now trying to tell women what to do with their bodies. Government is trying to tell us we can't own guns. Government has been trying to tell us we can't smoke weed by pushing their prohibition on marijuana for years. Yet, I can pull through the drive-thru at a liquor store, order whatever I want and even get a cup of ice to go. And then, I can drive my ass down the road with a cup of ice and all the liquor I want. Insane! Fuck you! I'll smoke as much fuckin' weed as I want. My brothers and sisters hear me. We have been abandoned. Revolution must be the next step. Today, when you fuck up and get a criminal record, there is no forgiveness or rehabilitation. Finding a good job with a criminal record is damn near impossible because ya won't be able to pass a background check. A person is left with the bottom of the barrel, which usually consists of labor and minimum wage—a non-livable wage. A person can no longer vote with a criminal record. Why? It's because your voice, your thoughts no longer matter. Now, I understand that if you're a murderer or rapist or something like that, your right to vote should be taken away—among other things. Again, I get it. But dealers or addicts and the like? That's because they don't want people who can think for themselves. They want cattle. They? The authoritative, the religious, the corporate, the educational, the political institutions—they decide these things. Today, everyone thinks they have the answers. There is too much hate and divisiveness for any answer to be found. Today, families are divided more than ever. And over what? Politics? Religion? Vaccination? Whatever. Today, no one gives a fuck. The bottom line? Money! Today, life is a manipulation. I think it always has been. Today? Fuck, I don't know. You tell me.

My conclusion? I'm happy to be alive. I tell you this: take measure of what you have. Use it. Be thankful you have it. Don't worry about muthafuckers hating you because you like the conveniences of living in the twenty-first century, in a first-world country. Live life! You're not guaranteed tomorrow. Earn and experience the love of a Rottie—an alpha-male Rottie. Experience driving down beautiful backroads with a beautiful woman next to you, sunroof open, cold beer, and plenty of smoke. Make sure you tell the people that you really love and care for that you really love and care for them. Tell them as often as you can that you love them.

My conclusion? Do you. Be you. Be kind. Be patient. Watch. Learn. Teach. Strive for righteousness and justice. Humble yourself. Be a part of the solution, not the problem.
My conclusion? I've already told you my conclusion. But I will say this again: I'm happy to be alive!

A List of Revolutionary Artists

I believe the following list of artists and bands have the voice of our kind. I'm not talking about the drugs. I'm talking about the revolutionary thought process. These artists speak to us and to those who KNOW. We are the ones who are awake, for our part. We have an understanding that most do not, an outlook and a vision that only we understand. Most of us cannot describe this sight, foresight, vision, and understanding that we see and comprehend. Yet, we know it exists because we have these elite artists who can not only put it in words for us, but they can absolutely put it in sound as well. I speak, of course, of music. And those who know what I speak of, know what I'm saying. Right? For me, music was the first thing I ever fell in love with. Don't get me wrong, my life is a gift. My family and friends are gifts. But, besides The Father, music was and is the gift that has gotten me to this exact moment. It is through music that I have the gifts I have today: life, my family, my friends (who are family); and The Father, who provided it all. It is my understanding of music—a level of communication that cannot be duplicated—that has brought me to this point. Does that make sense? Sometimes words and thoughts come at me so fast that I cannot write them down quickly enough. Wait. Did I just say that out loud? Go fuck yourself! Anyway, I thought I would take an opportunity to express that these artists got me through tough times—or you could say through the stages of my life—and they inspired me. I'll probably miss some. That's not intentional. These are the cats who come to me immediately. And, of course, how my high and currently drunk ass is remembering them during this writing. As I sit here, the Violent Femmes just came into my rotation. Note to self: add to following list. (Oh, and obviously, this list is in no order.)

Alice in Chains, Tool, Nonpoint, Soulfly, Mudvayne, Slipknot, Deftones, Staind, System of a Down, Jay Z, Lamb of God, Eminem, A Perfect Circle, Stone Sour, The Game, Puscifer, Post Malone, Waylon Jennings, Willie Nelson, Blake Shelton, Charlie Daniels, Johnny Cash, Ängie, The Band, Bill Withers, Chris Stapleton, Jelly

Roll, John Cougar, Bone Thugs-n-Harmony, Brad Paisley, Curtis Mayfield, Prince, Shooter Jennings, Shuggie Otis, Tobe Nwigwe, Jimmy Buffet, Tom MacDonald, Childish Gambino, Justin Timberlake, Lenny Kravitz, Lynyrd Skynyrd, Ludacris, Lo-Pro, Atomship, Lizzo, Kenny Chesney, Kendrick Lamar, Jurassic 5, John Mayer, Ed Sheeran, Metallica, Incubus, Flaw, Violent Femmes, Everlast, Eric Church, Mariah Carey, Dua Lipa, DMX, Dolly Parton, Dave Matthews Band, Bobby Womack, Alanis Morissette, Aerosmith, Al Green, David Bowie, Hank Williams, Jr., Limp Bizkit, Halsey, Jason Aldean, Joe Walsh, Merle Haggard, Miranda Lambert, Neil Young, The Notorious B.I.G., Outkast, Red Hot Chili Peppers, Steely Dan, Steve Miller Band, Ice T, Wu-Tang Clan, Jane's Addiction, NIN, Clutch, Cyprus Hill, Megadeth, and Grandmaster Flash & The Furious Five.

www.ingramcontent.com/pod-product-compliance
Lightning Source LLC
Chambersburg PA
CBHW022050290426
44109CB00014B/1049